D0801634

BLUSTER

PETER R. NEUMANN

Bluster

Donald Trump's War on Terror

OXFORD

UNIVERSITY PRESS

Oxford University Press is a department of the
University of Oxford. It furthers the University's objective
of excellence in research, scholarship, and education
by publishing worldwide.

Oxford   New York

Auckland   Cape Town   Dar es Salaam   Hong Kong   Karachi
Kuala Lumpur   Madrid   Melbourne   Mexico City   Nairobi
New Delhi   Shanghai   Taipei   Toronto

With offices in

Argentina   Austria   Brazil   Chile   Czech Republic   France   Greece
Guatemala   Hungary   Italy   Japan   Poland   Portugal   Singapore
South Korea   Switzerland   Thailand   Turkey   Ukraine   Vietnam

Oxford is a registered trade mark of Oxford University Press
in the UK and certain other countries.

Published in the United States of America by
Oxford University Press
198 Madison Avenue, New York, NY 10016

Copyright © Peter R. Neumann 2019

All rights reserved. No part of this publication may be reproduced,
stored in a retrieval system, or transmitted, in any form or by any means,
without the prior permission in writing of Oxford University Press,
or as expressly permitted by law, by license, or under terms agreed with
the appropriate reproduction rights organization. Inquiries concerning
reproduction outside the scope of the above should be sent to the
Rights Department, Oxford University Press, at the address above.

You must not circulate this work in any other form
and you must impose this same condition on any acquirer.

Library of Congress Cataloging-in-Publication Data is available
Peter R. Neumann.
Bluster: Donald Trump's War on Terror.
ISBN: 9780190099947

Printed in the United Kindgom on acid-free paper by
Bell & Bain Ltd.

CONTENTS

CONTENTS

ACKNOWLEDGEMENTS

While writing this book, many people helped me in sharpening my ideas, finding sources and information, or pointing out mistakes and contradictions. I am indebted to my research assistants Amelia Birt and Maria Samsik, who sifted through a huge number of publications, as well as interviews, speeches, and statements made by Trump and his administration. Without their commitment and diligence, the book would have taken much longer to complete. I also benefited from conversations with experts and political insiders, such as Mark Freedman, Daveed Gartenstein-Ross, Jamie Geller, Joshua Geltzer, Matt Levitt, and Stephen Tankel. Especially helpful was Mark Stout, who read several versions of the manuscript and corrected many mistakes.

I am grateful to Kim Campbell, Sir Lawrence Freedman, and Bruce Hoffman, my academic and professional mentors, who have given me so much support over many years without ever expecting anything in return. This is also true for my colleagues at the International Centre for the Study of Radicalisation (ICSR) at King's College London, such as Shiraz Maher and Katie Rothman, as well as Joana Cook, John Holland-McCowan, and Charlie Winter, who read various drafts or helped me look at my topic from different perspectives. I should also mention Thomas Hegghammer, who allowed me to present my ideas at a research conference in Norway; all my interviewees, who spoke openly and were generous with their time; and the anonymous reviewers, who provided useful feedback. Needless to say, the mistakes that remain are my fault alone.

ACKNOWLEDGEMENTS

Finally, none of this would have been possible without the encouragement of Michael Dwyer at Hurst, and the support of Andrew and Orly Wolfson at the Charles Wolfson Charitable Trust, which—literally—bought me the time to pursue this project. The person I am most indebted to, however, is my partner Zora, who put up with my moods, read numerous drafts, and challenged many of my ideas and assumptions. Without her, this book would have never been finished.

INTRODUCTION

The first jihadist attack on American soil during Donald Trump's Presidency took place on Halloween. Shortly after 3pm on 31 October 2017, a grey pickup truck veered into a bike lane along the Hudson river in Manhattan, New York, killing eight cyclists and pedestrians before crashing into a bus. Police identified the attacker as Sayfullo Saipov, a twenty-nine year old immigrant and unemployed truck driver. Though Saipov had not been trained or directed by the group, Islamic State (which is also known as ISIS) later issued a statement claiming he was a "soldier of the Caliphate".

Unlike other Presidents, who have responded to terrorist attacks by calling on Americans to unite, stay calm, and pray for the victims, Trump's reaction was furious. Over the following four days, he mentioned the attack in nineteen tweets, several phone calls to foreign leaders, and in public comments before a Cabinet meeting. Within minutes, he posted several tweets in which he called Saipov "a very sick and deranged man", and warned that Islamic State "must not [be allowed] to return, or enter, our country".[1]

When it emerged that Saipov had been born in Uzbekistan, a country in Central Asia, Trump lashed out against vetting procedures and blamed the Democratic Party for "importing Europe's problems".[2] The next day, he described the American judicial system as "a joke", and suggested that Saipov, who had survived the attack, should be sent to the prison camp in Guantanamo Bay, receive capital punishment ("DEATH PENALTY!"), and that Islamic State would have to "pay a big price" for attacking America.[3] Meanwhile, Vice President Mike Pence told reporters that "there's nothing about President Trump's [counter-terrorism] policies that mirror the last administration".[4]

As it turned out, none of Trump's announcements were true or relevant. Despite claiming that Islamic State was being hit "ten times harder",[5] the American military did not increase their strikes against the group, whose base in Syria and Iraq was already on the verge of being defeated. Immigration screening procedures played no role, because Saipov did not radicalise for years after entering the United States.[6] Sending him to Guantanamo would have complicated the judicial process.[7] And the death penalty would have been more likely had Trump not jeopardised Saipov's chance of a fair trial by tweeting about it.[8] In the end, Saipov wound up being tried in exactly the same way he would have been tried under the previous administration. Apart from Trump's bluster, and contrary to Pence's statement, nothing seemed to have changed.

President Trump's response to the Halloween attack was part of a pattern. Since the first days of his campaign, Trump has portrayed himself as tougher than tough. He has told supporters that defeating Islamic State justified any means, and that he would authorise whatever plan "gets the job done". He has spoken in favour of waterboarding, torture, indiscriminate bombings, and the killing of terrorists' families. He has linked terrorism with Islam, warned of "Muslim immigration", and accused American Muslims of celebrating jihadist attacks. Other than the border wall with Mexico, there is no other topic which Trump has deployed more frequently, strategically, and with more vigour and excitement, especially during the election campaign and the early days of his Presidency.

As in Saipov's case, however, the policy impact of his outbursts has been limited. Although some rules and processes have changed, the basic operational framework that has guided counter-terrorism since President George W. Bush's second term remains in place.[9] Many of the people who executed Obama's War on Terror are now in charge of Trump's. In terms of what Joshua Geltzer and Stephen Tankel have called *actual counter-terrorism*—"the day-to-day grind of civil servants, diplomats, military, and other dedicated officials"[10]—the continuities are greater than the differences. Indeed, many Washington insiders have dismissed Trump's statements and his unpredictable style as irrelevant.[11] According to General David Petraeus, for example, "What you should follow... is the troops, the money and the substance of policies, which [can be overlooked] if we get too mesmerised by reading tweets".[12]

At the same time, it seems wrong—and impossible—to ignore Trump. He is, after all, President of the United States, and every time he expresses his views in an unscripted remark or tweet, it has an immediate impact on the political debate, sets expectations, dominates the news cycle, and forces bureaucrats and political leaders to respond. It also affects foreign audiences, and shapes their attitudes and actions towards America.[13] Not least, it creates chaos within his own administration: in foreign policy especially, it has at times been difficult to know who speaks for the President, what the government's positions are, and how long they will hold. As the journalist Derek Thompson put it: "Politics is downstream from persuasion, and law is downstream from language... No matter how often journalists and politicians dismiss Trump's words, the words matter".[14]

In short, there is no easy way to make sense of Donald Trump and his "War on Terror". Is it all bluster, aimed at mobilising his base, or does it represent a genuine shift from previous administrations in Washington? What are his core convictions, and to what extent do they correspond with substantive changes in counter-terrorism policies? How will his words and actions affect communities, civil liberties, and the relationships with other countries? Most importantly, is it going to make America—and the world—safer?

* * *

This book builds on the many debates about American counter-terrorism that have taken place since the September 11, 2001, attacks. The idea of a "War on Terror", which President George W. Bush declared in the aftermath of the attacks, has frequently been criticised for its vagueness, potentially open-ended nature, and the extent to which it has played into terrorists' hands.[15] Although President Barack Obama stopped using the term, scholars like Michael Glennon or Jason Ralph have shown that nearly all of the legal powers as well as military and intelligence programmes that were associated with it remained in place.[16] As a consequence, "War on Terror" has become shorthand for the American campaign against terrorism since September 11, 2001, and this is how I intend to use it.

One of the challenges in studying the War on Terror is that it crosses many disciplines and fields of research, including political science, international relations, law, history, and area studies. Despite this enormous diversity of approaches, and the huge number of books and articles that have been written about it, most of the scholarly attention has converged around two overarching themes.

The first is the projection of American power abroad. Many analysts have conceptualised the War on Terror primarily in "kinetic" terms, that is, as a war-like conflict in which the United States has deployed force in order to destroy terrorist networks, eliminate terrorist safe havens, neutralise state sponsors of terrorism, and transform political conditions that were believed to be conducive to terrorism. During the Bush years, for example, many scholars studied the consequences of the wars in Afghanistan and Iraq, and the implications of the so-called Bush Doctrine, which called for "preventive wars" and democracy promotion by force. They asked: To what extent were these wars necessary, legal, and justified?[17] Did they reduce or increase the threat from terrorism?[18] Was it possible to promote democracy through force, and what—if any—relationship existed between particular forms of governance and the spread of terrorism?[19] While Obama's election initially compelled analysts to focus on other issues, such as the use of drones[20] and non-kinetic ways of combating terrorism,[21] many of the more traditional debates returned to the fore as a consequence of the conflict in Syria and the rise of Islamic State.[22]

The second major theme is about ideas and values. In the early years, many academics studied and discussed what they believed were the two most egregious examples of how America had betrayed its core values: the detention camp in Guantanamo Bay, where suspected "enemy combatants" were held without trial, and the use of "enhanced interrogation techniques", such as waterboarding, which critics regarded as torture.[23] Other issues were primarily domestic in nature. Under Bush, there was an extensive debate about the Patriot Act, which restricted civil liberties in the name of fighting terrorism,[24] and the targeting of Muslims by law enforcement and intelligence agencies in the aftermath of September 11.[25] During Obama's Presidency, attention focused on surveillance by the National Security Agency (NSA),[26] and the use of so-called "sting operations", a controversial law enforcement practice.[27] Virtually all these debates revolved around similar questions: Have government responses to terrorism been excessive and/or discriminatory? Is the War on Terror causing more harm than good? And, to what extent has it compromised freedom and democracy—if not the very idea of America?

Although there have been a number of important scholarly books on counter-terrorism and the Wars on Terror in general,[28] the amount of analysis on Donald Trump's policies in particular was limited at the time of writing.[29] The purpose of this book is to offer a first assessment that seeks to understand how Trump's War on Terror differed from those of previous administrations. In doing so, my objective was to be as comprehensive as possible, and—unlike much of the existing literature—integrate both foreign and domestic aspects.[30] The themes that I concentrated on are those suggested by the secondary literature: the projection of "hard power", and trade-offs between security and American values.

In contrast to books by policy insiders, such as political journalists or former officials, I am not invested in the American political debate, and have no ulterior motive for being critical of Trump. Nor do I feel obliged to defend the counter-terrorism legacies of the Obama and Bush administrations, which will be referenced throughout the book. Indeed, I believe that many of Trump's policies can only be understood in the context of his predecessors' failings and omissions, and that—ultimately—Trump and his War on Terror are symptoms of a wider crisis about America's identity and role in the world.

Furthermore, this book is not primarily about processes or institutions. Although I have lived and worked in Washington, DC, I am not a lawyer, policymaker, or someone who can claim to have special expertise in the mechanics of the national security process. I also sense that, with Trump, this matters less than under previous Presidents. The most dramatic changes he has announced have emerged not from within the bureaucracy, or as a result of subtle shifts in power or opinion between Washington's national security agencies. While I have no doubt that "traditional" policymaking will once again become more important after Trump leaves office, for the time being, a more compelling story can be told by focusing on people and—especially—ideas.

In contrast to much of my previous research, which involved getting into the minds of terrorists, there was no shortage of publicly available sources and material on Trump and his administration. Not only have Trump and his closest advisers given numerous speeches and lengthy interviews, the President has shared his ideas and thoughts in real time, and on a daily basis, via Twitter.

Rather than finding relevant information, the challenge has been to organise the plethora of views and opinions that Trump and his supporters have articulated since announcing his intention to run for office in June 2015, and—to a lesser extent—before. In addition to interviews, speeches, and statements on social media (Twitter and Facebook), I have relied on media reports, policy papers, academic articles, official publications, and Congressional testimony. Between April and September

2018, I also conducted thirty interviews with experts, journalists, and policymakers.[31]

With few exceptions, most of the information that I required was available from open sources. Thanks in part to social media, leaks, and the many people who have by now left the administration, there are few internal fault lines or divisions which have not been publicly exposed. Though never intended that way, Trump may, in fact, be one of the most transparent Presidents in history.

Argument

My overall conclusion is that, in terms of what Tankel and Geltzer labelled "actual counter-terrorism", Donald Trump's War on Terror is not fundamentally different from those of his predecessors. One of the principal reasons for this continuity is not policy alignment, but—rather—Trump's administrative weakness. He entered office as a complete outsider, with neither the people nor the policies that would have enabled him to extend his political will across the federal bureaucracy. In practice, his most radical ideas—from torturing terrorist prisoners to "banning Muslims"—have been rejected or watered down by national security officials who had internalised the lessons from fifteen years of the War on Terror and sought only gradual changes from the status quo.[32]

At a more fundamental level, however, Trump's counter-terrorism doctrine—which can be summarised as "killing terrorists" and "keeping Muslims out of the country"—has been deeply at odds with established views on "American values" and America's role in the world. American policy elites are not opposed to "killing terrorists", but—unlike Trump—like to believe that America has a unique, benign, and more ambitious role in shaping the international order. They are not against restricting immigration, but resent the idea of restricting the supposedly universal "promise" of America to people of certain ethnicities or religions in such a blatant way. From a mainstream perspective, Trump's doctrine has not just been radical and different, but "un-American".

This is not to claim that Trump has had no tangible impact. Since taking office, American counter-terrorism has become more militaristic and less interested in causes and consequences. Far-right extremists feel powerful and emboldened. The biggest shift, however, has been the systematic conflation of terrorism, immigration, and Islam, which has weakened the idea of America as an ethnically and religiously diverse "nation of immigrants". Arguably, much of what Trump has said about Muslims and terrorism had little to do with countering terrorism, but used people's fear of terrorism as part of an ideologically-driven effort to "break" the mainstream consensus on immigration and promote a different, less "exceptional" and more aggressively nationalist idea of America—"America First".

Where the national security establishment has asserted itself, such as in the military campaign against Islamic State, changes have been more gradual and outcomes less negative. But successes in tactical counter-terrorism—the capabilities that have enabled American security agencies to thwart plots and dismantle terrorist networks—can only be sustained if they are held together by a coherent strategic framework. Trump has failed to provide such a framework and his entire approach has systematically eroded its foundations. In contrast to his predecessors, Trump's responses to terrorism have frequently contradicted (his own) government policy, undermined resilience, and sown division. In the event of a major attack, the government's greatest potential liability will be the President himself.

Like driving in the wrong gear, Trump's War on Terror looks strong and powerful in the short term, but will cause damage over time, as every short-term advantage is outweighed by negative, long-term consequences. Ultimately, the man who has pledged to defeat terrorism has not only made the world less safe but has also undermined America's greatest "soft power" asset—the very idea of America.

To demonstrate this, Chapters 1 and 2 will outline Trump's counter-terrorism doctrine, and describe the political dynamics that have amplified it. Chapter 3 will explain what I mean by "administrative weakness" and develop a typology of Trump's national security team. Chapter 4 analyses the so-called "Muslim travel ban", the purest and most significant policy application of his doctrine. Chapters 5 and 6 deal with changes in America's "kinetic" approach, especially the campaign against Islamic State in Syria and Iraq, and illustrate the tension between Trump's radical instincts and his "generals'" more traditional conservatism. In Chapter 7, I analyse the impact of Trump's approach on foreign partners and conflicts, while Chapter 8 looks at domestic counter-terrorism and Trump's role in "enabling" and emboldening the extreme right. The Conclusion will answer the questions mentioned earlier and highlight how Trump has changed America's War on Terror—not despite but because of his bluster.

1

THE TRUMP DOCTRINE

In December 2017, the Trump administration published its National Security Strategy. To no one's surprise, the 55-page document, which officials at the National Security Council (NSC) had worked on all year, contained "Trumpian" elements. Its guiding principle was "Making America Great Again". Borders had to be secure and foreign interventions avoided. Overall, however, the document was remarkably mainstream. It emphasised the role of "competitive diplomacy", described Russia and China as geopolitical rivals, and committed America to spreading its values—nothing that previous administrations would have fundamentally objected to.[1]

On terrorism too, there was hardly any change. Al-Qaeda and Islamic State were named as "the most dangerous terrorist [threats] to the Nation", but there was no mention of "radical Islamic terrorism", Trump's favourite phrase. Rather than "bombing the shit out of them", which Trump had demanded during the campaign, the document struck a careful balance between military (and paramilitary) action, diplomacy, countering jihadist ideology, and addressing root causes ("denying violent ideologies the space to take root"). Under the guise of "promoting stability" and "denying terrorist safe havens", it even committed the government to forms of nation-building, which Trump had frequently criticised as a waste of money.[2]

The contrast between the carefully crafted document and the President in whose name it was written became clear when

Trump introduced it to the public. Addressing an audience of national security professionals, he praised Russian President Vladimir Putin, and talked at length about his election victory, tax cuts, and success in cutting regulations. He also criticised previous administrations as "disastrous", "weak", and "incomprehensibly bad", while mimicking fascist language by talking about himself as the leader of a "great awakening"—a "rebirth of patriotism, prosperity, and pride".[3] There was little in his speech that reflected the document's content or sober tone.

Mainstream commentators, who had cautiously welcomed the document, were confused. Writing for *Newsweek*, Ilan Goldenberg, a former Obama official and fellow at the Center for a New American Security (CNAS), questioned the whole exercise:

> [The] president is the policymaker equivalent of the Tasmanian Devil. His advisers seriously deliberate on important options, only to have Trump enter and turn everything wildly upside down. The idea that in this environment an administration can put out a… national strategy that will have any impact whatsoever is pure fantasy.[4]

Thomas Wright, a senior fellow at the Brookings Institution, gave a similar assessment: "The National Security Strategy is a stunning repudiation of Trump, and Trump's speech was a stunning repudiation of the National Security Strategy".[5] Indeed, it later transpired that Trump had declined several opportunities to contribute to the document.[6] One of his spokesmen refused to say whether he had even read it.[7]

The episode raised fundamental questions. What, if anything, did the President believe? And why were those beliefs not reflected in the document? Conventional wisdom suggested that Trump was a blank canvas who would say or do whatever he believed was popular or suited his narcissistic instincts. There was no point in looking for a doctrine, as Trump was too fickle and self-absorbed to develop anything resembling a consistent approach or set of principles.[8] Even Joshua Green, the bestselling author who wrote an influential account of Trump's political education, concluded that the President had no consistent philosophy or convictions:

> Trump doesn't believe in nationalism or any other political philosophy—he's fundamentally a creature of his own ego. Over the years, Trump repeated certain populist themes… [But] these were expressions of an attitude—a marketing campaign—rather than commitments to a set of policies.[9]

In my view, this is only partly true. There can be no doubt that Trump is a narcissist, that he likes to stir things up and makes certain comments because he believes they are popular, and that his beliefs are not particularly sophisticated. After all, there is no evidence that he reads much or has been interested in political ideas.[10] At the same time, he has articulated similar positions for years, if not decades. The fact that they are neither complex nor informed by continuous intellectual engagement does not make them any less sincere. They are consistent enough to be distilled into a "doctrine"—a system of principles and overarching ideas that guide policy.

Trump's doctrine, which is anchored in various strands of populism, nationalism and the so-called Alternative Right, is a radical break with recent American approaches towards countering terrorism. Trump is not interested in addressing underlying conditions, causes or conflicts, and he believes that commitments in foreign countries are rarely helpful or necessary. He also thinks that terrorism is linked to immigration, and that Islam is alien to America. In Trump's mind the solution to terrorism is self-evident: terrorists need to be killed, and Muslims kept out of the country.

Before Trump

During the first fifteen years of the War on Terror,[11] Presidents George W. Bush and Barack Obama pursued counter-terrorism approaches that reflected their (very different) worldviews and perceptions of the threat. But they used many of the same methods and types of operations, and shared convictions that are fundamentally at odds with those of Donald Trump.

When George W. Bush launched the War on Terror, the United States was reeling from the 9/11 attacks. He decided to mobilise all instruments of national power for a wide-ranging campaign against al-Qaeda, the jihadist movement, and—ultimately—terrorism itself.[12] At one level, this involved an aggressive campaign against terrorist networks and their supporters, starting with the Taliban government in Afghanistan, which had hosted al-Qaeda and refused to hand over the group's leader, Osama bin Laden. Bush re-organised homeland security and intelligence, tightened border controls, and poured hundreds of billions of dollars into surveillance and the military. Not least, he authorised the creation of "black sites" and the prison camp in Guantanamo, where suspects were detained without trial and subject to "enhanced interrogation techniques", such as waterboarding.[13]

Bush also pursued an ambitious political agenda. Having identified "tyranny" as the principal cause of terrorism,[14] he set out to overthrow hostile dictators and spread America-friendly democracies across the Middle East. This is where he got stuck. In Iraq—the first of several countries he wanted to liberate—the toppling of Saddam Hussein was followed by civil war, years of "occupation", and open hostility to American-style "regime change". With, at times, more than 150,000 American troops deployed in the heart of the Middle East, the war not only diverted America's attention and drained its resources, but also provided jihadist groups—including the predecessors of Islamic State—with a new cause and battlefront.

Barack Obama entered office in 2009 as a fierce critic of the War on Terror. In his view, the Iraq War and the brutal tactics that Bush had used in the name of making America safer, had—in fact—created more terrorists. Instead of being liberators, Americans had come to be seen as occupiers and oppressors. Obama promised to end the foreign wars and increase efforts to counter terrorism by working "with and through" foreign partners.[15] He wanted to convey a humbler, less aggressive image of America, avoid human rights violations, and actively reach out to Muslims. Importantly, he stopped using the expression "War on Terror", discarded the idea of defeating terrorism as a whole, and focused on the group that had attacked America. His National Security Strategy from 2010 stated: "We are at war with a specific network, al-Qaeda, and its terrorist affiliates who support efforts to attack the United States".[16]

As it turned out, President Obama maintained virtually all of the laws and covert programmes that had been authorised during the Bush years. He failed to close Guantanamo, increased the number of drone strikes, and helped launch military campaigns in Libya and Mali.[17] The basic operational framework—intelligence cooperation, working through foreign partners, domestic prosecutions, and targeted killings—was identical to the counter-terrorism approach during Bush's second term, when Obama's predecessor had dropped the policy of regime change and closed down the black sites.[18] As former officials Robert Malley and Stephen Pomper confessed, "We stopped calling it a global war on terror, [but] in many respects we continued conducting the campaign [as] if it were one".[19]

The narrower focus on al-Qaeda enabled the systematic targeting of the group's leadership in the tribal areas of Pakistan, as well as the killing of bin Laden and one of its most influential propagandists, Anwar al-Awlaki. But it may have led Obama to underestimate the rise of Islamic State. By the end of his first term, he seemed convinced that al-Qaeda was defeated, and that the peaceful revolutions of the Arab Spring had brought in a "new wave [of freedom and dignity]" in which terrorism was "old news".[20] He clung to this narrative well into his second term, when Islamic State was becoming bigger and stronger and, eventually, took over large parts of Syria and Iraq. In January 2014, he compared the group to an amateur sports team, commenting that "if a [Junior Varsity] team puts on Lakers uniforms, that doesn't make them Kobe

Bryant".[21] It was only in August of that year that he fully acknowledged the threat and started assembling a global coalition to defeat the group.

Despite their differences in rhetoric and strategy, Bush and Obama—though not necessarily every member of their administrations—represented a powerful mainstream consensus on "American values" and America's role in the world, which informed their understanding of terrorism and how it should be fought. Though it was necessary to kill or capture terrorists, they believed that terrorism could not be resolved through military or "kinetic" means alone, and that countering it involved addressing the political, social and economic conditions that made people susceptible to extremist ideologies.[22] They agreed that America had to remain an open, outward-looking, and globally engaged society, as terrorists would be able to "cross the most defended borders".[23] And they subscribed to the idea of America as a multi-cultural "nation of immigrants", which people from different backgrounds, religions and ethnicities could become part of. Not least, they refrained from linking terrorism with Islam, stressing that Islam was a "religion of peace",[24] and that America was not at war with the world's 1.5 billion Muslims.[25]

Trump holds none of these convictions. He is infatuated with military power, and believes that it can be used bluntly and for its own sake. He is also sceptical of foreign commitments, and has no interest in addressing the underlying causes or conflicts. And he has come to understand the rise of jihadist terrorism as part of a civilizational conflict between America and Islam.

Trump's ideas on terrorism are not only different from Obama's, as one would expect, but represent a radical break with the first fifteen years of the War on Terror as a whole. Their closest historical inspiration is what the historian Walter Russell Mead has called the "Jacksonian tradition",[26] a nationalist and hawkish yet inward-looking strain of American politics that is named after Andrew Jackson—a former President (1829–37) whom Trump has referred to as an inspiration.[27]

THE TRUMP DOCTRINE

Killing Terrorists

The starting point for understanding Trump's doctrine is his long-standing hostility towards foreign commitments. Unlike Bush and Obama, he is not an "internationalist" who believes that America has a special role in protecting the international order or maintaining international institutions. In Trump's view, there are few—if any—advantages that America has gained from doing so. As early as 1987, when he briefly—and for the first time—considered running for President, he took out full-page advertisements in which he complained about foreign countries making "huge profits" while America was protecting their access to international trade routes. He demanded: "Make Japan, Saudi Arabia, and others pay… 'Tax' these wealthy nations, not America".[28] Nearly thirty years later, he applied the same principle to countering terrorism. In early 2016, he told foreign policy experts that America should always help countries that are "threatened by the rise of radical Islam", but added: "This has to be a two-way street. They must also be good to us".[29]

Not surprisingly, Trump has been sceptical of ideas like "nation-building" or "democracy promotion" through which other Presidents have attempted to remake the world in America's image.[30] Though he briefly—and opportunistically—supported the Iraq War, he quickly concluded that the whole venture was "a mess",[31] and that military operations which had objectives other than pursuing America's immediate interests were doomed to fail. In August 2004, he gave a scathing assessment of Bush and his policy of "regime change":

> Does anybody really believe that Iraq is going to be a wonderful democracy where people are going to run down to the voting box and gently put in their ballot, and the winner is happily going to step up to lead the country? C'mon. Two minutes after we leave, there's going to be a revolution, and the meanest, toughest, smartest, most vicious guy will take over.[32]

Throughout the 2016 election campaign, Trump described the Iraq war and its aftermath as a disaster.[33] The entire

Middle East, he later said, was a "troubled place", where no amount of American effort or commitment could guarantee a positive outcome.[34]

Yet Trump is no pacifist.[35] Like the Jacksonians, Trump believes that enemies need to be crushed, and that military power is the rawest, most immediate expression of American strength.[36] With few exceptions,[37] he has supported American wars and interventions, as long as their purpose was clear and they involved no major military, political or financial commitments. This has also guided his thinking about terrorism. Other than his views on Islam and immigration (see below), he has never articulated a theory on how people become radicalised, or shown any interest in the conflicts or underlying issues that have empowered jihadist groups. His ideas on fighting terrorism are almost entirely coercive, and typically revolve around killing terrorists and "showing strength", which he believes is the only way of gaining an opponent's respect.[38] The academic Stephen Walt has described this aspect of Trump's doctrine as "Cheneyism"—a reference to the often "crude and bellicose" views of Bush's Vice-President, Dick Cheney.[39]

One of the core elements of Trump's doctrine has been military aggression. In the years following the September 11 attacks, he routinely called on Bush to be tougher and more decisive: "Whatever happened to [General] Douglas McArthur", he asked in 2003, "He would go and attack. He wouldn't talk".[40] Twelve years later, he applied the same criticism to Obama. According to Trump, the conflict with Islamic State required a quick "military solution", which the President was failing to deliver.[41] In November 2015, he claimed that "we are not bombing", despite American forces having bombed the group's territory for over a year.[42] Throughout the election campaign, he rarely mentioned the need for a political settlement in Syria and Iraq, and never expressed any concern about "collateral damage".[43] Instead, he constantly demanded that the military be deployed more forcefully. In Trump's mind, "bombing the shit out of them"[44] was not the first stage of a more sophisticated plan—it *was* the plan: "You should be killing people", he reportedly told his generals in a meeting about Afghanistan, "You don't need a strategy to kill people".[45]

Another theme has been the empowerment of autocrats. While Bush and Obama believed that oppression and the absence of freedom had allowed extremist movements to thrive, and that democracy and open societies were the answer, Trump drew the opposite conclusion. In his view, democracy promotion in "troubled" regions like the Middle East, Africa, or parts of Central Asia had produced instability and weak governments, making it easier for terrorist groups to emerge. According to this logic, "strong leaders", who curtailed freedoms and suppressed dissent, were not part of the problem, as Bush and Obama believed, but part of the solution: Muhammar Qaddafi, the Libyan dictator, was "really bad", "but at least [he] killed terrorists";[46] Saddam Hussein may have been a tyrant, but he "killed terrorists like nobody";[47] the Syrian ruler, Bashar Assad, was great at "killing ISIS".[48] From Trump's perspective, it was precisely because they were so ruthless that they deserved America's support.

The most striking element of Trump's doctrine has been his enthusiastic support for torture. Unlike Obama, who opposed torture as a matter of principle, and Bush, who defended it as a last resort, Trump embraces torture as a form of "payback" and punishment.[49] Echoing Jacksonian notions of honour,[50] he believes that enemies only deserve as much respect as they are willing to show, and that groups like Islamic State, which have killed and tortured Americans, should be given the same treatment. What motivates Trump, in other words, is not the opportunity to obtain information, but seeing America's enemies humiliated. Terrorists, he told supporters in late 2015, should be waterboarded not because "it works", but because "they deserve it".[51] More than anything, this illustrates how Trump's thinking has been rooted in the notion of "an eye for an eye".

BLUSTER

Keeping Muslims Out

While Trump's belligerence and hostility towards foreign commitments are long-established, his views on Islam and immigration are more recent. In the immediate aftermath of the September 11 attacks, Trump talked about "being tough" on terrorism, and repeatedly blamed President Bush for failing to bring its perpetrators to justice, but never once mentioned their religion, or made any connection between Islam and terrorism.[52] When he criticised Saudi Arabia, it was because of its reliance on America's protection rather than the country's promotion of its ultra-conservative form of Islam or the fact that most of the hijackers on September 11 were Saudi nationals.[53] At no point before 2011 did he cast suspicions on American Muslims, or call for travel or immigration bans based on people's faith or country of origin. If anything, he refused to engage in the Islamophobic rhetoric which had become commonplace among conservative Republicans.

This changed when Trump became involved in the so-called "birther movement"[54] and started associating with Stephen Bannon, the editor of the *Breitbart* news website.[55] The first time Trump publicly spoke out against Islam and immigration was in an interview with Fox News in March 2011. Asked about immigration, he complained that the Mexican border was wide open, and that people were coming in, "selling drugs [and] killing people all over the place".[56] The solution, he said, was to shut it down completely: "You either have a line and a boundary or you don't".[57]

His views on Islam were equally strident. While *some* Muslims were "fabulous people", he said:

> There is something out there that brings a level of hostility that I have never seen in any religion. I mean, you can say what you want about the Koran. You can say what you want, but there's something there. There is tremendous hatred and tremendous hatred of us. I look at Iraq… They hate us. They hate us.[58]

When asked whether he thought there was a "Muslim problem [in the world today]", he responded: "Absolutely. I don't notice Swedish people knocking down the World Trade Center".[59]

Far from being random, the ideas that Trump was beginning to articulate were associated with a movement that later came to be known as Alternative Right. While the academic George Hawley defined the alt-right as essentially racist,[60] others, such as the journalist David Neiwert, viewed it in broader terms, accommodating a wide range of mostly young, internet-savvy conservatives whose political views were ultra-nationalist, anti-establishment, anti-political correctness, anti-immigration, and anti-Islam.[61] What alt-right supporters shared was a focus on preserving America's "European identity", which they believed was under assault by the political and intellectual establishment—which they referred to as "cultural Marxists"—and liberal immigration policies, which they regarded as every bit as insidious and deadly in their political and cultural impact as foreign "invasions".[62]

While not all of the alt-right's ideas were openly racist, it easily accommodated those that were.[63] The deliberately vague language by people like Bannon and his *Breitbart* website—whom Hawley described as "alt-lite"[64]—made it possible to bypass complex and potentially divisive issues such as race in order to unite as many factions of the extreme right as possible. For example, by talking about "culture" and "identity" instead of "race", Trump was able to describe groups that were not white and/or Christian as undesirable without referencing their ethnicity or colour of skin. At the same time, *actual* racists such as the former Ku Klux Klan leader David Duke understood perfectly well that concepts like "culture" were (more or less) compatible with their own, explicitly racist interpretations of who should be American. (Duke has frequently used "white" and "European", as well as "race" and "culture", interchangeably.)[65]

The most widely known expression of this ambiguity was "America First", Trump's campaign slogan, which has been used by the Ku Klux Klan and other white supremacist groups since the late nineteenth century.[66] While Duke immediately recognised the historical connotations of the slogan and welcomed its adoption by Trump,[67] Trump dismissed the idea that he was appeasing racists. When he was challenged about its origins, he said: "I don't care".[68]

The resulting doctrine—be it "alt-right" or "alt-lite"—not only made no effort to distinguish Islam from terrorism, but deliberately conflated the two. Since his 2011 interview on Fox News, the only times Trump has talked about Islam were in the context of terrorism, and the only occasions when he has discussed terrorism have been in relation to "Islamic" terrorism. When doing so, he consistently portrayed Islam as a monolithic belief system that was alien and hostile to the American way of life. While occasionally walking back his own statements ("I love the Muslims"),[69] the vast majority of his comments echoed the views of Bannon and the alt-right. During the election campaign, he "recycled" his line about the September 11 attackers "not being Swedes",[70] frequently talked about "the Muslim problem",[71] and repeated the exact words he had used in 2011, saying: "I think Islam hates us. There's something there... There's a tremendous hatred of us".[72]

A closely related element of Trump's rhetoric has been the coupling of terrorism and immigration. Since 2011, he has consistently argued that terrorist attacks within the United States were "caused" by immigration, and that America would be safer if no more immigrants entered the country. He specifically singled out Muslim immigration, which he said should be suspended "until [we] figure out what is going on".[73] In doing so, his definition of "immigrant" appeared to be loose: he often failed to distinguish between legal and illegal immigrants, and repeatedly confused "recent arrivals"—including refugees and naturalised citizens—with second generation Americans, who had been born and bred in the United States (see Chapter 3). For Trump, anyone with a non-"European" background could potentially be an "immigrant" and—therefore—a terrorist.

In summary, Trump's doctrine was traditionally Jacksonian in relation to the use of force and military aggression, the reluctance to engage with the world, its generalised suspicion of outsiders, and the narrow, inward-looking conception of America that it promoted.[74] Yet it also reflected more recent trends and currents, especially the so-called alt-right, whose emphasis on preserving "identity" accommodated openly racist views. The strongest indicator of his nativism were Trump's views on Islam, which he came to believe was dangerous, un-American, and needed to be kept out of the country—be it by building walls, banning Muslims, or suspending refugee programmes. Unlike Bush and Obama, who regarded Muslim Americans as "assets" and described them as "valued parts of the American family",[75] Trump regarded them as disloyal and potentially dangerous. In this respect, his views were the exact opposite of the mainstream consensus on religious neutrality and America as a "nation of immigrants" that permeated mainstream policy circles in Washington DC.

2

THE CAMPAIGN

When Donald Trump launched his presidential campaign, the jihadist threat, which many believed had been subdued by the time of the 2012 election, seemed stronger and more threatening than ever. The reason was a group which few had taken seriously just a few years earlier: Islamic State, which had split from al-Qaeda in 2013–14,[1] and quickly established itself as a major player in the civil wars in Syria and Iraq. Within months, it captured large parts of eastern Syria and Iraq's north-eastern provinces, flying its flag from town halls and mosques on both sides of the border. At its peak, the territory it controlled was the size of Great Britain[2] and had a population of 8–10 million. No jihadist group had ever accomplished anything on this scale.[3]

From the very beginning, Islamic State was more than just a local or regional phenomenon. It projected its "brand" of ultra-violent jihadism across the internet, with tens of thousands of social media accounts, feature-length videos, and magazines in every conceivable language.[4] It also recruited more than 30,000 foreigners—so-called "foreign fighters"—who had left their home countries in order to become part of the group's jihadist "utopia".[5] Not least, it proclaimed a Caliphate—an Islamic empire—which effectively declared war on the entire world. Standing at the pulpit of the Great Mosque of Mosul on 4 July 2014, its leader, Abu Bakr al-Baghdadi, told supporters that the group was "remaining and expanding", that every righteous Muslim in every part of the world had to "obey" his orders, and that all other Islamic states, authorities, and institutions were null and void. In this war, he later added, the Caliphate was leading "the people of faith against the people of disbelief".[6]

By early 2015, Islamic State's advance in the Middle East had been stopped. Despite this, people in America and Western Europe felt that the group was getting stronger and physically closer. One of the reasons was the migration of more than a million (mostly) young Muslim men from the countries in which Islamic State was active to the West. While the vast majority were genuine refugees, they also included a small number of Islamic State supporters, who had taken advantage of the chaotic situation in order to smuggle themselves into Europe.[7]

Another factor was the increasing number of terrorist attacks in the West. Islamic State's online propaganda had promoted the idea that every target in a Western country was legitimate, and that even the simplest tactics—using knives or cars, for example—could produce stunning effects. The result was what came to be seen as be an unrelenting series of assaults, with improvised stabbings in small towns as well as multiple, coordinated attacks in major cities like Paris and Brussels. According to Europol, the European police agency, 2015 and 2016 were the worst years for jihadist attacks in Europe in over a decade.[8] In America, the group claimed responsibility for shootings in San Bernardino, California, and Orlando, Florida—the two deadliest jihadist attacks in the United States since September 11, 2001.[9]

It is easy to understand, therefore, why terrorism and immigration became major issues in the election campaign. Beginning with the primaries, practically every townhall event featured questions about Islamic State. The topic was particularly prominent among Republicans, who have traditionally been more concerned about terrorism, more hostile towards Islam and immigration, and more likely to favour "tough" solutions than Americans as a whole.[10]

For Trump, this represented an advantage, because his core message—that terrorists had to be killed, and Muslims kept out of the country—seemed relevant and resonated strongly. Despite having no political experience or specific programme, Trump consistently beat his Republican rivals in polls on who was best at defending the country against terrorism.[11] Indeed, during the general election period, when conventional political wisdom would have dictated moderating his positions and "pivoting towards the centre",[12] Trump's rhetoric not only remained unchanged, but escalated.

As this chapter will show, the election campaign represented the clearest, most radicalised articulation of Trump's doctrine. It was driven by an electoral strategy that required Trump to constantly up his own ante in order to attract attention and mobilise the narrow segment of voters to whom his message appealed. This involved dropping the distinction between Muslims and terrorists, depicting Muslim Americans as "enemies within", incorporating the threat from (Islamic) terrorism into a grand narrative on the dangers of immigration, and pledging to restore "respect" for America.

Outrage

From the outset, Trump's campaign was different from those of his competitors. Unlike his rivals, he had never been part of any political "machine" and had no institutional support from within the Republican party. This meant that no one could tell him what to do, and that, for most of his campaign, he had to pay no attention to Republican stakeholders, consultants, policy advisors, or mega-donors. In other words, he could say whatever he wanted—or, indeed, whatever he thought would dominate a news cycle, or create attention on social media. This helps explain how "outrage" became the defining principle of Trump's campaign, and why his best—and only—chance of winning the election was to mobilise a comparatively narrow segment of white, mostly working class, conservative voters in rural areas and the Midwest.

At a deeper, more structural level, Trump's rise was connected to the changing demographics of America. For years, white, ethnic "Europeans" had been declining as a share of the population, while the percentage of Latinos and other non-European immigrant groups was increasing. Republican leaders understood that a party which failed to appeal to those "new Americans" would find it increasingly hard to win majorities. In 2004, George W. Bush was the first Republican President to engage in systematic outreach, and won 44 per cent of the Latino vote—more than any other Republican presidential candidate before or after him.[13] The turning point came in 2012, when Mitt Romney lost to Obama. The party's so-called "autopsy", a 100-page report commissioned by the party's then Chairman Reince Priebus, concluded that Romney's negative stance on immigration had cost him the election. Its main recommendations were for the party to be champions of "immigration reform", avoid divisive rhetoric, and project a more balanced, welcoming image to minorities.[14] By 2015, it had become a "quasi-religious belief" among the party's establishment that its "existing demographic base could not stretch far enough to encompass a winning coalition", and that its next presidential candidate had to be someone who was seen as "inclusive".[15]

Trump was on the opposite journey. While he used to be popular with Latino and African-American audiences at the time of his television show, *The Apprentice*, which frequently featured minority contestants in positive, ambitious roles,[16] this started changing when he embraced the "birther" conspiracy, which many Americans considered a racist slur. During the early 2010s, Trump gradually transformed into a hard-right populist whose main supporters were on the fringes of the Republican party. Instead of projecting the idea of a multicultural, changing America in which people from different races and backgrounds had equal opportunities to achieve the American Dream—which, in Trump's case, meant "getting rich"—his core message became one that primarily appealed to those who were overwhelmed by the economic and cultural change they experienced, felt abandoned by the elites, and believed they had nothing to gain from the more diverse, more multi-cultural America that shows like *The Apprentice* were seeking to promote.[17]

Trump quickly identified what seemed like their principal concern. One of his longest serving aides, Sam Nunberg, recalled that Twitter became Trump's "focus group", and that immigration was clearly—and by far—the biggest issue: "Every time Trump tweeted against amnesty [for illegal immigrants] in 2013, 2014, he would get hundreds and hundreds of retweets".[18] The people who got fired up by this message, and who believed that Trump would somehow "bring back the jobs" or reverse the latest wave of immigration,[19] were not radically different from Republican voters as a whole: in the end, more than 90 per cent of voters who defined themselves as Republican voted for Trump.[20] But, as various studies have shown, they tended to be slightly older, slightly less educated, and more likely to be based in rural areas and Midwestern states—the so-called "Rust Belt"—which had suffered from structural change and the decline of traditional industries.[21] They were also more hostile towards "political correctness" and strongly opposed to what the political scientist Matt Grossmanm described as "group-based claims of structural disadvantage"; in other words, the idea that white men engaged in racism and discrimination.[22]

Taken together, they did not constitute a majority of the American electorate—after all, Clinton won the popular vote by nearly 3 million votes—but were heavily located in "battleground states" and more likely to turn up at the polls than Clinton's supporters. Contrary to what Trump has claimed, his victory was neither decisive nor "crushing", but with small majorities in several large (and previously Democratic) states such as Michigan, Wisconsin, Ohio, and Pennsylvania, he gained just enough votes in the Electoral College to get elected.

Strategy

Trump's media strategy was revolutionary by the standards of presidential campaigns. Yet, for him, it was—more or less—what he had been doing for years. As a result of *The Apprentice*, he had become a national celebrity whose name recognition went far beyond New York or the people who were interested in his colourful private life. According to the historian Victor Davis Hanson, the show helped him establish his political brand:

> Each week, he fired the incompetent. He rewarded the supposedly more hard-working, talented and thus deserving—instantaneously, without appeal, filibusters, motions, votes, or bureaucratic consensus. For a country sick of Washington gridlock and stasis, the idea of a firer in chief seemed intriguing.[23]

Trump had also built up a vast following on social media—with more than seven million "fans" on Twitter and Facebook[24]—and become a regular feature in the "parallel universe" of right-wing talk radio and websites,[25] which echoed his political views and suited his "hyper-aggressive" style.[26]

His campaign consisted of the same elements, albeit on a bigger scale. In the run-up to the election, his social media presence grew from seven to nearly thirty million followers, and practically every tweet he posted created an avalanche of news stories and reporting in other media. The alt-right channelled its online networks into promoting Trump's latest stunts, recognising that he was an "icebreaker" who "violated conventions [and] helped normalise nativist narratives".[27] Most importantly, he came to dominate the election coverage on cable news. Whenever he staged one of his "mega-rallies", Fox News and CNN broadcast his entire speeches, followed by several hours in which clips of the event were replayed and debated. In many instances, the only way for his rivals to get airtime was by responding to something Trump had said or proposed.

From Trump's perspective, the advantage of this strategy was clear: it capitalised on his name recognition and required virtually no institutional support, which meant that no one in the party had any influence over him. Crucially, it was also very cheap. While his competitors spent millions of dollars on commercials, Trump received an estimated five billion dollars' worth of free media—more than nearly all of his competitors combined.[28]

Ultimately, the reason his strategy worked was because its was driven by outrage, and because the channels through which he communicated—especially social media—were ideally suited to amplifying it.[29] "If I was presidential", he told supporters at one of his rallies, "only twenty per cent of you would be here. And it would be boring as hell".[30] Yet, it also meant that pivoting towards the centre was not an option. The only way Trump stood a chance of maintaining an advantage over his better organised, better funded rivals was by feeding his voters' rage.[31] Bannon summed it up perfectly: "[Our campaign] was pure anger. Anger and fear is what gets people to the polls".[32]

Enemies Within

One of the issues that was guaranteed to rile up Trump's "base" was Islam. Throughout the campaign, Trump not only linked Islam with terrorism, but consistently portrayed it as a hateful ideology whose followers were implacably opposed to the American way of life. More so than before the campaign, he focused on Muslim Americans, suggesting that they were complicit in jihadist terrorism and could not be trusted to be loyal to their country. In Trump's rhetoric, they were an "outgroup"[33]—people who had no place in the American narrative, except as enemies.

In this respect, Trump's rhetoric was the exact opposite of Obama's. His predecessor rarely mentioned Islam in discussions about terrorism, and refused to identify groups like al-Qaeda and Islamic State by labels such as "Islamist", "Islamically inspired", or "jihadist". He was also careful never to question the loyalty of Muslim Americans, or blame them for violence that jihadist groups had perpetrated in their religion's name. In Obama's view, terrorism had nothing to do with religion, and jihadist groups' claims to represent Islam were false and flawed. He believed that, by associating terrorists' "warped ideologies"[34] with Islam, Western policymakers were not just insulting one of the world's great religions, but also falling into the terrorists' trap, as they granted them legitimacy and embraced their narrative of civilizational conflict. In his own words: "[Terrorists] are not religious leaders—they're terrorists. And we are not at war with Islam. We are at war with people who have perverted Islam".[35]

Long before Trump declared his candidacy, Obama's refusal to discuss—or even mention—Islam in relation to jihadist terrorism had attracted criticism, including from fellow liberals.[36] The main argument was that his position was factually questionable, and that denying the Islamic nature of jihadism was "disempowering" mainstream Muslims. As many experts have argued, while the interpretations of groups like al-Qaeda and Islamic State did not follow any of the established schools of Islamic theology, they were undeniably rooted in Islamic texts, operated with Islamic concepts, and followed Islamic rituals.[37] Though they clearly did not "represent Islam", or the world's 1.5 billion Muslims, it was more difficult to demonstrate that they were not "Islamic"— especially for someone like Obama, who was not a Muslim and had no theological authority. If anything, the critics argued, Obama's stance had discouraged mainstream Muslims from confronting the jihadists' religious narratives, and created a vacuum of (nuanced) discussion.[38]

Trump was not alone, therefore, in calling for "radical Islam" to be "named" and talked about. The idea that "you can't defeat an enemy you can't name" was a standard line in the stump speeches of practically every Republican primary candidate. Even Clinton started referring to "violent Islamism" and "jihadist terrorism" during the general election. Yet, no one did so with as much verve and enthusiasm as Trump. For Trump, leading chants of "radical Islamic terrorism" was not just a stunt, or something that was meant to make Muslims look bad, but the calculated breaking of a (perceived) taboo. As much as it was directed against Muslims, it targeted Obama and the "culture of political correctness", which he claimed had prevented people from speaking the truth: "With Hillary and Obama, the terrorist attacks will only get worse", one of his tweets on the subject read, "Politically correct fools, won't even call it what it is—RADICAL ISLAM".[39]

Moreover, with the possible exception of Ted Cruz, Trump was the only candidate who made virtually no distinction between "radical Islam" and whatever he might have thought was "mainstream" Islam. This echoed the ideas of advisors like Walid Phares who were close to—or officially associated with—the Center for Security Policy (see Chapter 3).[40] They believed that Islam had a single—and unchanging—essence, that the Quran had to be read (more or less) literally, and that those who believed in the Islamic faith—and practised it correctly—were bound to be hostile towards the West. It was impossible, in their view, to reconcile belief in an intolerant, supremacist "ideology"—Islam—with being a good citizen of a secular democracy. Islamic State, they insisted, was not an outlier, but the "true face" of Islam.[41] Strictly speaking, it made no sense, therefore, to single out "radical Islam". The real problem—the real "enemy"—was not "radical Islam", but Islam.

Indeed, in December 2015, the Center for Security Policy published a (widely debunked)[42] poll, which claimed that a quarter of American Muslims supported terrorist attacks against their own country, and that more than half wanted to see the Constitution being replaced with "sharia law". The Trump campaign repeatedly cited these figures to justify the "Muslim travel ban",[43] and Trump referred to them on several occasions: "Large portions of a group of people, Islam, large portions want to use very, very harsh means", he said in one of the television debates, "A lot of them [hate us]. I mean a lot of them".[44]

Muslim Americans

From saying that "real" Islam was, in fact, "radical" and there-fore incompatible with Western democracy, it was only a small step to questioning the loyalty, patriotism and "Americanness" of American Muslims. Unlike all other candidates, Trump did so systematically and consistently. Instead of drawing a clear line between jihadist terrorists and the 2.5 million law-abiding American Muslims, as Bush and Obama had done, Trump portrayed American Muslims as a "fifth column" who could not be trusted to support their country.[45] As Farah Pandith, who served in senior positions in the Bush and Obama administrations, told me:

> [Trump] has sown a very particular story together that abso-lutely insists that there is a right kind of American. And for him, being a Muslim is not a way to also be an American, even though Islam… has been part of this country since the very beginning.[46]

During the campaign, Trump effectively portrayed Muslim Americans as "enemies within". One of the earliest examples was Trump's claim that "thousands" of Arab Americans had celebrated the September 11 attacks. Speaking at a rally in late November 2015, he said:

> I watched when the World Trade Center came tumbling down. And I watched in Jersey City, New Jersey, where thousands and thousands of people were cheering as that building was coming down. Thousands of people were cheering.[47]

When the mayor of Jersey City and local police chiefs made it clear that none of this had happened, Trump was defiant: "It did happen. I saw it. It was… on television. I saw it".[48] He pointed out that Jersey City had a "large Arab population", and that local officials were denying the story because "it might not be politically correct… to talk about it".[49] Yet, there was no evidence of the television reports he had mentioned, and even though a handful of retired police officers later came forward saying that they had witnessed "Arabs" celebrating, this had happened in different locations and involved not thousands but "dozens of people".[50] In fact, many surveys have shown that Muslim Americans' overwhelming reaction to the attacks was not joy but fear of a backlash.[51]

Following the terrorist attack in San Bernardino on 2 December 2015, which involved a married Muslim couple shooting dead fourteen health care workers at a Christmas party, Trump made similar claims. Speaking at a townhall event, he alleged that local Muslims had known about the attack and done nothing to stop it:

> In San Bernardino, people knew what was going on… They had bombs on the floor. Many people saw this, many, many people. Muslims living with them, in the same area. They saw that house. They saw that.[52]

Again, there was no evidence for this allegation, except from an unnamed source who had heard something from a local resident, who—in turn—had been told by someone else.[53] None of the law enforcement agencies that investigated the attack uncovered any foreknowledge, yet Trump not only continued talking about "bombs on the floor", but widened his attack to implicate Muslims as a whole. At a rally later that month, he said:

> We have Muslims—they're wonderful… But there's something going on there. They have to turn in… these people in California. People knew [that the male attacker] had bombs all over the floor, people knew it, why didn't they turn him in? … Because it's their culture, they're around each other, they knew each other.[54]

Such remarks were typically tied to proposals which targeted American Muslims because of their faith, such as the idea of a "Muslim registry",[55] or the "surveillance of mosques".[56] "We're having problems with the Muslims", he said on one (of many) occasions, "You have to deal with the mosques, whether you like it or not".[57]

The most brazen attempt at questioning the loyalty of American Muslims was Trump's smearing of the "Gold Star" family of Army Captain Humayun Khan, who had died while serving in Iraq. Khan's parents, who had emigrated from Pakistan, delivered a speech at the Democratic Convention in July 2016, in which his father talked about the sacrifice of their son, and criticised Trump's proposal to ban immigration from majority Muslim countries. In one of the campaign's most memorable moments, he stood next to his wife, waving a copy of the Constitution and telling Trump that the "brave patriots" who were buried at Arlington Cemetery "were of all faiths, genders, and ethnicities".[58] When Trump responded, instead of talking about the family's loss, praising their patriotism, or addressing their criticism of his policies, he attacked the mother's silence, (falsely) implying that her husband—a practising Muslim—had not allowed her to speak: "If you look at his wife", he said, "she was standing there. She had nothing to say. She probably—maybe she wasn't allowed to have anything to say".[59]

"Snakes"

Although Trump talked about Islam and the threat of "radical Islamic terrorism" as topics in their own right, they formed part of a wider narrative about the dangers of immigration. According to Trump, in the same way that Muslim immigrants were causing terrorism, Latino immigrants were linked to crime. Throughout the election campaign, he portrayed both groups as immigrant "others" who could not be trusted, and whose cultures were fundamentally alien to the American way of life. Just like the alt-right, he called for an end to (non-European) immigration, and argued that the idea of a diverse, multi-cultural America was a dangerous myth.

That immigration became such a big issue in Trump's campaign was no surprise. In his June 2015 announcement speech, he said:

> When Mexico sends its people, they're sending people that have lots of problems, and they're bringing those problems with

[them]. They're bringing drugs. They're bringing crime. They're rapists. And some, I assume, are good people.[60]

This set the tone for the rest of his campaign. Instead of moderating his rhetoric, he stuck to the idea that, with few exceptions, Latinos were "bad" people, and that immigration was a grave physical and cultural threat to America. At practically every rally, he claimed that "killers and rapists [are] coming into this country", and that "immigrant crime" was soaring.[61] In many instances, he recounted the stories of victims—often young, attractive, white women—who had been raped or murdered by Latino immigrants, making it clear that this was a conflict between "us" and "them".

Unlike other Republican candidates, who were keen to stress that America was a "nation of immigrants" and that the only immigration they opposed was "illegal" immigration, Trump's definition of who was an immigrant often reverted to ethnicity. The clearest case was his confrontation with a federal judge who was presiding over a law suit against one of his companies. Trump called him a "hater", "very unfair" and "totally biased",[62] and asked for his dismissal because he "happens to be, we believe, Mexican".[63] The judge was not Mexican, of course, but descended from Mexican labourers who had emigrated to Indiana in 1946. He was born in the United States, the son of American citizens, and—in many ways—a prime example of the American Dream. While other candidates would have embraced his story, for Trump and his supporters, he was simply a foreigner.

Against the background of the European migration crisis, it became easy to make similar arguments about Muslims. Islamic State was the rhetorical "device" which enabled Trump to present Muslims as a threat, and argue that America's policy of accepting refugees from war-torn countries like Syria and Iraq was not just costly, but dangerous.[64] From saying that he was willing to accept "a small number" of refugees, who needed to undergo a process that he labelled "extreme vetting", his position shifted towards a ban on *all* refugees following the Paris attacks in November 2015.[65] One month later, the refugee ban became a "Muslim travel ban", with Trump announcing that, if elected, he would stop *all Muslims* from entering America until "we have figured out what the hell is going on".[66]

During the general election, his policy evolved again, this time towards restricting immigration from *countries* that were "tied to Islamic terror".[67] The common denominator, however, remained Islam and keeping Muslims out. Indeed, at the same time as "watering down" the "Muslim travel ban" by referring to countries rather than religion ("I'm [now] talking territory instead of Muslim"),[68] he framed the Orlando nightclub shooter, a native Floridian, as an immigrant, and falsely claimed that "hundreds of immigrants and children of immigrants" had been involved in terrorist attacks against the United States.[69] Not least, the original campaign pledge—including his full statement on "preventing Muslim immigration"—remained on his website until May 2017.[70]

Moreover, Trump increasingly portrayed the confrontation with Islamic State as a civilizational conflict, which involved not just a terrorist group threatening to kill Americans, but people from an alien culture trying to "conquer" the (Christian) West. "It's so dangerous", he told TIME magazine in December 2015:

> Paris is not Paris anymore. Not because of [the attacks]. Paris wasn't Paris before this event. They [the Muslim immigrants?] have taken over Paris and destroyed it. Wait till you see what happens to Germany. Okay. Wait till you see what happens to Germany.[71]

In his set-piece policy speech on "terrorism and immigration" in Youngstown, Ohio, in August 2016, he talked about "ISIS killers [invading] a Christian church", "Christians driven from their homes", and Islamic State "rounding up… the 'nation of the cross' in a campaign of genocide",[72] creating the impression that the conflict in Syria and Iraq was primarily one between Christians and Muslims. His rhetoric was the exact opposite of Obama's: instead of trying to separate terrorists from ordinary Muslims and downplay the extent to which the former represented the latter, Trump sought to conflate them.

Trump's most comprehensive policy statement did not come in a speech or declaration, but in the form of an obscure 1960s song, whose full lyrics he started reciting at campaign events from January 2016. In Trump's reading, "The Snake" was a metaphor for immigration, which sought to convey the idea that all immigrants were dangerous, and that even the seemingly most legitimate immigrant may, in the end, turn out to be a "killer". Many of his supporters knew it by heart.[73]

The implications were clear. Rather than embracing the idea of a "nation of immigrants"—a narrative that every other candidate shared and embraced—Trump regarded immigrants as a threat to the nation. Like the "Muslim travel ban" and "The Wall", "the Snake" expressed his determination to reverse the idea of multi-culturalism and radically transform the mainstream definition of America.

Respect

As well as attacking Islam and immigration, much of Trump's campaign rhetoric dealt with how he would defeat Islamic State. Against the background of a military campaign that was successful and sustainable but seemed excruciatingly slow (see Chapter 6), Trump positioned himself as the candidate who would defeat Islamic State faster and more conclusively than everyone else. He often criticised Obama for fighting a "politically correct war", which he claimed had empowered America's enemies,[74] and promised to stop interfering with the decisions of military leaders.[75] "ISIS will be gone if I'm elected president", he said in a foreign policy speech, "And they'll be gone… very, very quickly".[76]

He also frequently mentioned a "secret plan", which he said would "be decisive and quick, and it would be very beautiful".[77] The reason it was secret, he claimed, was to keep Islamic State in the dark and preserve the element of surprise ("you want to have a little bit of guess work for the enemy").[78] Yet, whenever he was asked to explain how a highly motivated and territorially entrenched enemy like Islamic State could be defeated within weeks, as he had repeatedly claimed,[79] most of his responses revolved around dropping more bombs in more places—in short, "knocking the hell out of ISIS".[80] In many regards, there-fore, his position was similar to that of other Republican candi-dates. (Cruz had promised to carpet bomb Islamic State "until the sand glows".)[81]

The most significant difference between Trump and his rivals was the emphasis he placed on restoring "respect". As he explained in several interviews, "being tough" was a way of getting an opponent's respect, and it was the absence of respect that had allowed Islamic State to be so brazen. "I don't think you're going to be successful [in fighting Islamic State] unless they respect you", he told a journalist, adding: "They have no respect for our president, and they have no respect for our country right now".[82] This was consistent with statements from before the campaign in which he had stressed values like "hon-our" and "respect" over international norms, conventions, and even the American government's own rules of engagement. It also offered a somewhat deeper, more philosophical justification for the ruthless—and frequently illegal—methods that he advo-cated in fighting Islamic State. In Trump's mind, if Islamic State had humiliated America by beheading its citizens and killing innocent people in places like San Bernardino and Orlando, America had to be equally strong and vicious. "They're chopping off heads. These are animals", he told his supporters, "You have to knock them off strong".[83]

It was this logic which produced an extraordinary list of pro-posals that sought to punish and humiliate Islamic State in return for what Trump's supporters perceived as the group's humiliation of America. They included the use of torture ("We're worried about waterboarding as our enemy, ISIS, is beheading people and burning people alive"), targeting terrorists' families ("When they say they don't care about their lives, you have to take out their families"), and even nuclear weapons ("[Let's assume] somebody hits us within ISIS—you wouldn't fight back with a nuke?").[84] While some of these ideas may have been "outbursts" that were meant to gain attention, they signalled that, unlike his rivals, he was not content with merely increasing the war's tempo and intensity. For Trump, fighting a war against a "lawless" enemy such as Islamic State required America to be bold and overwhelming. "[ISIS has] no respect for U.S.A. or our 'leader'", he tweeted, "If I win, it will be a very different story".[85]

The most graphic illustration was a story he repeatedly told at his rallies.[86] It recounted how John Pershing, a renowned American general, had allegedly dealt with Muslim rebels during the American-Philippine war at the turn of the twentieth century. According to Trump:

> They were having terrorism problems, just like we do, and [Pershing] caught 50 terrorists who did tremendous damage and killed many people. And he took the 50 terrorists, and he took 50 men and he dipped 50 bullets in pigs' blood—you heard that, right? He took 50 bullets, and he dipped them in pigs' blood.

> And he had his men load his rifles, and he lined up the 50 people, and they shot 49 of those people. And [to] the 50th person, he said: You go back to your people, and you tell them what happened. And for 25 years, there wasn't a problem. Okay? Twenty-five years, there wasn't a problem.[87]

In Trump's view, it did not matter that executing prisoners was a war crime, and that assaulting the religious beliefs of adversaries was the opposite of what America stood for. Nor was it important that the story was an urban myth, as no historian had ever found any evidence to support it.[88] By telling it, Trump conveyed the idea that he would make America strong and ruthless, and that no enemy would dare to challenge the country if he were President.

In line with his doctrine of "killing terrorists" and "keeping Muslims out", Trump presented a fundamentally different idea of countering terrorism than his electoral rivals. In its most radicalised version, he portrayed the confrontation with Islamic State as a civilizational conflict, which involved not just defeating a terrorist group, but classified Muslims as part of an immigrant "out-group", described Islam as fundamentally incompatible with the American way of life, and legitimised virtually any means of achieving victory. It was the kind of "nationalist and racialist demagoguery" that the historian Robert Paxton had identified as a precursor of fascism.[89]

3

POLICY AND PEOPLE

Donald Trump was not the first President to enter the White House with new ideas. Like Bush, Obama and virtually every other President before them, he came to Washington with a strong motivation to do things differently, only to find out that turning his ideas into political reality was more complicated than he expected. Many of the constraints he has encountered since taking office—Congress, the courts, public opinion, or the federal bureaucracy—were part of the constitutional checks and balances that apply to every President. Others, however, have been unique to him.

Only three days after his victory, Trump fired the head of his transition team, former New Jersey Governor Chris Christie, who had spent the previous six months preparing for a possible handover by recruiting 300 candidates for senior positions in the administration.[1] With Christie gone, Trump entered the transition period with virtually no preparation and hardly anyone to take over. According to the journalist Michael Lewis:

> On the morning after the election, the hundreds of [Obama officials] who had prepared to brief the incoming Trump administration sat waiting. A day became a week and a week became a month ... and no one showed up. The parking spots that had been set aside for Trump's people remained empty, and the briefing books were never opened. You could walk into almost any department of the U.S. government and hear peo-

ple asking the same question: where were these people who were meant to be running the place?[2]

The contrast with previous transitions could not have been starker. When Bush declared his candidacy in 1999, he was already one of the biggest names in Republican politics, and had secured the support of national security "veterans" from several Republican administrations, including Dick Cheney, who had served as Defense Secretary in the 1990s, and Donald Rumsfeld, a Defense Secretary in the 1970s. Obama started with a smaller group of advisers, but expanded into his party's establishment after defeating his Democratic rival, Hillary Clinton. By the time of his victory, Obama's national security team comprised what former CIA director Michael Hayden described as "a legion of seasoned Washington hands".[3] Like Bush, he was not just a successful candidate with personal ambition, a political vision and electoral appeal, but the leader of a government in waiting.

Trump, on the other hand, remained a complete outsider, who had never held public office and only joined the Republican party in 2012. Before announcing his candidacy in the summer of 2015, he had conducted no outreach, and had hardly ever travelled to important primary states like Iowa or New Hampshire. He had no relationships with important stakeholders, barely knew any of the key players in the Republican party, and had raised no money. Not least, he had little knowledge of policy, and—apparently—no interest in learning about it.[4] Many mainstream Republicans regarded his involvement in the birther conspiracy and his remorseless, often personal attacks on President Obama as "profoundly toxic".[5]

Well into the primary season, and despite leading in all opinion polls, much of the talk among "politicos" in Washington DC was not about a Trump presidency, but his campaign's inevitable failure.[6] Even as he became his party's nominee, large sections of the "policy elites" in his party, government, and the Washington think-tanks withheld their support, hoping that he would eventually lose.[7] When he did win the election, he might have become America's most famous person, but in terms of administrative power—the capacity to turn ideas into law or government action—he was weaker and more vulnerable than any President in recent history.

As this chapter will show, Trump had neither the policies nor the people to turn his doctrine into reality. Many of the decisions in his War on Terror were taken not by "true believers", who subscribed to his doctrine, but by career officials and mainstream Republicans—"the generals"—whose personal loyalty and commitment to his political ideas were limited.

Policy

Throughout the election campaign and the transition, officials across the federal bureaucracy scrambled to understand what exactly Trump wanted to do as President. Everyone had listened to his speeches and read his tweets, but no one knew what exactly those statements would mean in practice. As Hayden, who kept close contact with former colleagues, recalled:

> [Between the party conventions and election day,] we normally see massive policy teams turning out papers on a variety of issues. That didn't happen with the Trump campaign. Nada. Nothing…

> [During the transition, a senior intelligence official told me that] the incoming team was as weakly anchored on facts and on the artefacts of governance as any he had ever seen… It was some of the wackiest stuff… So ignorant of the institutions and processes of government, it seemed like the Wild West.[8]

Many of my interviewees confirmed this impression. One, a career official who served on the National Security Council during the transition, told me that, except for the slogans that Trump had used in his speeches, Trump's "people" came in with no clear agenda: "There was [no] sense of 'right, now we are in office, [here's] what we want to do and [here's] what… we want to do differently'". The result was that, for the time being, many counter-terrorism policies remained "on auto-pilot", with few immediate changes in policy or practice.[9]

To a large extent, this was Trump's own fault. Being a Jack-sonian populist, who favoured "simple solutions",[10] rejected elites and held intellectuals in contempt, Trump thought of "policy development" as overrated and unnecessary. Not only did he consider himself smarter than everyone else,[11] he believed that mastery of detail was secondary to the deal-making skills he had described in his 1987 book, *The Art of the Deal*.[12] In Trump's mind, the two million people across the Federal government could be run like his real estate business in New York:[13] "It's playing the game…", he reportedly said "I'm good at the game. Maybe I'm the best".[14]

Another reason was that most policy intellectuals and think-tanks in Washington DC disagreed with his doctrine, which challenged their beliefs on immigration and America's role in the world. The few policy institutes that sympathised with one part of it typically rejected the other. The libertarian think-tank CATO, for example, shared Trump's scepticism of foreign commitments, but disagreed with him on immigration, whereas Heritage, the conservative foundation, supported his stance on immigration, but disliked his views on American global leadership.[15] In short, there were no "Trumpian" think-tanks or policy intellectuals that would have helped translate his counter-terrorism doctrine into a viable programme for government. Nationalist populism did not (yet) have an intel-lectual "infrastructure" in Washington DC, and Trump had made no effort to build one.

Indeed, none of the organisations that have been credited with "inspiring" Trump's world view played a consistent or meaningful role in the process of policy development. Scholars at the small, California-based, Claremont Institute, for example, had long articulated "paleo-conservative" beliefs about culture, immigration, and the "tyranny" of political correctness. With their fluency in conservative political thought, they could have provided a coherent ideological framework for his ideas.[16] But

Claremont did not operate like a Washington think-tank, nor did it consider itself a "policy factory". Its principal mission was to promote education and stimulate intellectual discourse: "Policy battles are important", its President once said, "but they are not the most fundamental thing".[17] Many of its supporters had deep reservations about Trump, whom they regarded as a "buffoon" and a "fake conservative".[18] In fact, it was only in September 2016 that Michael Anton, one of its leading contributors (who later joined the National Security Council), came out with a less than enthusiastic endorsement. "Trump is worse than imperfect", he argued, "So what?"[19]

Bannon's *Breitbart* was the opposite. Its attitude was aggressive rather than scholarly, and its writers had no hesitations about backing Trump. Yet, like Claremont, *Breitbart* was of little use when it came to developing policy. While Bannon was able to articulate the broader, underlying ideas of the "alt-right", his website was not a "policy shop". Though it supplied Trump with news stories and snippets of "evidence" that he used in speeches,[20] no one at *Breitbart*'s office on Capitol Hill wrote policy papers or drafted executive orders. If anything, being exposed to *Breitbart* reinforced Trump's binary views and prevented him from considering the difficult trade-offs that were involved in running a vast bureaucracy.

The only exception was the far-right Center for Security Policy, whose work focused on Islam. In the early 2010s, it started promoting the idea that the highest levels of the Obama administration had been infiltrated by the Muslim Brotherhood. It also launched a nationwide campaign against the (alleged) proliferation of Sharia law in the United States, which resulted in referendums on the banning of "foreign laws" in several states.[21] Despite the outlandishness of many of its claims—in 2013, one of its associates alleged that CIA director John Brennan had "secretly converted to Islam"[22]—the Center continued having access to influential right-wing Republicans, and briefed several candidates during the 2015 primaries. While its director Frank Gaffney, a former official in the Reagan administration, initially signed up with Trump's rival Ted Cruz, some of his colleagues supported Trump.[23] In retrospect, there can be no doubt that the Center and several of its associates played an important role in shaping Trump's views on Islam, including some of the policies that he eventually adopted.[24]

People

The most tangible indicator of Trump's lack of "administrative capacity" has been his difficulty in filling the 4,000 or so politically appointed positions through which new Presidents impose their will—and political programme—on the federal bureaucracy. Two years into the Trump presidency, only half of the 700 "key positions" that required confirmation by the Senate had been filled—nearly 30 per cent less than during the Obama and Bush administrations.[25] At several national security agencies, the figure was as low as one third.[26] Meanwhile, staff turnover was higher than in any other recent administration. According to the Brookings Institution, more than half of the President's initial core team had resigned or been fired by the summer of 2018, with numerous positions left open for long periods of time or filled with other appointees, thereby creating vacancies elsewhere.[27]

While Trump claimed that many of his nominees were held up in the Senate for party political reasons, the far greater—and much more obvious—problem was that he did not have enough suitable candidates to begin with. When journalists started asking him for the names of people who influenced him on foreign and security policy in early 2016, he struggled to answer. "My primary consultant is myself", he replied in an interview, "I have a good instinct for this stuff".[28] Shortly afterwards, he presented a group of advisers, which he said would form the nucleus of his foreign policy team. Apart from Keith Kellogg, a retired general with a solid reputation in military operations, it included four individuals whom many national security experts had barely heard of. The better known ones were Walid Phares, a foreign policy analyst with hostile views on Islam,[29] and Joe Schmitz, a former mid-ranking appointee at the Department of Defense who had co-authored a controversial Center for Security Policy report.[30] The other two were Carter Page, an energy consultant with commercial interests in Russia, and George Papadopoulos, a twenty-nine year old former intern and freelance author. Even before it emerged that Page and Papadopoulos had improper contacts with Russian intelligence,[31] many Republicans thought of the group as "embarrassing", "quirky", and/or "third rate".[32]

What's more, by the summer of 2016, 172 of the country's most experienced foreign policy and security experts, as well as 75 former diplomats, had signed letters stating that they would under no circumstances serve in a Trump government.[33] These so-called "Never Trumpers" included large parts of the Republican foreign policy establishment, which any Republican President would have called upon to populate the senior ranks of their administration. On national security issues, this effectively left Trump with a combination of less prominent Republicans, who had no commitment to him or his political doctrine, as well as "true believers" and "know-nothings", who often turned out to be "wacky" and/or ineffective (see Table 1).

Table 1: Key Characteristics of Trump National Security Appointees

	Personal Loyalty	*Political Alignment*	*Administrative Competence*
Know-Nothings	+	~	−
True Believers	+	+	−
The Generals	−	~	+

Know-Nothings

Far from being limited to the early days of his campaign, "know-nothings"[34] have been appointed in all agencies and at all levels of the Trump administration. Instead of having relevant qualifications, they were typically connected to the Trump campaign as volunteers or through family members. They also included some television personalities (whom Trump had spotted while "watching the shows")[35] and several outright imposters.[36] Responsible for their recruitment was the Presidential Personnel Office, which—itself—was under-staffed and filled with campaign volunteers who had never worked in politics or human resources. (The person in charge of vetting senior nominees for the Department of Defense, for example, was a twenty-nine year old reservist, who had been arrested for assault and disorderly conduct, and lied about his education and employment history).[37]

The most powerful "know-nothing" has been Jared Kushner, a real estate developer from New Jersey who is married to Trump's daughter. Kushner had no government experience or background in diplomacy, intelligence, the military, or international affairs, and had repeatedly failed to obtain a "top security" clearance until Trump ordered his officials to give him one.[38] Yet, as a senior advisor to the President, he has assembled a vast portfolio of important, complex, and highly sensitive assignments, such as the United States' relationships with China, Mexico, and Saudi Arabia, as well as brokering peace between Israel and the Palestinians. The journalist Michael Wolff described him as "the chief work-around to institutional diplomacy", enabling foreigners with an interest in changing U.S. policy "to avoid the State Department, the foreign policy establishment, the intelligence community, and virtually every other normal diplomatic process or restraint".[39] Apart from personal loyalty, his only qualification for this role seemed to be the President's belief that he was a good negotiator: "He is a natural talent", Trump told a reporter, "everyone likes him".[40]

True Believers

The only reliably enthusiastic supporters of the President's doctrine were "true believers" who often found it difficult to work—and/or function—within the federal bureaucracy. Their undisputed leader was Bannon, the *Breitbart* editor who had first met Trump in 2011 and served as his campaign manager during the months leading up to election day. While Bannon thought of himself as a visionary, his knowledge of political theory was eclectic, and he spent little time considering how to translate his—often grandiose—ideas into practical policy.

Unlike James Mattis, the Defense Secretary, who was conservative in the sense of wanting to *preserve* things, Bannon saw himself as a revolutionary who believed that the only way of "saving America" was to break what he regarded as a broken system. According to Green:

> Bannon was a radical who aimed to aggressively transform politics, not just in the United States but across the globe… [He was] an outsider with no experience operating the levers of government, a man with a gift for making enemies, and someone whose habit it was to feud bitterly with those with whom he disagreed.[41]

By making him his "Chief Strategist", Trump gave Bannon a role that allowed him to float freely between different areas of interest and responsibility. It quickly became clear, however, that someone with his background and personality would never be able to adjust to the daily grind of government work. When he left the White House in the summer of 2017, even Trump had lost faith in him.

One of Bannon's "soul mates" was Michael Flynn, who had resigned as Director of the Defense Intelligence Agency (DIA) in 2014. Among colleagues, Flynn was seen as a brilliant officer with a difficult personality. Hayden described him as "aggressive, iconoclastic, intolerant of bureaucracy, and impatient with people and institutions".[42] As head of the DIA, other intelligence chiefs accused him of a "chaotic management style" and leaving the agency "in turmoil".[43] Flynn disputed these allegations, claiming he had been the victim of a political plot, and that Obama officials wanted to punish him for talking about the rise of Islamic State and "radical Islam".[44]

Within months of leaving government, Flynn teamed up with Bannon and *Breitbart*, where his views became "increasingly radicalized". He started speaking about the need to defend "European identity" and surrounded himself with alt-right activists.[45] Evidence of their influence could be found in a 2016 book in which he denounced political correctness, wrote about Islam as "an ideology", and proclaimed the existence of "an international alliance of evil countries and movements".[46] When he took up his position as Trump's National Security Advisor, he said he wanted to purge the entire system.[47] Few in the intelligence community shed any tears when he had to resign after just twenty-four days in his post.

Despite their short periods in office, Flynn and Bannon positioned many of their followers in security agencies across government. They became known as "Flynnstones"—"a motley crew of former military and intelligence operators, craven agitators and political operatives with no government experience".[48] Examples included Richard Higgins, the National Security Council's director for strategic planning, who accused the national security bureaucracy of being in cahoots with Islamic radicals (see Chapter 8);[49] Ezra Cohen-Watnick, Flynn's former assistant, who prolifically leaked information about so-called "Obama holdovers";[50] and Sebastian Gorka, a former *Breitbart* editor, who served as Deputy Assistant to the President and presented himself as Trump's leading counter-terrorism "strategist".[51] The only person in this category to have survived—and thrived—in government is Stephen Miller, a far-right activist and immigration hardliner, who became Trump's head of speechwriting and has successfully inserted himself into many policy discussions, especially on immigration and security (see Chapter 8).[52]

The Generals

Trump also appointed many mainstream Republicans who had not signed the "Never Trump" letters. Throughout this book, I refer to them as "generals", because many of them had backgrounds in the military and intelligence. Although most held conservative views, they did not necessarily share Trump's doctrine or respect him as an individual. (One of my interviewees, a deeply conservative Republican, described Trump as "a very strange man".)[53] Instead, their outlook was shaped by their own experiences in the War on Terror, and a strong—though largely apolitical—commitment to the nation, which sometimes involved "defending the country, to some extent, *from* the President".[54] Prominent examples included Dan Coats, whom Trump made Director of National Intelligence, and Tom Bossert, his first Homeland Security Advisor, as well as numerous actual generals, such as John Kelly, Trump's former Chief of Staff and Homeland Security Secretary, H.R. McMaster, Trump's first National Security Advisor, and James Mattis, the former Defense Secretary.[55]

Mattis was undoubtedly the most influential "general".[56] Although supportive of Trump in increasing the defence budget and loosening the restrictions that Obama had imposed on air strikes and other "kinetic" operations (see Chapter 5), he repeatedly refused to carry out Presidential orders that he considered reckless or irresponsible.[57] For nearly two years, he also prevented Trump from withdrawing troops from Syria and Afghanistan, which Trump had wanted to do from the start.[58] The most profound difference between the two men was in respect to international partnerships. In his resignation letter in December 2018, Mattis stressed how important it was to "advance international order" and "maintain the solidarity of our alliances." It concluded by saying that Trump "deserved" to have a Secretary of Defense whose views were "better aligned".[59]

"The generals", in turn, populated their bureaucracies with like-minded individuals who were known for their competence and professionalism, but rarely for their personal allegiance to Trump or his political programme. One such person was Chris Costa, the National Security Council's Senior Director for counter-terrorism, who summed up his attitude and achievements as follows:

> I am very proud that we didn't allow counterterrorism policy work to be weaponised, meaning to be politicised. We maintained our professional sensibilities. I would say that is the most important legacy my whole team had... And I think that is a story [that] resonates with the Americans I talk to. They are really happy that ... despite what they hear from the various news outlets, there are people who are quietly doing the work of CT [counter-terrorism].[60]

Together with the many career officials, who continued serving in "acting" positions because Trump struggled to find enough candidates, people like Costa formed the core of what Trump supporters criticised as the "deep state" (which, in turn, had been empowered by Trump's lack of preparation and administrative capacity.)

The collective weight of "the generals"—both in terms of numbers and professional experience—meant that Trump's doctrine, his political programme, and—indeed—Trump himself could, at times, seem irrelevant. In an interview, Gorka recalled what it was like to be a "true believer" on the National Security Council:

> You sit there as a newly appointed political, and you listen for two hours on a big issue—ISIS, Russia, whatever it is—and not one participant mentions the name of the President or what he said yesterday in Warsaw, or what his objective is given that specific issue. And you see this happen again and again and again, and you're the guy at the end of the conversation... who says, "Excuse me, ladies and gentlemen, you do know what the President said about x yesterday. Can we actually do that?"[61]

On another occasion, Gorka described the experience of entering the White House as a "hostile takeover", arguing that "many people inside the building... would have been comfortable inside a Hillary Clinton administration".[62] This view was echoed in many of my conversations with "generals" and career officials, who told me to "ignore" what was coming out of the Oval Office, and "never pay attention" to anything the President said, except when he was reading from a script.

This does not mean that Trump and his ideas had no impact, or that the categories were static. During his first two years in power, media organisations like *Politico*, *The Hill*, or *Axios* published endless stories about the shifting balance of power between "true believers" and "the generals", and—more recently—the rise of a fourth category—the "uber-hawks"—which included CIA Director, now Secretary of State Mike Pompeo, and McMaster's successor as National Security Advisor, John Bolton.[63]

Yet, despite those changes and fluctuations, it seems clear that "true believers" have never been a majority, and even by mid-2019—nearly three years into his first term—Trump had failed to fill a third of the political positions at the State Department, and more than half at Homeland Security.[64] The problem, therefore, remained essentially unchanged: Trump may have won an election, but lacked the policies and people that would have allowed him to turn his doctrine into reality.

4

BANNING MUSLIMS

Given Trump's insistence that he was going to "Make America Great Again", one of the most unexpected criticisms of him was that his policies were "un-American". Yet, nearly all of Trump's rivals, at one point or another, accused him of betraying the spirit, if not the interests, of the country he was seeking to lead. They criticised his foreign policy as "isolationist", and argued that his support for torture contradicted American "values". The strongest objections, however, concerned his statements on immigration and Islam. Trump was not only trying to end (most) immigration, and—thereby—reverse the idea of America as a multi-cultural "nation of immigrants", but proposed to ban people based on their religion. When Trump first articulated what became known as the "Muslim travel ban" in December 2015, even conservative Republicans were united in their condemnation. Former Vice-President Dick Cheney said that it went "against everything we stand for and believe in".[1] Mike Pence, who later became Trump's running mate, called it "offensive and unconstitutional".[2]

The extent to which these policies were truly "un-American" was, of course, a matter of debate. Scholars such as George Hawley have argued that today's multi-cultural consensus, which thinks of America as a post-racial society in which freedom and liberty are available to all, is contrary to most of the country's history: "Despite the egalitarian rhetoric of the Declaration of Independence, the United States operated as a defacto white supremacist nation for most of its history".[3] Similarly, Samuel Huntington and Francis Fukuyama stressed that, although America was a "nation of immigrants" in that nearly everyone's ancestors had at some point migrated to the country, its dominant culture, values and ethos had always been Anglo-Saxon and Protestant.[4]

Indeed, Trump's hawkish and occasionally xenophobic nationalism was perfectly consistent with a segment of that dominant culture, the so-called Jacksonian tradition, which Mead had identified as one of the four major strains in American politics. While Jacksonians have never been popular—according to Mead, their views were "the most deplored abroad, [and] the most denounced at home"[5]—their claim to be regarded as "American" was as strong and historically valid as all others'. Not least, they had "flocked to the colours", and were over-represented in "patriotic" professions such as the military and the police. "Without Jacksonians" and their readiness to fight for the country, Mead argued, "the United States would be a much weaker power".[6]

Trump's agenda, therefore, was not as outlandish and ahistorical as his rivals made it seem. But it clashed with how America had come to be understood by mainstream politicians and those in powerful national institutions such as the media, the federal bureaucracy and the courts. *Their* idea of America was that of a culturally diverse nation, which practised religious neutrality and accommodated people regardless of race, ethnicity, religion, or how recently they or their ancestors had arrived. The notion of banning Muslims based on their religion—and, in doing so, excluding an entire group from the promise of America—was the opposite of what they believed America stood for.[7] It was this mainstream consensus, rather than the idea of America per se, that Trump and his policies challenged.

The "Muslim travel ban"—which Trump referred to as the "travel ban" and his officials described as a "travel moratorium"—was the high point of implementing Trump's "Jacksonian" idea of America, as well as the purest policy expression of the alt-right philosophy that Bannon had promoted in the years before Trump took power. But it also revealed his movement's weaknesses. The original Executive Order, which had been crafted by a small group of "true believers" with no experience in policy development or implementation, plunged the country's immigration system into chaos. More tellingly, it was so clearly at odds with the mainstream consensus on religious liberty that its true intention—"keeping Muslims out"—had to be concealed. To become lawful, the "Muslim ban" had to stop being a ban on Muslims.

As this chapter will show, there is no evidence that the "Muslim travel ban" or the idea of "extreme vetting", which Trump has presented in similar terms, were workable or made the country safer. Although Trump justified them as counter-terrorism measures, they are best understood as part of an ideologically-driven effort to "break" the mainstream consensus on immigration, and in so doing re-define the idea of America.

The Travel Ban

Long before Trump started talking about travel bans, travelling or emigrating to America had become more difficult. One of the immediate consequences of the September 11, 2001, attacks was a complete overhaul of the immigration system, resulting in additional checks on visitors and immigrants.[8] Obama not only maintained this more restrictive system, but imposed additional constraints. After two Iraqi refugees, whose fingerprints had previously been found on a bomb in Iraq, were caught planning a terrorist attack in America, he ordered a review of the entire refugee screening process. He also tightened vetting procedures for citizens of eleven, mostly Muslim majority, countries, and required visitors under the so-called Visa Waiver Programme who had recently been to Iraq, Iran, Syria, Yemen, Libya, Somalia, or Sudan to undergo enhanced background checks.[9] Even so, neither he nor Bush ever imposed outright bans, or excluded people based on their religion or nationality alone.

By contrast, Trump's initial Executive Order, which he signed just seven days after taking office, banned all citizens from the seven countries that Obama had identified as "high risk" in relation to the Visa Waiver Programme. It also stopped all refugee admissions on a temporary basis, and suspended those from Syria permanently.[10] While making no mention of "Islam" or "Muslims", the countries it singled out were all predominantly Muslim.[11] It was impossible, therefore, to separate the Executive Order from Trump's campaign pledge for a "total and complete shutdown of Muslims entering the United States".[12] The Cato Institute documented at least twelve occasions between the election and the inauguration on which Trump reaffirmed his intention of banning Muslims because of their faith.[13] One was a request to Rudy Giuliani, a former prosecutor, New York City mayor, and close supporter of Trump, to show him "the right way to do it legally".[14]

From the moment that Trump signed it, the Executive Order caused widespread chaos at airports and border crossings. Relevant agencies, such as Customs and Border Protection (CBP), had received no prior warning.[15] There was virtually no guidance on how to deal with entire categories of people, such as dual nationals, lawful permanent residents (so-called "green card" holders), or people with valid visas. The whole drafting process had been limited to "true believers", especially Bannon and Miller, with no significant input from counter-terrorism or immigration experts, or the very departments and agencies that were meant to implement it.[16] John Kelly, Trump's (then) Secretary for Homeland Security, only became involved at the final stages, while his Department's General Counsel, who might have spotted many flaws and oversights, received it less than an hour before it came into effect.[17]

Bannon later claimed that the chaos had been intentional, as he wanted the "[liberal] snowflakes [to] show up at the airports and riot".[18] But few officials and policymakers believed this.

The general consensus was that he and the other "true believers" had botched it, because they lacked government experience and had underestimated the many difficulties and pitfalls that came with passing a measure of this magnitude. In the words of a senior Trump appointee:

> That was chaos. You don't roll out a policy like that without thoroughly vetting it with all the affected departments, ensuring that it is going to be smooth, thinking about unintended consequences. Are people going to be stopped in the air? What's going to happen at the airports? Are [Customs and Border Protection] officers going to know how to implement this? The "A Team", if they had been in position, would not have done that, and I think this had some negative consequences for the administration.[19]

Alberto Fernandez, a former diplomat and defender of the ban, shared this view. He believed that the lack of professionalism by Trump's team had weakened an otherwise reasonable policy: "The whole thing was a disaster", he told me, "The way they rolled it out was really stupid, because you could make a very logical case for it".[20]

Politically, the Executive Order undermined global perceptions of America and damaged relationships with key allies. While there has been no systematic polling, the reception in Muslim majority countries was overwhelmingly negative. Rukmini Callimachi, a *New York Times* journalist who was in the Iraqi city of Mosul at the time of the announcement, reported that the only locals who welcomed it were supporters of Islamic State, because it proved "that America really does 'hate' Islam".[21]

For the Iraqi government, the ban was a major embarrassment, given its long-standing partnership with America and active support for the Global Coalition against Islamic State. Members of Congress and Trump's own Cabinet pleaded with Trump to remove Iraq from the country list, so that local translators, fighter pilots, and others, who had served with American forces, could continue to travel to the United States.[22] The late

Senator John McCain argued that the ban not only sent a terrible signal to the "thousands of Iraqi men and women" who
were fighting alongside America, but also played into Islamic
State's hands and strengthened Iran's influence within Iraq.[23]

The same happened with Chad. The religiously mixed African country (more than 40 per cent of its population are Christian) was added to the ban in September 2017, despite its long
history as an American ally and participation in numerous missions against jihadists belonging to al-Qaeda, Boko Haram, and
Islamic State. According to the State Department's own reporting, very few Chadians had joined terrorist groups.[24] Given the
tiny number of immigrant visas issued in recent years (40 in
2016; 24 in 2017),[25] blacklisting the country's entire population
was widely seen as "draconian" and "knee-jerk".[26] Chad's government, which had received no warning, responded by saying
that Trump's decision had tainted the country's image in the
eyes of the world and damaged "the good [bilateral] relations".[27] In the end, both Chad and Iraq were removed from
the list, but not before significant—and entirely avoidable—
political damage had been done.

By far the most serious problems were legal and/or constitutional in nature. Just days after the announcement, half a dozen
states launched lawsuits against the federal government, causing
the ban to be suspended nationwide. The revised version, which
came out in March 2017,[28] was meant to "fix" the problems of
the first, as it exempted dual nationals, "green card" holders and
those in possession of valid visas. But it was struck down as well,
prompting Trump to tweet that his government should have
"doubled down" on the original ban—making it "far larger,
tougher, and more specific"—instead of adopting a "politically
correct version".[29] Many courts regarded such statements as evidence of his actual intention—that is, to ban Muslims. One of
the appeals courts concluded that the entire policy "[dripped]
with religious intolerance, animus and discrimination".[30]

The third—and final—version of the ban was issued in the
form of a Presidential Proclamation in September 2017 and

approved by the Supreme Court nine months later.[31] It was a significantly watered down version of the two Executive Orders that had been published earlier. By adding North Korea and Venezuela, while removing Sudan,[32] the country list became less explicitly Muslim. It also no longer dealt with refugee admissions, which were resumed—albeit at a much lower level—in the following month. Not least, it contained a long list of exemptions, which had been imposed by the courts. Citizens of banned countries who could demonstrate "bona fide" links to the United States—say, through family or business ties— were allowed to travel. Depending on the country, exemptions also applied to students, children, and people attending "significant business or professional obligations".[33]

As a result, the practical consequences of the "travel ban" were not as severe as initially expected. As mentioned above, visitors and immigrants—especially from Middle Eastern or African "countries of concern"—had long faced restrictions when travelling to America. More so than previously, however, the burden of proof shifted towards the applicants: instead of American authorities having to find reasons to refuse admission, citizens from the listed countries had to make a stronger case for gaining it. Moreover, considering the many caveats and reservations that the Supreme Court expressed in its ruling—including a reminder that Presidents had to "espouse the principles of religious freedom and tolerance"[34]—it was unlikely that Trump would carelessly expand the list or attempt to turn it into the kind of outright "Muslim ban" that he had originally envisaged.

Trump did not, therefore, shut the door as firmly as his supporters might have liked. The main difference was the message that he conveyed about America's attitude towards immigration, especially from non-European and/or Muslim countries. In contrast to his predecessors, Trump no longer talked about immigrants as people who had escaped oppression or sought the chance to start a new life, but portrayed them as potential threats.[35] The extent to which he has succeeded in "normalising" this narrative is evident in refugee admissions, which have been cut to the lowest level in recent history without much debate or public opposition.[36]

From Trump's perspective, the damage to America's global standing and Americans' self-perception as a "nation of immigrants" was not only acceptable, but intentional and desirable. As well as energising his "base", talk about the "Muslim ban" has powerfully projected a different, more Jacksonian idea of America. In the words of Reince Priebus, his former chief of staff, it was "the big signal" in what America First was all about.[37]

False Assumptions

Regardless of its legality, Trump's original idea—that is, to ban all Muslims from entering the United States—would have been unworkable. Its underlying premise was that being Muslim was a precursor to becoming a terrorist, and that "keeping Muslims out" would therefore reduce the threat from terrorism. This reflected the (flawed) thinking of groups like the Center for Security Policy and advisors such as Phares, which Trump had been exposed to in the years running up to the election.[38] It assumed that all (practising) Muslims were equally likely to turn to (Islamic) terrorism; that Islam was a monolithic and never-changing set of ideas and practices; and that someone's (Islamic) faith was a powerful predictor of radicalisation. In reality, of course, radicalisation had multiple causes; Salafi-Jihadism—the specific theological strain that had produced Islamic State and al-Qaeda[39]—was adhered to by only a small percentage of Muslims; and other, more mainstream schools of Islamic thought strongly rejected it.

More importantly, there was no reliable way of identifying Muslims—never mind, Muslim terrorists—by name, race, ethnicity, appearance, or country of origin.[40] Some of the highest per capita rates of radicalisation—measured, for example, in the number of jihadist foreign fighters compared to the Muslim population—could be found among converts from other religions[41] and in predominantly non-Muslim countries such as

Belgium and Denmark.[42] Even if someone's Islamic faith could somehow be determined, banning them from the United States based on their faith alone would have produced an absurdly high number of "false positives"—at least 250,000 for every actual terrorist[43]—making it less effective in counter-terrorism terms than, for example, banning all males between the ages of fifteen and thirty-four.[44]

Yet, even when Trump's policy shifted away from banning Muslims to banning the citizens of (Muslim majority) countries, much of the information that was used to justify it was misleading or outright false. The original Executive Order asserted that "[n]umerous foreign-born individuals have been convicted or implicated in terrorism-related crimes since September 11, 2001".[45] Four weeks later, Trump claimed that "the *vast majority* of individuals convicted of terrorism and terrorism-related offenses since 9/11 came here from outside of our country" [emphasis added].[46] The data he relied on were figures compiled by the Department of Justice, which were later published in a joint report by the Departments of Justice and Homeland Security.[47] Their central claim was that, out of 549 individuals who had been convicted on "international terrorism-related charges in U.S. federal courts" between September 2001 and October 2017, nearly three quarters (73 per cent) were born abroad.[48]

As many experts have pointed out, the way this figure had been produced—and, especially, how it came to be used—was highly misleading. It included over a hundred individuals who had never lived in the United States, made no distinction between terrorist attacks in America and abroad, understated the extent to which many people had radicalised after entering the United States, and counted a range of "terrorism-related offenses" that had virtually nothing to do with terrorism.[49] Not least, while the report focused on "international"—that is, jihadist—terrorism, Trump and his supporters presented its findings as if they related to all forms of terrorism, ignoring that "domestic extremism", such as attacks by White Nationalists and Sovereign Citizens, had caused nearly as many deaths since September 11, 2001, as "international terrorism".[50]

Almost a year after the report's publication (and nearly two years after Trump had first used the figures), the Justice Department conceded that the information could have been "better present[ed]".[51] According to Benjamin Wittes, a respected journalist and Trump critic, this was "as close as the administration is going to get" to conceding that it had "used a formal government report to distort data to slime Muslims and immigrants".[52]

Many career officials who had been asked to work on Trump's policy were deeply unhappy about the way the administration sought to make its case. One of the country's most senior counter-terrorism officials, who had served in the Trump, Obama, and Bush administrations, told me:

> The intelligence community was wilfully misused in the policy development process of the travel bans. It was not a case of "Let's understand the threat and then, from the threat that we understand, let's devise a set of measures". It was "We have the answer, now let's work back our way into the supporting intelligence-driven justification". In many cases, we couldn't or wouldn't do that.[53]

Indeed, an internal memo by the intelligence branch of the Department of Homeland Security (DHS), which was leaked in March 2017, contradicted Trump's claims. It stated that, based on its own research, citizenship was "unlikely to be a reliable indicator of potential terrorist activity", and that more than half of the eighty-two individuals that had been prosecuted for jihadist activity in America since the beginning of the Syrian conflict in 2011 were "native-born United States citizens", while the others had come "from 26 different countries, with no one country representing more than 13.5 percent of the foreign-born total".[54]

The memo's findings were in line with virtually every rigorous open source and/or academic study that has been published on the jihadist threat in America. This included two recent studies, which covered similar periods to the Department of Justice report:

- In "The Origins of America's Jihadists", Brian Jenkins of the RAND Corporation analysed 178 jihadists who were involved in planning and executing attacks on American soil between September 2001 and late-2017. He found that nearly half (48 per cent) were native-born, while another quarter had been naturalised. This meant that nearly three quarters (74 per cent) were American citizens.[55]
- In "Jihadist Terrorism 16 Years after 9/11", Peter Bergen and a team of researchers at the New America Foundation looked at 472 American residents who were charged with jihadism-related offences between September 2001 and mid-2018. In addition to the domestic plotters and attackers that Jenkins had focused on, this included individuals who had travelled to places like Syria and Somalia as foreign fighters or become involved in terrorist activity abroad. The results were similar: of the 472 individuals, 49 per cent (207) were native-born American citizens. With naturalised citizens, the non-immigrant total rose to 70 per cent.[56]

In short, contrary to what Trump and the "true believers" tried to show, the terrorist threat in America was largely home-grown, and "travel bans" were never, therefore, going to be *the* solution. As the senior counter-terrorism official explained:

> The President strongly believes, as an article of faith, that the threat that we face inside the United States from a terrorist attack is tied to people from overseas. He clearly believes that... but it is not true. I always had to be careful about not going too far in saying: "This stuff, this immigration policy is crazy because it doesn't make us any safer".[57]

Given the very few foreign-born terrorists that have entered the US since September 11, 2001 (see below), and the (already) small number of visas that were granted to citizens of "high risk" countries, no expert believed that banning them altogether would have any measurable impact on the terrorist threat. As a result—and despite his grandiose rhetoric—Trump's "Muslim ban" had effectively morphed into a policy instrument that was, at best, inconsequential.

Extreme Vetting

Trump's other big idea was a tightening of immigration vetting procedures. During the election campaign, he often created the impression that people from places like Syria and Libya could just walk into the country, and that "vetting failures" had allowed dozens, if not hundreds, of foreign terrorists to enter the United States.[58] In his August 2016 policy speech in Youngstown, Ohio, he called for entirely "new screening procedures", and promised that he would "only admit into this country those who share our values and respect our people".[59] Since taking office, he has claimed to have made major progress, and that vetting was "getting tougher each month".[60] But there is little evidence that vetting has fundamentally changed—or that it needed fixing in the first place.

Needless to say, Trump was not the first President to have tackled the issue of immigrant vetting. In the aftermath of the September 11, 2001, attacks, President Bush merged all of the agencies concerned with immigration under the newly created Department of Homeland Security (DHS), and increased their funding—in part, to create large, inter-operable databases with biometric data such as photographs and fingerprints. He also initiated programmes that registered and interviewed individuals from two dozen "high risk" Muslim countries, and deported thousands of foreigners who had overstayed their visas or were thought to pose a terrorism risk.[61] Not least, he created the governmental "infrastructure" through which visa and immigration applications could be vetted. In addition to "admitting agencies", such as the State Department and DHS, which received applications and carried out interviews, this comprised the Terrorist Screening Center, which was located at the Federal Bureau of Investigations (FBI); the National Counter-Terrorism Center (NCTC), which maintained the Terrorist Identities Datamart Environment (TIDE); and the DHS-based National Targeting Center, which integrated the other agencies' efforts.[62]

Far from relaxing this system,[63] Obama increased vetting procedures across all types of visitors and immigrants. Even citizens of visa waiver nations, which included America's most trusted allies such as Britain and Australia, were compelled to submit biographical information and go through a screening process. He also oversaw a massive expansion of the "black-lists" and terrorism databases, which have grown to include more than a million names. The so-called "No Fly" list alone increased from 4,000 to over 40,000 entries during Obama's Presidency.[64]

The strictest procedures applied to individuals under the refugee resettlement programme. Obama tightened screening procedures for refugees from eleven predominantly Muslim countries in 2011, and deployed "big data" software in order to make it easier to search across the entire holdings of the intelligence community. The process became so rigorous that it would take several years for someone from a Middle Eastern country to be resettled in the United States.[65] This was especially true for Syrians. In the words of a former director of US Citizenship and Immigration Services: "Refugees get the most scrutiny, and Syrian refugees get the most scrutiny of all".[66]

As a consequence, very few terrorists have escaped the American vetting system, especially in the post-September 11, 2001, period. As CATO's Alexander Nowrasteh has shown, out of more than two billion visitors and immigrants who entered the United States in the thirty year period between 1975 and 2015, 154 were charged with terrorism offences.[67] Only seventeen of them had entered the country after September 11, 2001,[68] and just five carried out deadly attacks. None were refugees.[69] In statistical terms:

[T]he chance of an American being murdered in a terrorist attack caused by a refugee is 1 in 3.64 *billion* per year, while the chance of being murdered in an attack committed by an illegal immigrant is an astronomical 1 in 10.9 *billion* per year. [original emphasis][70]

This contradicts many of the misleading figures that have been used by Trump and members of his administration, including a claim by former Homeland Security Secretary Kirstjen Nielsen that 3,000 (suspected) terrorists had illegally crossed the border with Mexico in 2018 alone, which has since been exposed as false.[71] It also means that, unlike Europe, there was no "asylum-terror nexus", which right-wing terrorism analysts had argued was a risk.[72]

Indeed, even the foreign-born individuals who did become terrorists were not necessarily "vetting failures", because nearly all of them radicalised after entering the United States. Mohamed Mohamoud, for example, a Somali American who was convicted of wanting to bomb the Christmas Tree lighting ceremony in Portland, Oregon, in 2010—and whose case Stephen Miller cited in defence of the "Muslim travel ban"[73]—came to America at the age of two. Dzokhar and Tamerlan Tsarnaev, the brothers who attacked the Boston marathon in 2013, entered the country as children and were drawn into jihadism in their late-teens. Sayfullo Saipov, the Uzbek-born terrorist who killed eight cyclists and pedestrians in New York City in 2017, likely turned to jihadism while he was a resident of Paterson, New Jersey. As much as they were immigrants, their turn to extremism took place in America.

In short, there was no empirical basis for Trump's claim that terrorism in America had been caused by "vetting failures". On the contrary, the evidence that has been put forward by Nowrasteh and others[74] demonstrated that the system through which visitors and immigrants were screened before entering the United States had worked exceptionally well. In Nowrasteh's view, Trump's fixation on vetting was not only mistaken but generated significant opportunity costs:

It is a waste of government resources. If human life is equally valuable… then every additional Dollar we spend on vetting is a Dollar that could be spent saving somebody's life in a different way. Maybe more effective immigration screening in other places, maybe something that has nothing to do with immigration. Maybe law enforcement or police or something else.[75]

Silver Bullets

Once in power, the administration started exploring different ideas for making the vetting process "tougher". Trump's initial proposal, which he had articulated in the Youngstown speech, was to introduce a system of "ideological testing". He said:

> In the Cold War, we had an ideological screening test. The time is overdue to develop a new screening test for the threats we face today. In addition to screening out all members or sympathizers of terrorist groups, we must also screen out any who have hostile attitudes towards our country or its principles—or who believe that Sharia law should supplant American law. Those who do not believe in our Constitution, or who support bigotry and hatred, will not be admitted for immigration into the country.[76]

While this may have sounded reasonable, no one with any insight or experience in immigrant admissions believed that such a system could be made to work.[77] Questions about "provable facts", such as past or present involvement in terrorism, genocide or torture, have long been part of the application process. Likewise, expressions of hostility towards America, or open support for "bigotry and hatred", would already result in a negative outcome. (A former consular officer told me: "[If such comments came up during a visa interview,] almost any consular or CBP [Customs and Border Protection] officer would reject their application".)[78] Beyond this, immigration officials rarely have time to engage in free-flowing discussions about political ideas, the Constitution, or attitudes towards American society. The only way of incorporating elements of "ideological testing" into the process would be through (additional) standardised questions.[79] But such questions would quickly become public knowledge and, therefore, easy to anticipate. The chances of identifying extremists or future terrorists would be virtually zero.

Another idea, which DHS has labelled "lifecycle vetting", was to create a system whereby the government would continue screening people as long as they stayed in America—potentially, that is, for the rest of their lives. Central to this idea was a (yet to be developed) software which officials hoped would make automatic assessments about immigrants' "intention to commit criminal or terrorist acts" and their overall "contribution to society".[80] A policy document by Immigration and Customs Enforcement (ICE) explained that the objective was to generate 10,000 leads per year for further investigation and review.[81]

As with ideological screening, many experts have raised doubts about the project's viability. In an open letter, more than fifty leading computer scientists and technologists argued that the idea of making a "positive contribution" to society was so vague, subjective, and difficult to "operationalise" that no algorithm would produce accurate results—especially in relation to terrorist radicalisation, which follows no single pattern or pathway and is, at best, loosely related to people's "contribution to society".[82] It said:

> Even the best automated decision-making models generate an unacceptable number of errors when predicting rare events… Terrorist acts are extremely rare. Even the most accurate possible model would generate a very large number of false positives…

> Data mining is a powerful tool. Appropriately harnessed, it can do great good… But the approach set forth by ICE is neither appropriate nor feasible.[83]

Civil rights groups worried that, if it ever came into existence, the algorithm would be based on crude and empirically flawed assumptions about religion and income, leading to an increase in prejudice and discrimination[84]—and probably result in a Chinese-style "social credit system", whereby immigrants' every behaviour would be constantly "scored".[85] Although DHS has not officially abandoned "lifetime vetting", there is no sign that any system is ready to be deployed.

Arguably, the most pressing issue was what DHS referred to as "social media exploitation".[86] Under Obama, the government had started asking visitors and immigrants to provide social media handles, and launched a pilot programme, which sampled them to see what information could be generated, and how—and to what extent—it might be scaled.[87] It also created eight "Homeland Security Investigations" stations across the world searching applicants' accounts for connections with terrorists.[88] Even so, Congress and other critics had long argued that Obama was moving too slowly.[89] This became a major issue when it was revealed that the Pakistani wife of the San Bernardino shooter had openly stated her support for jihadist groups on social media, and that none of this information had been seen or considered during her visa application.[90] It was in this context that "extreme vetting" became one of Trump's talking points.

Two years into Trump's term, there was no evidence that social media screening had significantly improved. Although "social media exploitation" was included as a requirement in virtually all relevant tenders and policy statements, technology experts doubted that the existing software could perform this task reliably and "at scale", and that automated content analysis tools were sufficiently developed to "parse the nuanced meaning of human communication, or to detect the intent or motivation of the speaker".[91]

Indeed, in the absence of a technological solution, large-scale "social media exploitation" would have required substantial increases in resources and staff, which Trump has failed to commit. According to Seamus Hughes, a former NCTC official, "It's one thing to want to check the social media accounts for everyone who gets a visa, it's another thing to have enough people to look at them… [Unless you put resources behind it,] you get a larger haystack and have no ability to look for the needle".[92]

Trump's only tangible initiative in relation to vetting has been the creation of a new bureaucratic structure, the National Vetting Center, which he announced in February 2018. Having criticised earlier administrations' vetting efforts for being "ad hoc", the White House claimed that the new centre was going to provide better "coordination".[93] But neither Trump nor any of his officials were able to explain what this meant. A year after its announcement, it remained unclear why a new structure was necessary, and how its mission would differ from the National Targeting Center, which had been created for the same purpose and was widely seen as successful.[94] Matt Levitt, a former FBI and Treasury official with decades of counter-terrorism experience, told me: "[T]hey are doing useful work, but much of it was being done already".[95] In the absence of a distinct mission, the centre's *raison d'être* was little more than to feed "the [administration's] false narrative that there was an influx of terrorists related to weak immigration controls".[96]

In summary, all of my interviewees with relevant experience told me that, short of discovering a technological "silver bullet", the only feasible way to improve vetting was to do "more of the same", which meant consular officials spending more time with applicants and intelligence agencies performing deeper searches, increasing the number of layers and levels of connection that are investigated for each name and phone number they received. As the senior counter-terrorism official, who had served under Bush, Obama, and Trump, explained:

> You can spend hours and hours, and days and days, doing that work, and yet the return on investment… is still relatively modest. Outside of the political rhetoric about letting good people or bad people in, the [key question is:] "Just how much effort are you willing to go through"? Time. Energy. Expense.[97]

At the time of writing, there was no indication that the Trump administration had been willing to increase the levels of funding by amounts that would allow government fundamentally to transform the process. Nor is it clear that this would be necessary or useful. As noted earlier, the idea that "hundreds and hundreds" of foreign terrorists had entered America without being detected was demonstrably false. The only actual "vetting failure" since September 11, 2001, that had resulted in American deaths, was the wife of the San Bernardino shooter. While it was important to learn the lessons from this one case, it was mistaken to conclude that the entire system was broken.[98]

As it turned out, therefore, none of Trump's ideas on immigration were feasible or made Americans safer from terrorism. The reason was simple: immigration was not the principal problem, and existing systems for vetting immigrants worked as well as they could. For the "true believers", however, this had never been the point. Both the "Muslim ban" and "extreme vetting" were part of their (ideological) project of challenging multi-culturalism and the "nation of immigrants". The ultimate purpose was not to counter terrorism or protect the American people, but to promote "America First".

5

RULES OF ENGAGEMENT

In his famous treatise *On War*, the nineteenth-century Prussian general Carl von Clausewitz defined war as an "act of force to compel our enemy to do our will".[1] In theory, he argued, war was unlimited and unrestrained—like two wrestlers trying to knock down their opponent. But in practice, all wars were limited. They did not consist of a single blow, but of a series of engagements. And they were rarely conducted by military force alone. Unlike a wrestling match, war was guided by a "political object", and military force—though important—was just one of many ways in which it could be achieved. "[W]ar is not merely an act of policy", Clausewitz wrote, "but a true political instrument, a continuation of political intercourse carried on with other means".[2] This simple set of ideas—the primacy of politics and the instrumentality of military force—has shaped modern strategy, and taught political leaders that their role in war was both important and fundamentally different from the military. In the memorable words of Georges Clemenceau, a former French Prime Minister, war was "too serious a matter to be left to the generals".[3]

In America, the closest institutional expression of Clausewitz's ideas is the National Security Council. It brings together representatives from the military, the intelligence community, as well as more "civilian" Departments such as State, Treasury, and Homeland Security,[4] whose job is to integrate the different bureaucracies, instruments and sources of national power that are involved in pursuing national security objectives. It reports directly to the President, who is in charge of every aspect of a conflict and, therefore, responsible for its political outcome. Presidents, after all, not only authorise military (and paramilitary) operations, but manage alliances, lead diplomatic efforts, coordinate economic sanctions, maintain political support, and mobilise the public. As the strategist Colin Gray put it, military commanders "fight battles or conduct campaigns", while Presidents "wage war".[5]

Donald Trump's idea of war is profoundly different. As shown in Chapter 1, he conceives of wars predominantly—if not, exclusively—in terms of force, and believes that victory is entirely the result of firepower and military aggression. Rather than Clausewitz, his approach can be summed up in the words of Curtis May, a World War II general, who famously said: "[In war,] you've got to kill enough people, and when you've killed enough, they stop fighting".[6] Trump also believes that wars should be left to the generals, and that politicians must not interfere in their decisions. From Trump's perspective, having done so was Obama's main mistake, as he had "micromanaged" conflicts, imposed "politically correct" rules, and prevented the military from "getting the job done".[7]

Those who agreed with the scholar Michael Glennon, who had famously criticised the national security establishment under Obama as too "hawkish", expected things to get worse under Trump.[8] In their view, the new President had given "the generals" a blank cheque, which they were going to use in order to "unleash" the military and roll back the restrictions and safeguards that Obama had put in place.[9]

Yet this is not what happened. As this chapter will show, Trump's "generals" have moved the operational needle in the direction of a more heavily "kinetic" counter-terrorism approach, resulting in greater risks for soldiers and civilians, and lessening the extent to which policymakers were able to control the (political) consequences of military operations. Even so, and despite Trump's willingness to sign off on virtually anything, they also decided to keep many of the existing rules in place.[10] They maintained Obama's framework for distinguishing between war zones and other areas of conflict in which stricter standards applied; they preserved most of the standards and procedures for avoiding civilian casualties; and they rejected the targeting of terrorists' families, the introduction of torture, and the expansion of the prison camp at Guantanamo that Trump had called for on the campaign trail. Contrary to what Glennon might have expected, the national security establishment was more cautious and significantly less hawkish than the President they served.

Change

Obama, of course, had never been as "soft" on terrorism as Trump's rhetoric suggested. Especially during his first term, he pursued a highly aggressive campaign against the leadership of al-Qaeda. More than 70 per cent of the roughly 1,000 drone strikes that he authorised took place in the years between 2009 and 2012,[11] and nearly all targeted Pakistan's tribal areas, where al-Qaeda's leadership was hiding. By the time of the May 2011 special forces operation that killed bin Laden, he had effectively destroyed what used to be known as "al-Qaeda Central".[12]

In his second term, Obama placed greater emphasis on "regulating" the War on Terror—partly, no doubt, because he believed that jihadist terrorism, and the threat it posed to America, had been reduced. In May 2013, he issued the so-called "Presidential Policy Guidance", which spelled out stricter rules for targeted assassinations, and introduced a distinction between "areas of active hostilities" (war zones such as Afghanistan) and other conflicts (for example, Pakistan, Yemen, Somalia, and Libya), where higher standards applied.[13] He also ordered the CIA and the Department of Defense to be more transparent in relation to civilian casualties, and account for discrepancies between their own figures and those from non-governmental organisations.[14]

Yet, by the end of his Presidency, with the rise of Islamic State and the Caliphate, he once again moved towards a more aggressive campaign. In early 2016, his administration relaxed the rules for launching operations against Islamic State in Afghanistan, and classified the Somali group al-Shabaab as an "associated force" of al-Qaeda, making it easier to target them.[15] It also designated the Libyan city of Sirte as an "area of active hostility", and considered doing the same in relation to Somalia and Yemen.[16] Not least, it accepted a wider range of justifications for attacks on targets that were not "imminent threats" to the United States.[17] From this perspective, some of the changes that followed during the first year of the Trump administration were a logical consequence—or extension—of a process that had already begun.

New Rules

At first, however, the more gradual changes that eventually emerged seemed unlikely. During the campaign, Trump had frequently criticised Obama's efforts to regulate the War on Terror as "pointless" and "politically correct". He claimed that counter-terrorism operations were being "micro-managed" by liberal appointees who had never served in the military and did not understand how to run a war. (His campaign manager, Steve Bannon, claimed that Susan Rice, Obama's National Security Advisor, personally "picked the drone strikes".)[18] Within a week of taking office, Trump visited CIA headquarters and told the agency's leadership to defeat Islamic State by any means necessary: "If you can do it in ten days", he reportedly said, "get it done". When officials showed him footage of a drone attack in which the operator delayed a strike until the target had walked away from his family, Trump's response was: "Why did you wait?"[19]

The first opportunity to demonstrate what his approach meant in practice was a special forces operation in Yemen, which Trump authorised on 29 January 2017. It targeted the village of Yakla, where the leadership of al-Qaeda in the Arabian Peninsula (AQAP), a local al-Qaeda affiliate, was thought to be based. Although the operation was considered risky, and Obama had repeatedly postponed it, Trump signed off immediately and without showing much interest in the details. Consistent with his philosophy, he had total confidence in "the generals", and was keen to show that America "meant business" when it came to killing terrorists. At the crucial meeting, he allegedly said: "[T]hese guys, this is what they do. Let them do it".[20]

But the operation went wrong. It resulted in the deaths of a Navy Seal and an estimated thirty civilians. While more than a dozen AQAP fighters got killed, the group's leader, Qasim al-Rimi—who was believed to be the operation's "real" target— survived. Less than a week later, the group published an audio tape in which al-Rimi threatened America and taunted Trump as "the fool of the White House".[21] In propaganda terms, the operation was a victory for al-Qaeda.

In its initial response, the White House claimed that the raid had been a great success, as it had yielded "an unbelievable amount of intelligence".[22] When this was contradicted by senior sources from within the military,[23] Trump blamed the very generals whom he had sought to empower. In an interview with Fox News, he said:

> This was a mission that was started before I got here. This was something they wanted to do. They came to me, they explained what they wanted to do—the generals... And they lost Ryan [Owens, the Navy Seal].[24]

As far as Trump's idea of a hyper-aggressive military was concerned, the Yakla raid was a significant setback. Although the National Security Council proceeded with relaxing the rules for counter-terrorism operations, it did so more cautiously than Trump had originally intended. According to Charlie Savage and Eric Schmitt—two journalists who have closely followed the evolution of Trump's War on Terror—the

Yemen operation "broke the momentum" for a radical change from Obama.[25]

The new approach, which materialised over the course of the first six months of Trump's Presidency, was not as drastically different from Obama's as many had expected. The priority was to speed up operations and disrupt "malign terrorist networks" before they could develop into large, state-like structures—in other words, preventing the rise of another "Caliphate".[26] In practical terms, this translated into four changes:

- The first was an increase in the number of "areas of active hostility". This term, which dated back to Obama's "Presidential Policy Guidance", referred to "hot battlefields" in which the rules for using force or launching "kinetic" operations were less strict. In "areas of active hostility", commanders only had to be "reasonably certain"—not "near certain"—of avoiding civilians. They also no longer had to submit planned operations to a process of "interagency review".[27] In addition to Afghanistan, Iraq, and Syria, Trump placed Somalia and parts of Yemen into this category.

- The second change related to targeting rules. One of the new administration's first decisions was to relax the requirement that targets had to be "imminent threats" to the United States. This condition, which Obama had introduced as part of the "Presidential Policy Guidance", was meant to ensure that American forces would not get sucked into local conflicts. But it had often caused tensions with local partners, who resented the distinction between "first-class" and "second-class" enemies. According to Juan Zarate, a former deputy National Security Advisor: "[Our allies] were asking: 'Why are you viewing this enemy differently? This is a common enemy!'"[28] In war zones, "the generals" also removed "proximity requirements", which had obliged American assets—such as aircraft or special forces teams—to be at a maximum distance between themselves and a target.[29] Together with the deployment of American troops closer to the frontlines, Defense Secretary Mattis expected that this would enable more air strikes, "deny the enemy having the high ground", and make partner forces "bolder" by giving "them more opportunities militarily to take the fight to the enemy".[30]

- Related to this was a devolution of decision-making powers. Even Obama officials believed that the "level of attention to details of troop numbers and [operations]" had become "inefficient".[31] Members of Trump's team—especially those with military backgrounds—felt that the whole process needed to be reversed. As soon as Trump became President, they started devolving high-level operational decisions from the National Security Council to relevant agencies—mainly the Department of Defense and the CIA—while empowering lower-level operators within those agencies. In war zones, they dramatically reduced the number of issues that were subject to "interagency review", and pushed operational decisions "one, maybe two levels" down the chain of command.[32] Outside "areas of active hostility", they limited the National Security Council's role to drawing up yearly "country plans", which set out objectives and general parameters, but left it to departments and agencies to decide on specific targets and operations.[33]

- The least tangible change was an easing of political pressure, especially in relation to civilian casualties. Beyond the specifics of new rules and regulations, it seemed clear that the new Commander-in-Chief was not only less concerned about "collateral damage", but positively gung-ho about "bombing the shit" out of countries. As much as people like Mattis kept emphasising that America still cared about the loss of innocent lives and was obeying its own rules for avoiding "collateral damage" (see below), the President's rhetoric conveyed the opposite. As Daniel Byman, a professor at Georgetown University, told me, "getting yelled at [by someone] on behalf of the President of the United States" was a powerful deterrent;[34] yet, with authorities devolved and a President, who had consistently told audiences that he wanted the military to err on the side of action and pardoned service members who were guilty of war crimes,[35] this was less likely to happen.

Continuity

The degree to which the Trump administration has sought to accelerate "kinetic" operations is only part of the story, however. While reversing many of Obama's regulations, "the generals" also rejected Trump's most radical ideas, maintained basic standards in relation to civilian casualties, and preserved key elements of Obama's framework.

One of the overarching principles of Obama's counter-terrorism doctrine was easy to maintain. Instead of invading and occupying countries, as Bush had done, America was meant to pursue its objectives in partnership with local forces, while reserving the right to act unilaterally when vital interests were at stake. Though first mentioned in military documents in 2003, as a doctrine, it was fully articulated by Obama in the spring of 2014 and became known as "by, with, and through".[36] It meant that, in places like Yemen, Somalia, or—indeed—Syria, America would identify local partners, and provide them with training, intelligence, equipment, and tactical support, but generally stay behind the frontlines and play no visible role in combat or governance. For Trump, who had promised to reduce foreign "adventures" and sought no permanent foreign "footprints", it was an attractive formula. As much as he had accused Obama of "leading from behind", the idea of empowering local actors to tackle foreign enemies was exactly what he believed in. It was no accident, therefore, that Trump officials explicitly referred to "by, with, and through" as the guiding principle behind their Afghanistan strategy.[37]

The Trump administration also maintained a regulatory framework for the War on Terror. When Obama issued the "Presidential Policy Guidance" in May 2013, it was the first time that a President had formulated a comprehensive, global "play book" for the War on Terror, which distinguished between different theatres of operation. As mentioned before, Trump officials opposed many of these rules, and believed that the process for approving "direct actions" had become overly centralised and bureaucratic. But they agreed that such a framework was useful and necessary. While they "streamlined" or scrapped some of the regulations that were contained in Obama's "Presidential Policy Guidance" and ultimately replaced it with their own document, the underlying logic remained the same. Like its predecessor, the Trump administration's "Principles, Standards, and Procedures", which the President approved in September 2017, was a global framework for "kinetic" operations in the War on Terror that delineated areas of operation according to their "levels of hostility". According to Savage and Schmitt, even Obama officials "offered tentative praise", recognising that key aspects of their framework had survived.[38]

Arguably, one of the principal reasons for this continuity was the personal and professional experiences of the many former military and intelligence officers who were involved in re-drafting the rules. Although nearly all of them resented the Obama administration's excessive centralisation and were committed to making counter-terrorism operations more aggressive, they also rejected the mindless militarism that Trump had espoused in his speeches. They had spent enough time in places like Iraq and Afghanistan to realise that civilian casualties made it more difficult for them and their local partners to achieve their objectives. Even Michael Flynn, one of Trump's "true believers" who had served as a senior intelligence officer in Iraq, understood that "victory" was contingent on local support, and that killing the wrong people resulted in less intelligence and more enemy recruits. "[I]f we kill one of them", he wrote in his book, "ten new fighters rush to fill the void".[39] Unlike Trump, therefore, many members of Trump's national security team had learned that imposing limits on the use of force was not just a moral or legal imperative, but a practical one. In this regard, they were closer to their Democratic predecessors than their own Republican President.

Ironically, the unofficial leader of the pushback against Trump's militaristic instincts was Mattis, the Defense Secretary. Chris Costa, the senior official who oversaw the process of re-writing the counter-terrorism "play book" at the National Security Council, told me that the protection of civilians became a recurring issue, stressing that "U.S. obligations to the rule of law and American values remained unchanged".[40] Speaking before the Senate Armed Services Committee, Mattis pledged:

> [We] will never fight at any time, especially in these wars among innocent people, without doing everything humanly possible to protect the innocent that the enemy purposely jeopardises by fighting from in amongst them. That is something we will always take as an absolute, in terms of how we conduct our tactical events on the battlefield.[41]

In practical terms, Mattis rejected the opportunity to reduce civilian protections to the bare minimum, which Trump had authorised him to do.[42] While loosening targeting rules and scrapping Obama's accountability measures, he maintained all mitigation procedures that local commanders had to follow before launching a strike.[43] Not least, he empowered senior commanders to follow higher standards, wherever they believed this was politically necessary and/or desirable. In Somalia, for example, US Africa Command chose to continue observing the "near certainty" standard, despite the country's re-classification as an "area of active hostility".[44] Contrary to what Hanson, the military historian, claimed, Mattis and "the generals" never had any intention of "bombing the shit".[45]

The strength of the institutional pushback could also be seen in the fate of Trump's most contentious proposals. During the election campaign, Trump had routinely talked about the re-introduction of torture and suggested that terrorists' families should be targeted in drone strikes. While many commentators claimed that these were examples of "bluster" and that Trump had quickly reversed his positions,[46] he had mentioned them so frequently, in both public and private settings,[47] that it would have been unsurprising for his national security team to take some action. Yet, from what is known, none of these ideas were ever pursued. The reasons were similar to the arguments against "bombing the shit" out of countries: ethical and legal concerns, as well as perceived lessons from fifteen years of the War on Terror, which suggested that torture and excessive violence were going to undermine local support and jeopardise relationships with allies and local partners, especially in Muslim majority countries. Costa phrased it diplomatically: "[W]e always offered options and strongly weighed in on what we thought was helpful and what we thought would… make us more vulnerable. And… in the end, our recommendations often times prevailed".[48]

A good example was Trump's demand to re-populate the Guantanamo Bay prison camp, which Obama had pledged—but failed—to close down. During the election campaign, Trump repeatedly promised to "load it up with bad dudes" from foreign battlefields.[49] While in office, he even suggested it should be used for domestic terror suspects, such as the Halloween attacker Sayfullo Saipov (see Introduction). Yet, despite signing an Executive Order to keep the facility open, and repeatedly expressing his determination to increase its population,[50] not a single person had been sent there at the time of writing. On the contrary, in May 2018, the repatriation of a long-time detainee to Saudi Arabia reduced the number of inmates from 41 to 40—the lowest it has been since President Bush created the facility in 2001.[51]

In the eyes of most "generals", Guantanamo had become a dated and divisive institution, whose revival was neither necessary nor desirable.[52] As Savage pointed out, while there were disagreements over what should happen with the remaining detainees, everyone accepted that the camp had become a "propaganda tool" for America's enemies, and that Supreme Court rulings had eliminated most of the legal "advantages" the facility had once had.[53] In any case, the American military had long developed alternatives for dealing with "enemy combatants", involving interrogations on warships or military bases, followed by trials in allied countries or domestic courts.[54] It was no accident, therefore, that Mattis, whose department was in charge of the camp, ignored the President's demands and made only minor changes to the existing policy.[55]

In doing so, Mattis' mindset mirrored that of people like Costa, Zarate and other veterans of the War on Terror who believed that—having gone through a fifteen year-long process of trial and error—American counter-terrorism policies were, in Zarate's words, "fairly set, fairly consistent, and—frankly— have proven to be fairly effective".[56] From this perspective, many of Trump's ideas were not just unnecessary, but ignorant and potentially harmful.

Consequences

"The generals" were no pacifists, however. The trend towards more—and more aggressive—counter-terrorism operations under Trump was consistent across several conflicts and nearly all theatres of operations. In both Yemen and Somalia, for example, the immediate consequence of being classified as "areas of active hostility" was a dramatic increase in drone strikes. Compared to the previous year, their number more than trebled in 2017 (126 in Yemen; 35 in Somalia).[57] In Afghanistan, the number of air strikes doubled (615 in 2016; 1,248 in 2017),[58] while the average number of weapons per strike rose from 2.17 to 3.49, resulting in a threefold increase in the amount of ordnance that American forces dropped over the country.[59]

As significant as the number of strikes was the devolution of decision-making powers. Even at the time of the Yakla operation, before many of the changes had been formalised, Trump officials were eager to demonstrate that the era of "micromanagement" was over. As Costa recalled:

> When I was told on a Sunday morning at three or four o'clock in the morning that we lost someone… I went into the White

House, I called the DoD [Department of Defense], and I made sure they knew I was at my desk and I would be there all day long. But I didn't ask them for a lot of information, because it was too close to the operation having unfolded, and I knew that, in time, we would have the appropriate level of information to pass to our leadership.[60]

This, he said, had been a conscious decision:

It wasn't that we didn't care, quite the contrary, it was that we were going to let the department and agencies—in this case the DoD—pull together the information that we needed and, in time, we were satisfied with the information that we had... I didn't ask tactical questions; in fact, I would eschew the tactical questions... [That was] not what the National Security Council was here to do.[61]

How strongly committed "the generals" were to this new approach became clear in April 2017, when American forces in Afghanistan dropped a so-called Mother of All Bombs (MOAB)—the largest, non-nuclear bomb in their arsenal—on a complex of Islamic State-run underground tunnels in the east of the country. It was the first time the device had been used in a conflict, prompting speculation about America's ultimate intentions and strategy.[62] In reality, neither the President nor the National Security Council—nor even the Secretary of Defense—had been consulted before its use. Newspapers reported that "the commander who made the decision had been given prior authority to use the bomb if needed".[63] Mattis described it as a "tactical event in the field", stressing that the decision had been taken by a local commander.[64]

Far from being an escalation, "the generals" regarded these changes as consistent with earlier, more hawkish periods of the War on Terror. During Obama's first term, for example, drone operations were at similar levels to 2017,[65] while the number of US air strikes in Afghanistan was higher during each year of the early 2010s than in 2017.[66] At the same time, "taking a bit more risk", as Zarate put it,[67] clearly involved trade-offs. As well as exposing American soldiers to greater dangers, they also increased the likelihood of "collateral damage". In Afghanistan, for example, the United Nations Assistance Mission in Afghanistan recorded an 18 per cent rise in American-linked non-combatant fatalities during Trump's first year in office (from 165 in 2016 to 196 in 2017).[68] This was less than expected, given that the number of air strikes had doubled and the amount of ordnance had nearly trebled, suggesting that mitigation procedures continued to work, there was no breakdown of discipline, and military commanders did not feel empowered to act recklessly. On the other hand, it showed that the idea of a "clean war" remained an illusion, and that more bombs would ultimately result in greater civilian casualties.

Equally problematic was the scrapping of Obama-era accountability measures. Under Trump, the Director of National Intelligence stopped publishing his annual reports on discrepancies between the casualty numbers of American government agencies and other organisations. As a consequence, the Defense Department and the CIA were no longer required systematically to justify all instances in which their reporting had "under-counted" civilian casualties.[69] In places like Syria, where ground access was difficult, this resulted in vastly different accounts of the "collateral damage" that American military operations had caused. While non-governmental organisations, such as the Syrian Observatory on Human Rights, have documented more than 3,300 non-combatant deaths in the campaign against Islamic State since 2014, the American government has acknowledged just over 1,000.[70] In its four-month offensive to re-take the Syrian city of Raqqa during the summer of 2017, the Trump administration confirmed only twenty-three civilian deaths—a figure which Amnesty International described as "neither accurate, nor credible, or serious" (see Chapter 6).[71] In combination with other measures—such as the (less rigorous) "country plan" system and an increased role in drone operations for the (less transparent) CIA[72]—this has diminished the extent to which government agencies can be held accountable for causing innocent deaths.

In the short term, the greatest risk was accidental escalations. Everyone in the Trump administration agreed that Obama had imposed too many restrictions, and that operational decisions needed to be taken quicker and further down the chain of command. In Costa's view, doing so enabled "a quicker decision cycle", and gave military commanders a greater ability to respond to events.[73] Yet, it also increased the probability of accidents and miscalculations, given the many complex conflicts in the Middle East in which America was involved. As Tony Blinken, a former Deputy Secretary of State and deputy National Security Advisor in the Obama administration, explained:

> Any incident in this kind of environment can turn into something much larger, even though it may not be intended. There are more and more friction points where Iranians and Americans are very close together. In Iraq now, with all of the Iran-supported militias… In Yemen, with the Iranians supplying the Houthis, and the Saudis and the UAE pushing back. And then, of course, the Israel-Iran-Hezbollah dynamic… One spark, and everything goes off—especially since we [no longer have] good channels of communication to de-escalate.[74]

This has been a particular danger in Syria, where some of America's biggest geopolitical adversaries—not only Iran, but also Russia—have supported rival groups and were present with military "advisers" and personnel, sometimes in close proximity to American forces.[75]

In the long term, a greater emphasis on "kinetic" operations was likely to give rise to a more one-sided, purely repressive approach towards countering terrorism. "The generals" have denied this. Costa told me that the immediate priority of defeating Islamic State had required a more military response, but that everyone remained committed to an integrated, long-term approach, which involved not just military force, but diplomacy, working with partners, and stabilisation.[76] But there was no evidence of any investment in these areas. For most of

Trump's first two years in office, the State Department was hollowed out and neglected, with many positions remaining unfilled and money for stabilisation being cut. William Burns, America's most senior former career diplomat, described it as a "savaging of American diplomacy", which involved "the biggest budget cuts in the modern history of the department", a "terminally flawed 'redesign process'", and the "blacklisting of [highly experienced] officers" simply because they had worked on controversial issues during the Obama administration.[77] This has also affected the counter-terrorism approaches of America's foreign partners. According to the academic Stephen Tankel, "they no longer talk to U.S. diplomats. They go straight to CENTCOM [United States Central Command]".[78]

Nevertheless, "the generals'" approach did not represent a suspension or abandonment of the Clausewitzian understanding of warfare. Their idea of empowering military operators and incurring "a bit more risk" was based on a thoroughly political understanding of "kinetic" power. In applying the lessons from the past fifteen years of the War on Terror, and by choosing to remain within the framework that had been established by previous administrations, they accepted—and upheld—existing rules, structures, and institutions, while seeking to implement changes that would allow for earlier, faster, and more heavily "kinetic" interventions, and—thus—prevent the rise of another Caliphate. This more traditional type of conservatism stood in marked contrast to the President's radical instincts, which—if implemented—would have challenged the political and constitutional basis for how American governments have deployed military force.

6

DEFEATING ISIS

One of the most useful Clausewitzian concepts in making sense of terrorism and counter-terrorism is the "centre of gravity". It has long been part of the military doctrines of many armed forces and military organisations, including NATO and the US Army. Most conceive of it as a physical location in which an enemy's forces are densely concentrated.[1] But this is an overly narrow interpretation. In *On War*, Clausewitz defined it as "the hub of all power and movement, on which everything depends [and] against which all our energies should be directed,"[2] making it clear that it could mean an adversary's army, but also—and equally—a country's capital, the personality of a leader, or even public opinion. For Clausewitz, therefore, the "centre of gravity" was not merely about a physical location or enemy forces, but—rather—a way of thinking about an adversary's sources of strength, and how they could be curtailed.

In the case of Islamic State, any discussion about the group's centre of gravity will inevitably lead to the issue of territory. No jihadist group has ever held as much land or governed as many people. More so than ideology or tactics, it was Islamic State's emphasis on territory and state-building—the idea of an Islamic State—that differentiated the group from its jihadist brethren. Territory gave it access to local fighters, sources of income,[3] and a permanent place to train, recruit and organise. It was also the reason for Islamic State's enormous allure, which resulted in more than 30,000 men and women from a hundred different countries wanting to join it.[4] Unlike al-Qaeda, it was not just fighting against something, but offered the opportunity to become part of a utopia—the creation of a new and entirely different society.[5]

Its greatest strength, however, was also its greatest weakness. While territory gave it a permanent "address" that supporters could find and go to, this was also true for its adversaries. By transforming into a (proto-)state with a fixed location, it robbed itself of the greatest advantage that terrorist groups hold in their confrontations with more conventional adversaries. Moreover, territory had become so central to Islamic State's identity that any losses would cause supporters to question its legitimacy.[6] Depriving the group of its territory was not just about diminishing its military capability, therefore, but undermining the very idea on which its power and appeal rested.

The campaign to defeat Islamic State's Caliphate—primarily in Syria and Iraq, but also in external "provinces" such as Libya and Afghanistan—began more than two years before Trump's election. Even so, Trump's supporters have insisted that it was their President who defeated the group. Steven Emerson, for example, a right-wing terrorism analyst, claimed that Islamic State had been "totally destroyed, 99 per cent, under Trump", and that it was Trump—not Obama—who had deprived the group of its "allure" and sense of "being a winning team".[7] In fact, as early as March 2018, Trump himself told a Republican audience that "we've taken back almost 100 per cent, in a very short period of time, of the land", stressing that "it all took place since our election".[8] Nine months later, he publicly declared victory over Islamic State, posting a video in which he said: "We have won against ISIS. We've beaten them, and we've beaten them badly".[9]

None of this was true. Though substantially weakened, Islamic State remained undefeated, and it was not Trump, or—rather—Trump alone, who had achieved the military successes against the group. As this chapter will show, the campaign against Islamic State consisted of three distinct phases. After some hesitation, Obama made defeating Islamic State a priority, created a plan and structure, and executed a significant part of the military campaign. Trump's "generals" continued implementing this strategy, albeit with the new "rules of engagement" that involved greater risks in return for faster, more decisive operations (see previous chapter). Trump's personal involvement was limited to the last phase, in which he declared victory over Islamic State and announced a pull-out of American forces from Syria. In doing so, he contradicted his own administration's policy, alienated allies, strengthened America's adversaries, and emboldened the (nearly defeated) Islamic State.

Obama's War

Trump was right, however, in criticising Obama's slow initial response to the rise of Islamic State. Five months after the group had broken with al-Qaeda and publicly declared its presence in Syria, Obama still portrayed the conflict as "someone else's civil war", in which only "some of [Syrian President Bashar] Assad's opponents" were extremists.[10] In January 2014, he notoriously compared Islamic State to an amateur basketball team, insisting that the takeover of the Iraqi city of Fallujah—which had happened a few days earlier—was the result of "local power struggles and disputes".[11] Even in May 2014, after the group had seized control of the Syrian city of Raqqa and large parts of north-eastern Iraq, he refused to acknowledge its growing influence. Speaking at the West Point military academy, he talked at length about al-Qaeda's leadership and "al-Qaeda affiliates" with "agendas focused in [the] countries where they operate", but failed to make a single reference to Islamic State.[12] One month later, the group declared its global Caliphate.

Arguably, Obama's deep and persistent reluctance to deal with the emerging threat was no accident or oversight, but a logical consequence of his core beliefs and objectives. He had been elected, in no small part, because of his opposition to the Iraq intervention and other military "adventures". Rather than starting wars, he wanted to be the President who ended them.[13] In a recurring statement that could easily have been Trump's, he told audiences that it was "time to focus on nation-building here at home".[14] This resulted in two policy positions that (inadvertently) enabled the rise of Islamic State. One was the hasty withdrawal from Iraq, which left a deeply broken country to its own devices and gave Islamic State—whose predecessors had been close to defeated by 2010—a new lease of life.[15] The other was his unwillingness to do more than the bare minimum in Syria, even as it became clear that the country was descending into a vicious sectarian conflict and started attracting support from jihadists all over the world. Indeed, his instinctive response to complex and seemingly intractable situations in faraway places was "don't do stupid shit"[16]—which frequently translated into doing nothing much at all.

Another factor was Obama's own narrative, which revolved around a simplistic reading of the jihadist movement as consisting of a single organisation, al-Qaeda, and an equally simplistic—as well as empirically flawed[17]—expectation that the popular revolutions of the Arab Spring would remove the "cancers" of repression and authoritarianism which had created it. Following the killing of bin Laden, his consistent message was that al-Qaeda had stopped being "relevant",[18] that most of its affiliates were now pursuing "local" (as opposed to "global", that is, anti-Western) agendas,[19] and that the historical trajectory in the Middle East was pointing towards "a world that is more peaceful, more stable, and more just".[20] From this perspective, the rise of Islamic State was not just inconvenient, but virtually inconceivable.

When Obama launched his counter-Islamic State campaign in September 2014, it was largely in response to the Iraqi government's dramatic losses of territory and the beheading of the American hostage James Foley,[21] rather than as a result of serious planning or preparation. By officials' own admission, there was barely any intelligence from within the group's territories, nor did America have local partners with whom to coordinate its campaign.[22] It took another year to develop a full campaign plan, build an international coalition, forge a new relationship with the Iraqi government, develop deeper ties with the Syrian Kurds, and stand up a training programme for "moderate rebels" in Jordan.[23] According to Alexander Bick, who served on the National Security Council, it was only in October 2015—once "the objective was clear, the partners were clear, and the plan was clear"—that Obama was happy to sign off on troop increases and the deployment of special operators.[24]

The overarching aim of Obama's plan was to "degrade and ultimately destroy" Islamic State. As well as keeping America safe and countering the expansion of Islamic State into other territories, such as Libya and Afghanistan, this primarily meant re-taking Raqqa and Mosul—the two largest cities in Islamic State territory, which were believed to be key to unravelling the Caliphate as a whole. When Defense Secretary Ash Carter and his colleagues presented the final version of the plan, they produced "a map with two bright red arrows, pointed to Mosul and Raqqa", and explained the different steps that were required in order "to get there".[25] They also made it clear that defeating the group had to be prioritised over everything else, including the overthrow of Assad, which had been America's principal objective in Syria. Obama accepted this,[26] and Trump was wrong, therefore, to criticise his predecessor for trying to "fight Assad and ISIS simultaneously".[27] He did not.

The plan consisted of three main elements:

- The first was "Operation Inherent Resolve", a combined military air and ground campaign, in which America supported an eclectic (and politically challenging) group of local partners in accordance with Obama's "by, with, and through" doctrine. On the Iraqi side, the main partners were the Kurdish regional administration and the Baghdad government, whose sectarianism and dysfunction had been blamed for the rise of Islamic State. In Syria, it relied on "moderate rebels" who were prepared to turn their fire on Islamic State, and (what became) the predominantly Kurdish Syrian Democratic Forces (SDF), which Turkey regarded with suspicion because of its links with the separatist Kurdish Workers' Party (PKK). To varying degrees, these partnerships involved America providing training, equipment, weapons, and intelligence, as well as air strikes and small numbers of special forces (300 in Syria by mid-2016).[28]

- The second element was a diplomatic coalition through which America coordinated international efforts. By the end of Obama's tenure, it had more than seventy members, including practically all of America's allies in Europe, the Middle East, parts of Africa, as well as NATO and the European Union (but not Russia and Iran).[29] The purpose was to mobilise diplomatic and political support, share intelligence on foreign fighters and terrorist financing, and get Muslim majority countries, especially in the Gulf, more actively involved in debunking Islamic State's ideology. Equally important, the so-called Global Coalition was a vehicle for "burden-sharing", through which other countries could contribute militarily (for example, by participating in air strikes, surveillance missions, or providing weapons and equipment), financially, or by helping to run stabilisation and reconstruction projects.

- Finally, the guiding principle, which was meant to inform every aspect of the campaign, was the idea of sustainability. As Carter explained, "I had no doubt that our troops could have marched into Raqqa and Mosul and ejected ISIS" within a matter of weeks, but such a victory would have been "fleeting unless communities taken from ISIS could rebuild and secure themselves to prevent such extremism" from returning.[30] To achieve what Carter called a "lasting defeat" of the group required attention to civilian casualties, keeping American troops away from the frontlines, making sure that "liberated" areas could be held and defended by locals, as well as providing assistance for post-conflict stabilisation, reconstruction, and the resettlement of displaced persons. In the eyes of Obama officials, this reflected "the lessons of the

Iraq and Afghanistan wars",[31] where the use of "kinetic" power had on many occasions been counterproductive and military victories reversed.

While Islamic State continued to make gains until March 2015, America's local partners—particularly the Peshmerga in the Kurdish region of Iraq, the SDF, and the Iraqi Security Forces—gradually started holding their own. By 2016, they were taking back towns and cities in both countries, culminating in a six-month operation to capture Mosul—one of the campaign's key military objectives.[32] By the time Obama left office, his campaign had gained nearly 43 per cent of the group's territory, and freed more than 2.4 million people from its rule.[33] Most importantly, this had been achieved without ceding any "liberated" territories, and while only thirty-three American soldiers lost their lives. Although the official figure of 188 civilian deaths is almost certainly too low, it was significantly lower than corresponding figures for the Trump administration.[34]

The main criticism of Obama was not the campaign per se, but that it took him such a long time to get there. He only decided to act when Islamic State was (literally) marching on Baghdad and threatened not just Iraq and Syria, but the region as a whole. What's more, his reluctance to take risks meant that another year went by until the Coalition started inflicting major losses. While this may have made the campaign more sustainable, it also created a lag period in which America and the other members of the Coalition *claimed* to be at war with Islamic State, but large parts of the group's territory and infrastructure—including its ability to plot terrorist attacks— remained largely intact. It was during this period that the attacks in Paris and Brussels were being planned.

Obama also failed to anticipate some of his strategy's political consequences. In Iraq, his cautious approach prompted the government to seek help from Iran, which deepened the relationship between Baghdad and one of America's principal adversaries. According to Inna Rudolf, an expert on Shiite militias in Iraq:

When Mosul fell and the army collapsed [in June 2014], [the Iraqi Prime Minister Nouri] al-Maliki was seeking help from the Obama administration… Obama was trying to explain it would be a longer process, we need to get everyone on board, there has to be a structure, institutions, etc., and at that point, Maliki just gave up and contacted Iran.[35]

Months before Obama's intervention, the government in Tehran sent military advisers and assisted with the creation of militia groups. Though not all of the so-called Popular Mobilisation Units were dominated by Iran (and not all were exclusively Shiite),[36] many Iraqis credited them—and their Iranian sponsors—with defeating Islamic State. As Rudolf told me, Iraqis are convinced that, "in the hour of need, Iran was there for us".[37] America's contribution, on the other hand, has been barely acknowledged.[38]

In Syria, Obama's reliance on the SDF not only caused tensions with Turkey, but essentially created an embryonic Kurdish homeland.[39] Although American advisers were keen to broaden the group's composition, and portray it as democratic and multi-sectarian, the SDF always remained a primarily Kurdish militia with a strong commitment to the (Marxist) ideology of the PKK's founder, Abdullah Ocalan. While effective in combating Islamic State, its dominance over northern and northeastern Syria, including—eventually—the city of Raqqa, was unsustainable without American support. Despite its emphasis on the long-term, Obama's plan failed to confront this issue, or make any statement on Kurdish autonomy, independence, or even the future of the Syrian Kurds.[40] It effectively left the Kurdish question to the next administration to resolve.

The Generals' War

During the election campaign, Trump frequently criticised Obama for "not doing much" against Islamic State, and at one point even claimed that he was not bombing the country at all.[41] Trump also talked about a "secret plan", which he would implement once elected. In April 2016, he told his supporters: "We're gonna beat ISIS very quickly, folks. It's gonna be fast. [And] I have a great plan. They ask, 'What is it?' Well, I'd rather not say".[42] The clearest evidence that no such plan had ever existed came during the first month of his Presidency, when he ordered his "generals" to come up with an *actual* plan.[43]

The strategy for defeating Islamic State that "the generals" produced, and which Trump followed until December 2018, was—in essence—a modified version of Obama's plan. Initially, it was so similar that its publication had to be delayed several times in order to find ways to make it look "more different".[44] In the end, it reflected the "generals'" more military-centric view of the world, but kept in place Obama's main assumptions and lines of effort. Crucially, Trump seemed happy to let "the generals" run the campaign with minimal interference from himself. Consistent with his philosophy, he believed that it was his job to allow "the generals" to do theirs—which meant signing off on anything they thought would deliver the desired result.

Like Obama's strategy, the "Defeat ISIS Plan" sought to destroy Islamic State in its core territory, prevent the group's expansion, and protect America from terrorist attacks. Unlike Trump, who had predicted that it could be defeated within weeks, "the generals" articulated no overall timeline or specific date. Rather, they presented the aim of defeating Islamic State as an important, ongoing priority that would continue to consume significant attention and resources, while making clear that it was the new administration's intention to speed up military operations. They also maintained all the structures and partnerships that had been created under Obama. In accordance with the "by, with, and through" doctrine, American forces continued working with the same local partners—in some cases more extensively so—while the Global Coalition remained the diplomatic vehicle through which America coordinated international support.

Most tellingly, most of the key individuals that had created and implemented Obama's plan were allowed to carry on. On the military side, this included Joseph Dunford as Chairman of the Joint Chiefs, Joseph Votel as Commander of United States Central Command (CENTCOM), and Stephen Townsend as the Commanding General of Operation Inherent Resolve, while Brett McGurk, a diplomat, remained as head of the Global Coalition. It was clear, therefore, that Trump's generals did not share the President's assessment that Obama's plan had been a total disaster. Although they never publicly said so, the Operation's deputy commander, a general from New Zealand, was less cautious: "The strategy hasn't changed at all", he told *Business Insider* in mid-2017.[45]

Not everything stayed exactly the same, however. Given Trump's long-standing (and deeply felt) aversion to "nation-building", there were notably fewer mentions of post-conflict stabilisation and the idea of "sustainability". Although the National Security Strategy referred to "denying terrorist safe havens"—which insiders regarded as "code" for the kind of efforts that Trump despised—officials were eager to downplay American involvement in post-conflict reconstruction. Whenever asked, they argued that America's role in the fight against Islamic State was primarily military, and though American agencies were happy to "clear the rubble" and make sure that people in affected areas had water and electricity, anything more substantive had to be paid for—and run—by other countries.[46]

The second change resulted from the new rules for "kinetic" operations (see Chapter 5). While the status of Syria and Iraq as "areas of active hostility" remained unchanged, the Trump administration's new targeting rules, the deployment of American troops closer to the frontlines, and—especially—the devolution of decision-making powers facilitated faster and "riskier" operations. Although these changes applied across all missions and theatres of operations, and were not, therefore, specifically related to Syria, Iraq, and/or Operation Inherent Resolve, it was no secret that "the generals" understood them as a vitally important element of their plan for defeating the Caliphate.[47]

Finally, the Trump administration intensified their support for the SDF. Starting in May 2017, America provided the group not only with air support and training, as Obama had done, but more military "advisers", equipment, as well as "mortars, machine guns, ammunition, and light armoured vehicles".[48] To no one's surprise, Turkey, which considered the SDF—and, in particular, its Kurdish units—as part of the PKK, was strongly opposed. Yet, Trump officials believed that the SDF was going to be key in the battle for Raqqa—the second major military objective after the fall of Mosul. In addition to the devolution of authorities, Costa regarded the intensified partnership with the SDF as the "biggest example" of how the new administration accelerated and, therefore, changed the dynamics of the campaign.[49]

Two operations that McGurk described in a briefing at the end of 2017 illustrated the effects of these changes. The first was the operation to re-take Tabqa, a town in north central Syria, which is located next to a large dam. In mid-March, an SDF unit spotted a gap in Islamic State's defences and requested American support. According to McGurk, "They had to launch almost immediately. They said, if we can launch within days to hop over a body of water… and catch ISIS by surprise, [we] could seize [the city]".[50] During Obama's tenure, the operation would have been subject to "interagency review", and the approval—had it been given—might have come too late. Under "the generals'" leadership, the decision was taken immediately. Within days, 500 SDF fighters, supported by American air strikes and 500 Special Operations forces, started attacking Islamic State positions, leading to six weeks of intense fighting and the town's eventual "liberation".[51] While successful, the operation was not without risk: dozens of Islamic State fighters had hidden inside the dam, and repeatedly threatened to blow it up if attacked. Had they done so, the result would have been a humanitarian and environmental catastrophe.[52]

The second example was the operation to capture Islamic State's capital Raqqa, which began in early June and concluded by mid-October. It heavily relied on the (recently empowered) SDF, whose fighters served as the ground force guiding Coalition air strikes and artillery in what turned out to be a drawn-out, devastating battle with many civilian casualties (see below). The alternative, McGurk explained, "would have required [the deployment of]… tens of thousands of American troops", which he said was "a model that we do not want to return to".[53] By the end of the operation, 400 SDF fighters but not a single American soldier had been killed in action. The biggest difference was the approach to post-conflict reconstruction. McGurk admitted that there had been large-scale displacement, and that it would take "a very long time before people are able to return" to the city.[54] Yet, he made it clear that this was no longer America's problem: "We're in the business of stabilizing these areas… clearing landmines—basic water, basic health, electricity. We're not in the business of nation-building exercises and long-term reconstruction".[55]

Rush to Victory

By the end of 2017, the Coalition had taken back a further 50 per cent of the territory that Islamic State in Syria and Iraq had controlled at its peak, which was reduced to just 7 per cent of its maximum size, with another 5.3 million people freed from its rule.[56] Another year later, the Caliphate—which had once threatened the entire world—consisted of little more than a few villages in the Euphrates River Valley, amounting to less than 2 per cent of its territory in early 2015.[57]

Estimates of the number of remaining Islamic State fighters differed, because it was never clear how many of the people who had, at one point or another, fought for the group actually belonged to it, or to what extent "civilian" supporters of the group, such as local administrators, teachers or judges, should be considered "fighters".[58] In addition, many of those who were members may not have been killed or captured, but—instead—gone underground, waiting for the next opportunity to re-emerge and fight again. Although everyone agreed that the group had lost a significant proportion of its manpower, the United Nations and a report by the Pentagon's Inspector General estimated "up to 30,000" members by the summer of 2018,[59] while the Department of Defense's leadership—and the President—gave a figure of just 1,000.[60] Whatever the truth, no one doubted that Islamic State had incurred significant losses, and that its decline had accelerated since Trump's inauguration.[61]

While this seemed like good news, the campaign's rapid success also created problems. First among them was a rise in civilian casualties. In the case of Raqqa, this was routinely blamed on the "difficult urban environment", and the fact that Islamic State fighters had used civilians as "human shields".[62] But this was only part of the story. A significant number of the 4,000 Coalition air strikes relied on information from the SDF, which did not consistently apply US procedures for mitigating civilian casualties.[63] Moreover, an estimated 35,000 artillery rounds, which a US Marine Corps battalion had fired from a position more than twenty miles away from the city, only had an accuracy of 100 metres, meaning that "accidents" and "unintentional deaths" were all but guaranteed.[64] It is possible, therefore, that a significant part of the 3,000 or so civilian casualties that have been counted were caused by the Coalition, and that their actual number was much larger than the twenty-three civilian deaths that the Department of Defense initially admitted.

Following an investigation by the non-governmental organisation Airwars, which identified 1,500 civilians from Raqqa as killed by (Coalition) air strikes, the Pentagon increased the official count to seventy-seven.[65] When asked about the discrepancy, a Pentagon spokesman stated that "no one will ever know [how many civilians died in Raqqa]", while ignoring that his own administration had scrapped the accountability measures that might have explained it (see Chapter 5).[66]

Destruction on this scale bolstered the jihadist narrative. Even organisations like Raqqa is Being Slaughtered Silently, a civil society group which had courageously defied Islamic State's rule, condemned the Coalition's campaign as feckless and counter-productive. Abdalaziz Alhamza, one of its spokespeople, said:

> [People used to] fear Russian air strikes and Assad's forces. But then the strategy of the Coalition seemed to change. The strikes seemed more random, less accurate. They felt that the main goal was only to get rid of ISIS, without caring enough about thousands of civilians who are living there.[67]

Hassan Hassan, a Syrian analyst, believes that the disregard for civilian casualties helped jihadist groups reinforce the idea that Sunni Muslims were being oppressed rather than liberated. He told me:

> Jihadists are very good at telling a story. So what they do with people who don't agree with them, is to ask: "What's the common denominator between the destruction of Aleppo [by Russia], the destruction of Mosul, and the destruction of Raqqa [by the Coalition]? All the Sunni areas in Syria and Iraq are destroyed, and they were destroyed by forces that supposedly don't work with each other. Is that a coincidence?" Most people will say no, it was deliberate…
>
> They are simple people, they don't understand the differences between American and Russian military doctrine. All they see is the outcome, and the outcome is destruction. That's why conspiracy theories thrive in the region.[68]

Francois-Regis Legrier, a senior French officer, who had participated in the campaign, was one of the few Western military figures to criticise the Coalition's approach. In an article for *National Defense Review*, he confirmed Hassan's assessment: "We have massively destroyed the infrastructure and given the population a disgusting image of what may be a Western-style liberation".[69] In his view, this had been a result of "the generals'" rush to victory, but also—and equally—of the doctrine of "by, with, and through", which had perpetuated the idea that wars could be fought with minimal risks to Western troops, from the air and/or by proxies.[70]

The situation in Raqqa was made worse by a complete lack of preparation for the aftermath. Although the State Department had intended to put together an alliance of countries to support the reconstruction of "liberated" areas, and Trump was reported to have talked about it with King Salman of Saudi Arabia,[71] the victory in Raqqa happened too quickly for a coordinated—and well-funded—initiative to come together. The failure to find money elsewhere did not stop Trump from announcing that more than $200 million of American aid, which had been set aside for stabilisation efforts in Syria, would be cut.[72] As a result, large parts of Raqqa remained without water and electricity by the end of 2018, while most bridges and hospitals lay in ruins. American forces and civilian agencies maintained their presence, but focused on preventing Islamic State from returning.[73] At the time of writing, the money that America and other countries had committed to post-conflict construction in Raqqa was a fraction of what experts believed was needed—and much of it had not (yet) arrived.[74]

Not least, the rapid victories in Syria exacerbated the *political* problems that the new administration had inherited from Obama. By late 2018, the SDF had captured most of the territory in Syria that had been governed by Islamic State, with an estimated population of 2 million people. It relied on a contingent of 2,000 (mostly) American troops, which protected the territory against a return of Islamic State, attacks by the Syrian regime, but also—and crucially—Turkey in the north. In supporting the group, America was sponsoring an entity whose Marxist ideology was fundamentally at odds with its own, and which had virtually no legitimacy among the people it ruled. According to Hassan, Kurdish militia rule only increased the sense of paranoia and grievance among Sunni Arabs, who had no sympathy for either Assad or Islamic State, but now found themselves governed by a non-Arab group, which spoke a different language and whose ultimate motives were unclear.[75] Joshua Landis, a Syria expert, who has conducted fieldwork in the region for decades, described the local dynamics as follows:

The place is a hellhole. The Kurds hate the Arabs and vice versa. The different tribes are all stealing each other's land, and some were working with the [Assad] regime to out-compete the others. The Assyrians, Yazidis, and other minorities are trying to look out for themselves and escape the region, which is desperately poor and disadvantaged. It is right out of the barroom scene from Star Wars.[76]

There is no guarantee that a slower pace of operations would have avoided these problems.[77] But the "generals'" primarily kinetic approach, and the resulting failure to prepare for the political consequences of their "rush to victory", probably made them worse.

Trump's War

Until the end of 2018, Trump had largely left the counter-Islamic State campaign to his "generals". Other than his (failed) attempts to get other countries to pay for reconstruction, there is no evidence that he became closely involved or took any interest in what was happening. Earlier that year, Rex Tillerson, the Secretary of State, had given a detailed speech outlining America's objectives in Syria, which included not just defeating Islamic State and preventing the re-emergence of "ungoverned spaces", but the establishment of political institutions, the resettlement of refugees, as well as thwarting the ambitions of Assad and his Russian and Iranian allies.[78]

This dramatically changed on 19 December 2018, when Trump posted a tweet which said that "[w]e have defeated ISIS in Syria", and that American troops would pull out of the country.[79] Several hours later, he added a short video claiming that Islamic State *as a whole* had been beaten, and that "our boys, our young women, our men, they're all coming back".[80] Although subsequent messages were more guarded,[81] and both Pence and Pompeo made it clear that the mission had not changed,[82] Trump's sudden intervention overturned the administration's policy and jeopardised many of the gains that had been made since 2014.

Indeed, none of "the generals" agreed with the substance of Trump's assessment. During a Senate hearing in January 2019, leaders of the intelligence community, such as Dan Coats, the Director of National Intelligence, and Gina Haspel, the CIA Director, whom Trump himself had appointed, publicly contradicted his view that Islamic State was defeated. While agreeing that the Coalition had made gains, and that Islamic State was unlikely to capture new territory in the short-term, they pointed out that "ISIS still commands thousands of fighters" and was "perpetrating attacks… to undermine stabilization efforts and retaliate against its enemies".[83] They predicted that "any reduction in CT [counter-terrorism] pressure"—in other words, pulling out of Syria—would allow the group to "strengthen its clandestine presence and… [rebuild] key capabilities", including its ability to attack America and Western allies.[84]

They also emphasised that Islamic State had become a transnational network with global reach. Although the loss of territory had diminished the group's allure, many of its international supporters remained committed to the cause.[85] As Coats explained, "despite significant leadership and territorial losses", Islamic State still had eight so-called provinces outside of Syria and Iraq, as well as "more than a dozen networks, and thousands of dispersed supporters around the world".[86] In Europe alone, it had inspired a dozen terrorist attacks in 2018—significantly fewer than in 2017, but more than in any year before 2015.[87] Although Trump later ordered Coats, Haspel and other intelligence chiefs to "correct" their assessment, it was clear that none of them actually shared the President's view.[88]

So why did Trump make the announcement? Media reports suggested that he had been "talked into" it by the Turkish President, Recep Tayyip Erdoğan.[89] This resonated with the notion of Trump as an unprincipled buffoon, who would adopt the positions of whomever he had last met or had a conversation with. Yet, the idea of pulling out of Syria and declaring Islamic State defeated was neither new nor at odds with his long-standing convictions. Politically, it allowed him to deliver on one of his campaign promises—"beating ISIS"—at a time when fulfilling other pledges—especially the wall with Mexico—seemed more difficult. Ideologically, it aligned perfectly with his doctrine, which postulated that America must not be involved in occupations or "never-ending" wars, and that "killing terrorists" required no permanent military commitment. In fact, it was widely reported that Trump had asked his national security team to present him with scenarios for "pulling out of Syria" as early as April. When they did so, he immediately opted for "full withdrawal", in spite of warnings by Mattis and Dunford that doing so would be "catastrophic". Although he ultimately changed his mind, he told his "generals" that they would have no more than six months to "complete the mission".[90] In retrospect, therefore, neither the announcement nor the timing should have been a surprise.

Fallout

One of the most negative consequences of Trump's announcement was its impact on local partners, given that America effectively abandoned the Syrian Kurds, whose support had been essential to re-taking not just Raqqa but all of north-eastern Syria. Although the SDF had become a powerful militia, whose fighters were seen as "tenacious and effective",[91] it remained dependent on American air and ground support. Without it, most experts believed that the Kurdish administration would quickly collapse from within or under attack from Turkey. While this would "solve" the question of what to do with America's Kurdish "protectorate",[92] the Kurds regarded it as a profound betrayal. A Kurdish community leader in Europe told me, "Many feel that our [American] friends have let us down. People say, we shouldn't have fought for them. We shouldn't have fought for areas other than our own."[93] For the "generals", abandoning the SDF was not just a betrayal of the Syrian Kurds, but sent a terrible signal to any group or government that America was hoping to partner with in future. Mattis and McGurk felt so strongly about it that they resigned.[94]

Even if Trump's announcement has been partly reversed (in March 2019, the Pentagon announced that 1,000 troops would be staying beyond May of that year),[95] his intervention instantly changed the political and military dynamics on the ground. For Islamic State, it was the first piece of good news in nearly four years, as it indicated that the (combined) pressure from America and the SDF, which had nearly destroyed it, would soon diminish. In an official response, the group predicted a return of chaos and instability,[96] which it hoped would create opportunities for renewed radicalisation and recruitment.[97] Indeed, the SDF immediately redeployed fighters away from the campaign against Islamic State to what it regarded as its own priority—countering a military offensive by Turkey in north-western Syria. It also announced that it was planning to release 3,200 foreign jihadists whom it had arrested and held on behalf of their countries of origin.[98] Kurdish leaders, meanwhile, wasted no time in reaching out to Assad, seeking a "deal" that would offer protection in return for extending the influence of America's adversaries—the Damascus government and its Russian and Iranian allies—across Kurdish territories in the northeast.[99] As *Time* magazine put it, "With one tweet, Trump may have given Assad a path to victory".[100]

From a wider perspective, Trump's announcement was neither urgent nor necessary, considering that America's presence in Syria was small (2,000 troops), relatively cheap ($15 billion per year),[101] and had caused few American losses (only four deaths before his December 2018 announcement).[102] In making it, Trump contradicted his own government's strategy, and undermined the "by, with, and through" doctrine, which had become the principal basis for projecting American force in the War on Terror. Worst of all, he offered no realistic alternative to the (largely successful) partnership with the SDF.[103] In a February 2019 interview, he said:

> We'll come back if we have to. We have very fast airplanes, we have very good cargo planes. We can come back very quickly…

We have a base in Iraq… I've rarely seen anything like it. And it's there. And we'll be there.[104]

Few experts believed that adopting a strategy of "bombing the shit" was viable or adequate, or that America's relationship with the SDF, which had taken four years to build, could easily be replaced by air strikes and a tiny number of troops in theatre.[105] (In McGurk's view, Trump's plan would have exposed the remaining troops to even greater risks.)[106] Meanwhile, there was no plan for resolving the Syrian conflict, easing the tensions between the Syrian Kurds and Turkey, or making sure that the military gains against Islamic State could be sustained.[107] In the eyes of many, Trump was effectively repeating his predecessor's mistake, who had abandoned Iraq without a clear strategy or objectives at a time when Islamic State was nearly—but not entirely—beaten. Lindsey Graham, a Republican Senator, described it as "Iraq on steroids".[108]

This should not diminish the military success of a campaign which targeted—and effectively destroyed—the "centre of gravity" of a group that, four years earlier, had seemed like an all-powerful threat. Yet, this was achieved not because of Trump, but largely despite him. Although the contributions of Obama and "the generals" were not flawless—Obama's approach was too timid, "the generals'" too aggressive—they were based on the same, generally sound framework, which required an "enduring defeat" of Islamic State and foresaw a longer-term commitment to Syria. Trump's intervention not only contradicted this framework, but jeopardised the military gains that it had enabled. No doubt, short-term political interests—the desire for a "quick win"—played a role. More importantly, though, it was a reflection of his doctrine: even after two years in office, Trump's hostility towards foreign commitments, and his belief in fighting terrorism by brute force, remained unchanged.

7

FRIENDS AND FOES

During the Cold War, Presidents of the United States were often described as "leaders of the free world". Although the expression has become less popular in recent decades, it encapsulates what many Americans (still) believe makes their country "exceptional"—that America is better, stronger, and more powerful than other countries,[1] and that it represents an ideal—the idea of freedom—which it has a duty to uphold and promote. For President Abraham Lincoln (1861–65), the Declaration of Independence "gave liberty, not alone to the people of this country, but… to the world for all future time".[2] While Presidents have taken different approaches towards fulfilling this mission, few have denied or questioned their responsibility for doing so.[3] As the academic Kori Schake argues, it has allowed America to become a more benign hegemon, as other countries have generally been happy to follow its rules.[4] Spreading freedom, in other words, was not just about doing the world a favour, but in America's own, enlightened self-interest.

This has also influenced America's approach towards fighting terrorism. Immediately after the September 11 attacks, it was obvious to many Americans that their country had to lead a global effort to rid the world of terrorism—not only because it was fellow Americans who had been killed, but because the attack was consciously framed as an assault on freedom.[5] Although Presidents Bush and Obama had vastly different ideas of what it meant to be "leaders of the free world", they rejected the notion that terrorism could be defeated by "killing terror-ists" alone, and that "stability" without freedom was positive or desirable. Even if their efforts were not always consistent or successful, they sincerely believed that oppression was the "root cause" of terrorism, and that freedom was its natural antidote. In their minds, and in the minds of nearly every other President before them, promoting freedom was not only no contradiction to making America safe, it was America's ultimate aim and purpose, and the reason why America, rather than any other nation, had to lead the fight.

With the possible exception of his idol, Andrew Jackson, Donald Trump was the first American President who has never associated American exceptionalism with the idea of spreading freedom, and whose definition of American global leadership involved no moral or idealistic dimension. When the *New York Times* asked him when he thought America was "great", he talked about the early twentieth century and the 1950s—his-torical periods in which America experienced economic booms or had just won wars. In Trump's view, they were eras in which "we were not pushed around, we were respected by every-body... we were pretty much doing what we had to do".[6] His idea of "greatness", therefore, was more conventionally nation-alistic than that of his predecessors: it involved sovereignty (in the sense of not being shackled by international law, institu-tions, and relationships with other countries), and the ability to get one's way.

Indeed, Trump has rarely talked about relationships or alli-ances with other countries in positive terms, except when he knew that doing so would be popular with his audience (for example, in the case of Israel). The principal ways in which he has conceived of America's interaction with the world seems to have been in competitive terms—through wars and deals—none of which required sustained diplomatic engagement or a systematic foreign policy approach. This did not make Trump an isolationist, but it demonstrated the hostility, scepticism, and/or lack of interest with which he has approached main-stream notions of American global leadership.

FRIENDS AND FOES

As this chapter will show, Trump's approach to foreign policy has been shaped primarily by idiosyncrasies and his "know-nothing" advisers' ignorance. In Afghanistan, his idea of "doing a deal" with the Taliban may have sounded imaginative, but its execution has been hasty and half-hearted. In the Middle East, the effort to outsource American leadership to Saudi Arabia has made America dependent on an erratic partner with fundamentally different priorities, whose reckless behaviour in the region has drawn America into multiple new conflicts. Moreover, through his shameless promotion of foreign "strongmen", Trump has not just abandoned any pretence that America promotes freedom, but also removed all incentives for foreign partners to observe minimum standards in their own "Wars on Terror". Far from promoting stability, Trump's foreign policy has resulted in a vacuum of global leadership and greater opportunities for terrorist groups to gain support, take advantage of violent conflicts, and find safe havens.

Deals

The most compelling way to understand Trump's approach towards diplomacy is through his experience as a businessman. Trump, after all, never thought of himself as a politician—never mind a diplomat—and part of his electoral appeal, which he touted in practically every campaign speech, was that he would apply his business skills to Washington's problems. In Trump's mind, by far the most important of these skills was his ability to negotiate good deals. The most consistent theme in his rhetoric, starting with his first public interviews in the early 1980s, was the idea that America had been taken advantage of by other countries, and that American politicians and diplomats were terrible at negotiating on behalf of their country. When he declared his candidacy, he said: "Our country needs a truly great leader, and we need a truly great leader now. We need a leader that wrote *The Art of the Deal*"[7]—referring to his 1987 book, in which he described his experience as a property developer in New York.

Though it remains unclear how many of the events and inter-actions in *The Art of the Deal* actually took place—Trump's ghost writer described it as a "non-fiction work of fiction"[8]—it never-theless gives a good insight into how Trump thinks of negotia-tions.[9] Nearly all the deals it describes resulted from engagements with just one party, represented by one person, that he negoti-ated with over meals, via telephone, or—less often—in a more formal setting. Although other people, such as lawyers and bank-ers, are mentioned, their jobs typically involved fixing appoint-ments, writing up contracts or "crunching numbers", without playing any meaningful role in the negotiation itself. He dis-misses consultants and experts, whom he portrays as greedy and lacking his entrepreneurial "instincts".[10] Rather than relying on professional advisers, he recommends talking to ordinary people, friends, or cab drivers: "I [ask] everyone for an opinion... until I begin to get a gut feeling about something. That's when I make a decision".[11] To the extent that there is an overall argument, it is the idea that "deals" are games of perception, in which "fun-damentals" matter less than expectations, hopes and fears—and that virtually any means are justified to create or manipulate them.[12] Needless to say, Trump considers himself to be a master at this game: "Deals are my art form", he writes: "That's how I get my kicks".[13]

It was not only for ideological reasons, therefore, that Trump sought to marginalise the State Department. From his perspec-tive, politics—like business—was a never-ending series of deals, which did not require large bureaucracies, thousands of diplo-mats, and special envoys for issues like women and arms con-trol. (The person he appointed as his first Secretary of State, Rex Tillerson, was a former CEO of Exxon Mobile whom he described as a "world-class player and dealmaker".)[14] Nor, in fact, did he care about international treaties or multilateral organisations, which complicated the kind of bilateral negotia-tions he was familiar with and needlessly constrained America's ability to impose its will. When Mattis praised the "rules-based post-war international order" in a July 2017 meeting as "the greatest gift the greatest generation left us", Trump allegedly responded: "That's exactly what I don't want".[15]

Talking to the Taliban

One of the greatest tests for Trump's deal-making ability was Afghanistan. Although America had deployed up to 100,000 troops to the country, the Taliban proved to be a resilient enemy which neither Obama nor his predecessor were able to defeat. Beginning in 2011, Trump started arguing that the conflict was a waste of time, money, and American lives, and that American troops should come home. In one of many tweets that he posted during that period, he said: "Let's get out of Afghanistan. Our troops are being killed... We waste billions there. Nonsense! Rebuild the USA".[16] This remained his message throughout the election campaign, when he told supporters that America's "destructive cycle of intervention and chaos" had to end, and that American forces should not be in "[places] that we shouldn't be fighting in".[17]

Half a year into his Presidency, however, he seemed to change his mind. In a major speech on Afghanistan in August 2017, he acknowledged that his "original instinct" had been to "pull out", and that "historically, I like following my instincts".[18] But, having studied the situation, he concluded that doing so would be a mistake, as it "would create a vacuum" and allow terrorist groups to thrive. As a consequence, he had decided to step up the military campaign and increase, rather than reduce, the number of American troops. He also made it clear that there would be no "arbitrary timetables", and that America was going to stay as long as it was needed.[19]

In the media, the President's decision was celebrated as a major victory for the "generals", because it avoided a hasty withdrawal and delayed the question of what to do with the country.[20] What many did not realise: it also laid the groundwork for negotiations with the Taliban.[21] Mattis and the other "generals" had convinced themselves that, despite the group's success, the conflict had reached a "mutually hurting stalemate",[22] in which all parties were ready to settle for less than their maximum demands.[23] They also believed that the Taliban remained a largely local movement, which could be separated from global jihadists such as al-Qaeda and Islamic State. Against this background, an increase in military pressure and the commitment to staying sought to create incentives for the Taliban to come to the table.[24] In short, the new policy was meant to give America leverage.

At the time of writing, one of the main obstacles was the talks' bilateral format, which excluded the Afghan government.[25] While this may have suited Trump based on his personal experience, it ignored the lessons from previous rounds of negotiations, in which the Afghan and Pakistani governments had acted as "spoilers". In a 2013 report, which I co-authored with several colleagues, we concluded: "As much as Western governments would [like] to reduce the conflict to a simple confrontation between [the NATO-led International Security Assistance Force] ISAF and the Taliban, no peace deal will be possible without the involvement [of the two governments]".[26]

The biggest "spoiler", however, was Trump himself. Senior diplomats had spent over a year crafting and communicating a proposal which offered a full American withdrawal in return for guarantees that the Taliban would expel al-Qaeda and Islamic State. By December 2018, negotiators from both sides were ready to sit down for talks in Qatar, where the Taliban maintained an office. Yet, just when the formal negotiations were meant to get underway, Trump announced that he would withdraw 7,000 troops—nearly half of the American deployment. The decision, which media reports suggested was an angry reaction to Mattis' resignation,[27] had not been discussed with the Secretary of State or any of the diplomats involved in the process. In taking it, Trump not only confirmed his reputation of being a "force of chaos" within his own administration,[28] but—more importantly—eviscerated the negotiators' leverage.[29] Why would the Taliban agree to any concessions if Trump was going to "pull out" anyway?

Except for "thinking big", the Trump administration's peace initiative in Afghanistan ignored virtually all the rules of deal-making that Trump himself had stipulated in *The Art of the Deal*: there has been no effort to "maximise your options", "know your market", or "use your leverage", nor has there been any consistent long-term plan or objective. The sole driver was Trump's desire to "pull out", regardless of conditions and consequences, and if possible before the 2020 elections. As a senior American official told me: "It's not like we no longer have a timeline. We do. It's the worst kind of timeline. It's now".[30]

Outsourcing

Trump's wider critique of American global leadership has been as consistent as it has been radical. As mentioned earlier, one of his big themes was the idea that America was paying for the world without receiving anything in return. "For many decades", he said in his inaugural address:

> We've enriched foreign industry at the expense of American industry; subsidized the armies of other countries while allowing for the very sad depletion of our military; [and] defended other nation's borders while refusing to defend our own.[31]

The second, more radical part was an explicit break with American exceptionalism, as it had been articulated by virtually all Presidents before him. Despite his rhetoric, Trump essentially thought of America as a "normal" country, which should be allowed to pursue its interests without having to worry about values and ideas. He said:

> We will seek friendship and goodwill with the nations of the world—but we do so with the understanding that it is the right of all nations to put their own interests first. We do not seek to impose our way of life on anyone…[32]

In Trump's mind, this meant fewer "foreign adventures" in places that America did not understand or had no tangible interests in. On the other hand, it also signalled a more inward-looking America:[33] if Trump wanted to be reimbursed for every "service" that America provided, and if he was no longer interested in spreading freedom, or maintaining the multilateral institutions, such as NATO, which America had helped build, what was left of American global leadership, except its continued ability to project military power? Was America going to "bomb the shit" out of every country that refused to bend to its will? Why would anyone follow America rather than Russia, China, Europe, or any other major power that offered a "better deal"?

One way in which Trump hoped to resolve this conundrum was by outsourcing American leadership to regional powers. Just like Obama's "by, with, and through" doctrine—albeit on a grander scale—Trump was seeking to empower regional partners that were willing to "manage" parts of the world on America's behalf. In doing so, America would retain influence, while reducing its financial burden, bypassing international institutions, and having local powers take more responsibility for problems in their "backyards".

However appealing, this strategy also entailed risks. While potential partners were willing to be empowered, they also had interests and priorities of their own. As the case of Saudi Arabia showed, this was particularly dangerous for an administration, whose level of administrative competence was as low as Trump's, and which relied on "know-nothings" and "true believers" who lacked the required knowledge of diplomacy and international politics.

Saudi Arabia

Before Trump came to power, the relationship between America and Saudi Arabia had reached its lowest point in decades. The reason was Obama's rapprochement with the country's rival, Iran, which resulted in the so-called "Iran deal" and the partial lifting of sanctions against the country. There was broad agreement among members of Trump's team that Obama had gone too far in "appeasing" Iran, and that the regional "balance of power" needed to be reversed in favour of America's traditional allies, Saudi Arabia and Israel.[34] Yet, some of Trump's closest advisers, in particular Bannon and Kushner, wanted to go further. In their minds, not only should America help the Saudis pursue a more aggressive approach towards Iran, but Saudi Arabia should make a commitment to ceasing its support for (Islamic) extremism, lead an "ideological battle" against it, agree to take responsibility for "policing" their neighbourhood, and pay for everything from Syrian reconstruction to a possible Palestinian peace dividend. The aim was a deeper, more substantive partnership that had ever existed between the two countries, but one that—essentially—required Saudi Arabia to serve as America's proxy.

The idea that such a relationship was possible was linked to the rise of Mohammed bin Salman, also known as MBS—the young, hot-headed royal, who had talked about modernising his country and "destroying" Islamic extremism.[35] Kushner and Bannon had identified him as the "change agent" whom the new administration needed to embrace.[36] His most enthusiastic supporter was Kushner, who knew little about Middle Eastern politics, but was seen as a "great deal-maker" by his father-in-law and struck up a friendship with MBS during meetings in Washington and Riyadh. Side-lining the State Department and the National Security Council,[37] he became the administration's principal interlocutor with Saudi Arabia, who relentlessly promoted his "friend" and the idea of a "grand bargain". Against the advice of virtually every government agency, he also convinced Trump that his first trip abroad should be to Saudi Arabia.[38]

Trump's visit to Riyadh, which took place in May 2017, was meant to signal the beginning of the new partnership. As well as signing dozens of commercial contracts and memorandums of understanding—including a commitment for what would be "the largest arms deal in American history"—he announced the launch of a Terrorist Finance Targeting Center and opened the Global Center for Combating Extremist Ideology, which the Saudis had committed to funding.

In a speech to the leaders of fifty-five Arab and Muslim majority countries, Trump set out the terms of America's new relationship with Saudi Arabia and, by extension, the wider "Muslim world". First, he made it clear that America would no longer criticise others for their records on democracy and human rights, or "seek to impose our way of life". He said:

> We are not here to lecture—we are not here to tell other people how to live, what to do, who to be, or how to worship. Instead, we are here to offer partnership—based on shared interests and values—to pursue a better future for us all.[39]

The second part was about extremism, which Trump claimed was the main obstacle to stability and economic development in the Middle East. He called on Muslim countries to make sure "that terrorists find no sanctuary on their soil":

> A better future is only possible if your nations drive out the terrorists and extremists. Drive. Them. Out. DRIVE THEM OUT of your places of worship. DRIVE THEM OUT of your communities. DRIVE THEM OUT of your holy land, and DRIVE THEM OUT OF THIS EARTH.[40] [Emphasis in original]

Finally, he urged Muslim countries to unite in opposition to Iran, which he said had given terrorists "safe harbour, financial backing, and social standing":[41]

> Until the Iranian regime is willing to be a partner for peace, all nations of conscience must work together to isolate Iran, deny it funding for terrorism, and pray for the day when the Iranian people have the just and righteous government they deserve.[42]

For Bannon, the visit was a resounding success, as it had produced what he believed was a stronger, more honest—and more equitable—relationship with Saudi Arabia and the Muslim world in general.[43] Indeed, one month later, his and Kushner's biggest wish was granted, as the Saudi King deposed his designated successor, Mohammed bin Nayef, and appointed MBS as Crown Prince. The journalist Michael Wolff described it as "the Trump administration's first coup".[44]

It quickly became clear, however, that the administration had dramatically overestimated the extent to which MBS could—or wanted to—deliver. For example, there was no evidence of what Trump had claimed were $450 billion worth of trade deals (in 2018, all US exports to Saudi Arabia amounted to just $40 billion), and only about ten per cent of the alleged $110 billion arms deal ever came through.[45] Despite Trump's requests, Saudi Arabia did not pay for stabilisation and reconstruction programmes in Syria (see previous chapter), nor did it succeed in creating an "Arab force" with which to "police" regional conflicts.[46] (Hassan Hassan described efforts in this respect as a "shambles".)[47] While the Saudis did take a stricter line in relation to terrorist financing, this had predated Trump, the Riyadh summit, and the creation of the Targeting Center.[48]

Regarding extremism, although MBS's commitment to "return Saudi Arabia to moderate Islam" seemed sincere, it was ambiguous. While he has repeatedly defied the clerical establishment in relation to cultural issues and women's rights, the country's religious doctrine—Wahhabism or Salafism—continued to be the most rigidly conservative form of Islam.[49] Most of the clerics he has targeted in his "crackdown" on extremism were personal opponents rather than people with extreme views.[50] Indeed, MBS has typically blamed the rise of jihadism on hostile influences from the outside, such as the Iranian Revolution or the Muslim Brotherhood, but never questioned to what degree Wahhabism itself had been responsible for promoting intolerance and sectarianism.[51] It remained unclear, therefore, what Saudi Arabia's commitment to lead "ideological warfare" against extremism amounted to, and whether it would involve significant changes in its global promotion of Wahhabism. Nor was there any sign that its support for rebel groups in places like Syria or Yemen had fundamentally changed, or that Trump's intervention had caused it to alter its approach.[52]

In fact, two years after the Riyadh Summit, the principal outcomes of MBS's "reform agenda" were not moderation and modernisation, but increased authoritarianism and a progressively reckless foreign policy.[53]

Moreover, instead of following America's orders, it increasingly seemed like America was being used to advance Saudi Arabia's. This became obvious just two weeks after the summit, when MBS and his allies in the United Arab Emirates (UAE) felt empowered to confront Qatar—one of their regional rivals—over the recording of a speech by Qatar's leader (which later turned out to be fake). Saudi Arabia and the UAE launched a blockade, sought to topple its leader, and even contemplated a military invasion.[54] The Saudis told Trump and his advisers that Qatar had been funding extremism, and that America should get behind their campaign. Not realising that Qatar was the location of a major American air base, and that he himself had described the country as a "strategic partner" at the Riyadh summit, Trump's initial response was to support the blockade, and blame Qatar for "funding… Radical Ideology".[55] When Tillerson and Mattis became involved, Trump gradually backed down and started speaking in favour of Tillerson's attempts to mediate a compromise. But Trump's inner circle, especially Kushner, continued to side with Saudi Arabia and the UAE, who lobbied to have Tillerson fired.[56] Six days before MBS's first official visit to Washington in March 2018, Tillerson resigned.

The most embarrassing instance of American servitude to Saudi Arabia was Trump's defence of the assassination of the journalist Jamal Kashoggi, a Saudi dissident and long-time American resident. According to a finding by the CIA, MBS had personally ordered his killing, which took place in the Saudi consulate in Istanbul in early October 2018.[57] Yet, instead of condemning this grave violation of human rights and international law, Trump praised Saudi Arabia and smeared Kashoggi. In an official statement, he cited the Saudi claim that Kashoggi was "an 'enemy of the state' and a member of the Muslim

Brotherhood" before concluding that Saudi Arabia was a "great ally in our very important fight against Iran… and the largest oil producing nation in the world".[58] According to Wolff, Kushner was the source for many of the most outrageous leaks, alleging—for example—that Kashoggi had been a terrorist, or that Turkey had ordered his murder.[59] If anything, this showed that, in America's new relationship with Saudi Arabia, the (Saudi) tail was wagging the (American) dog.

Regional Conflict

The most dangerous consequence of America's dependency on Saudi Arabia—and MBS in particular—was the potential for an escalation of regional conflicts. Islamic State, after all, had not come out of nowhere. In both Syria and Iraq, it emerged in the context of sectarian civil wars in which the group had presented itself as the strongest, most fervent defender of Sunni interests against (non-Sunni) elites. For many of its local supporters, it was not Islamic State's theology, but its strength and raw sectarian appeal that made them join.[60] Yet, Trump's Riyadh speech completely failed to address the issue of sectarianism and how regional rivalries and proxy wars had promoted it.[61] By singling out Iran as the sole culprit for every problem in the region, Trump not only missed an opportunity to engage regional leaders in a more honest—and potentially productive—dialogue, but added fuel to the (sectarian) fire. In the words of Daniel Benjamin, a former Counter-Terrorism Coordinator at the State Department: "While Saudi Arabia is talking about dialling back extremism, the constellation of forces is going to promote conflict with Iran, which means there will be continued production of jihadis".[62]

Nowhere has this been more obvious than in Yemen, where a Saudi-led coalition has engaged in a devastating proxy war. In early 2015, during Obama's Presidency—and with his administration's support—MBS launched an air campaign to restore the country's internationally recognised government, which had been toppled by the Houthis a Shiite group. The Saudis promised that the war would be over in "just a few weeks", but it has continued for over four years, causing thousands of civilian deaths and more than ten million Yemenis to suffer from starvation.[63] In 2018, the United Nations described it as "the world's worst man-made humanitarian disaster".[64] While Western intelligence, weapons and logistical support may have helped to improve the accuracy of Saudi strikes,[65] the United States' full, continued—and largely uncritical—backing of an increasingly reckless campaign has replicated the conditions in which violent sectarian actors thrive.[66]

Indeed, there is mounting evidence that jihadist factions in Yemen have benefited from the conflict. While the Saudi-led coalition has carried out numerous strikes against al-Qaeda's Yemeni branch, an investigation by the Associated Press revealed that it also cut "secret deals" with the group. As well as allowing fighters to retreat, or paying them off, there have been instances in which jihadists were recruited into coalition-sponsored militias in order to fight against the Houthis. In one case, a US designated jihadist warlord reportedly "received millions of dollars from the coalition to distribute among anti-Houthi factions".[67] Another investigation, this time by CNN, showed that American military equipment had made its way to practically all of the factions participating in the conflict, including al-Qaeda and the Houthis. Although the Pentagon had imposed strict conditions on the distribution of its military hardware, the Saudis and their Emirati partners seem to have ignored them. In one instance, mine-resistant vehicles were given to a Salafist faction, while in another, American anti-tank missiles were simply airdropped into a city "where AQAP had been known to operate at the time".[68] Whatever the outcome of the conflict, thanks to the Saudi-led campaign, Yemen's jihadists will be among the best-funded and best-equipped in the world.

The greatest risk, however, was for America to be drawn into a direct military confrontation with Iran. With Israel,

Saudi Arabia and other (Sunni) Gulf states urging Trump to take a more confrontational stance,[69] and "Iran hawks" like Mike Pompeo and John Bolton, McMaster's successor as National Security Adviser, advocating what, in practice, amounted to a policy of "regime change",[70] it became harder for an inexperienced and administratively weak administration such as Trump's to withstand the resulting pressures—or even anticipate the consequences of its own actions.[71] In the words of Marc Lynch, a Middle East scholar at George Washington University:

> [Can people like Trump and Kushner] control all of this and keep it contained? Have they thought through the potential Iranian counter-measures? Have they thought through whether their international allies, the Europeans, will be on board? What will the Russians do? I don't get any real sense that they have done any of these things... I have zero confidence in the ability of the administration to maintain a coherent plan. Or to manage the fallout of all of this. They are in way over their heads.[72]

While Trump may have been sincere in wanting to reduce America's military commitments, one of the (unintended) consequences of his approach was to make a larger, region-wide conflict, with heightened sectarian tensions and the mobilisation of jihadist proxies on all sides, more likely.

Strongmen

One of the biggest contrasts between Trump and his predecessors has been his attitude towards democracy promotion. When Bush addressed the American people on the night of September 11, 2001, he started by saying that "our very freedom came under attack", and that America had been targeted because it was the world's "brightest beacon of freedom". In Bush's view, it was obvious that America not only had to find— and "bring to justice"—the terrorists who were responsible for the attacks, but pursue the greater—and more important—struggle of spreading freedom to the places from which they came.[73] Although Obama distanced himself from the Iraq war and rejected the idea of democracy promotion by force, he did not abandon America's historical "mission". In his June 2009 Cairo speech, he told his Egyptian audience that he had an "unyielding belief in… the ability to speak your mind and have a say in how you are governed", stressing that these were "not just American ideas, they are [universal], and that is why we will support them everywhere".[74] Like Bush, he linked freedom with peace and the absence of terrorism, arguing that "governments that protect these rights are ultimately more stable, secure, and successful".[75]

In empirical terms, however, the "democratisation hypothesis", which Obama and Bush—and many Presidents before them—had embraced was only partially correct. While democracies are indeed "more stable, secure, and successful" in the long-run, and terrorists have historically found it difficult to overthrow them,[76] this has not been true for the immediate aftermaths of revolutions or changes of regime. As many studies have shown, transitional periods, in which actors jockey for position, political institutions and security agencies are weak, and vacuums of power frequent, are often associated with instability and conflicts, which—in turn—facilitate terrorism.[77] They are particularly severe in countries where ethnic, religious or sectarian grievances have been suppressed, and new political actors—including militias and terrorist groups—try to gain support by seeking "payback" for wrongs that were committed in the past.[78] In short, there is little evidence that efforts to spread democracy lead to *immediate* security gains or reductions in terrorism.

At first sight, therefore, Trump's attitude seemed more sensible and realistic. From his perspective, both the Iraq war and the Arab Spring had demonstrated that, far from promoting freedom and stability, the introduction of democracy was producing chaos and extremism, and that stability and democracy promotion were not, as Bush and Obama had claimed, complementary and conducive to counter-terrorism, but mutually exclusive. Based on this reading, it was consistent—if not entirely logical—that Trump sought to curb American involvement in democracy promotion, and frequently stressed how America was no longer seeking to "impose our way of life".

The most clear-cut articulation of this policy was a memo by Brian Hook, who served as the State Department's Director for Policy Planning until September 2018.[79] Echoing an influential 1979 essay by Jeane Kirkpatrick,[80] which influenced Ronald Reagan's policy in Latin America, it argued that the only alternative to secular "strongmen" were Islamists and Communists, concluding that "human rights practices will [not] be improved if anti-American radicals take power".[81] The key recommendation was to institutionalise "double standards". With allies like Saudi Arabia, Egypt, and the Philippines, the administration would be "fully justified in emphasizing good relations for a variety of important reasons, including counter-terrorism",[82] while with adversaries such as China, Russia, North Korea, and Iran, human rights should be used in order "to impose costs, apply counter-pressure, and regain the initiative from them strategically".[83] Rather than articulating any trade-off between interests and values, which had characterised American foreign policy throughout history, Hook's memo was devoid of any ethical or moral considerations or sense of responsibility for America's historical mission. In foreign policy terms, it was the purest possible expression of "America First".

The contradictions of this policy became evident in the context of the State Department's terrorism prevention programme, also known as "countering violent extremism" (CVE). "True believers" and conservatives have always liked the idea of framing the struggle with jihadism, or "Radical Islam", as a battle of ideas, similar to the confrontation between Western democracy and Communism during the Cold War.[84] When Nathan Sales, the State Department's Counter-terrorism Coordinator, presented the Trump administration's CVE approach in May 2018, he duly talked about the Cold War, and how America defeated Communism by showing that its ideas "ran counter to the most basic human desires of freedom and dignity".[85] Yet, when speaking about the present, his notion of a "battle of ideas" was much narrower and more heavily circumscribed. Instead of promoting freedom of expression and the freedom to choose one's government, the most basic American liberties, he focused on challenging Islamic State's theology. It was a narrow and de-contextualised idea of the ideological battle, which completely ignored the social and political circumstances in which Islamic State had emerged. It also failed to play to America's strengths. As Sales conceded, the American "federal government is not a religious authority",[86] which meant that it was relying on foreign partners to convey its message. For an administration, which had boldly talked about "ideological warfare"[87] and criticised its predecessors for failing to wage it, the lack of enthusiasm with which it deployed its potentially greatest asset—the idea of freedom—seemed strange and curious.

Most significantly, rather than simply staying out of other countries' "business", Trump actively promoted "strongmen" and revelled in their abuses. A prime example was the Egyptian President Abdel Fattah al-Sisi, whom Obama had initially helped become President in 2013. Since then, al-Sisi has imprisoned tens of thousands of members of the opposition, including liberals, leftists, and supporters of the Muslim Brotherhood, staged mass show trials, and passed hundreds of death sentences against political activists. According to Amnesty International, today's Egypt resembles "an open-air prison" in which government abuses were "more extreme than anything seen in former President Hosni Mubarak's repressive 30-year-rule".[88] Trump has not just failed to condemn this, but lifted Obama-era restrictions, repeatedly expressed his admiration for al-Sisi and assured him of America's unconditional support, calling him a "great friend" who was doing an "outstanding job with respect to terrorism".[89] In his book on Trump, the journalist Bob Woodward described how the President got visibly excited after taking a phone call with al-Sisi, telling an adviser: "The guy's a f****** killer. This guy's a f****** killer… He'll make you sweat on the phone".[90]

In Libya, Trump supported the warlord Khalifa Haftar, a former Libyan officer who had turned against Ghaddafi and spent twenty years in exile, before returning to Libya to establish a power base in the eastern part of the country. While fighting against the United Nations and US-backed government, his forces have committed numerous human rights abuses. (In one instance, he literally ordered his troops to "take no prisoners".)[91] Backed by Russia, Egypt, Saudi Arabia, and the UAE, Haftar has taken an aggressive stance against the Muslim Brotherhood, and portrayed himself as someone who would rule Libya with an iron fist. This was what seemed to appeal to Trump: in April 2019, less than two weeks after Pompeo had publicly censured Haftar for "endangering civilians and undermining prospects for a better future", Trump released a statement praising his "significant role in fighting terrorism and securing Libya's oil resources".[92] In doing so, he not only endorsed a suspected war criminal, but—yet again—torpedoed his own administration's policy.

Another example was Rodrigo Duterte, the President of the Philippines. After his election in 2016, Duterte—a former prosecutor and mayor—declared a war on drugs, which has led to a brutal campaign resulting in an estimated 13,000 extra-judicial killings.[93] He has threatened journalists, encouraged soldiers to rape women,[94] and promised a "holocaust" of drug addicts, saying he was "happy to slaughter them".[95] When the southern Philippine city of Marawi was captured by Islamic State in early 2017, America provided special forces, intelligence, and logistical support for a tough, four-month battle, which killed 1,200 people and left half of the city destroyed.[96] At the time, Duterte described terrorists as "animals", and said that he would personally "eat [their]

livers… if you give me salt and vinegar".[97] Rather than criticise his rhetoric, Trump praised Duterte, saying that he had
done "an unbelievable job", and that the two countries
enjoyed "a great relationship".[98] He also invited him for an
official visit to the United States.

This is not to say that other Presidents had flawless records
in projecting "American values".[99] Throughout the War on Terror, the promotion of human rights and democracy has routinely been eclipsed by the harsh realities of an aggressive
counter-terrorism campaign. Yet, Trump's predecessors often
brought up concerns in private, periodically withheld aid or
weapons, or at least made sure that allies who shared America's
values were treated better, and were offered a visibly different
and deeper relationship with America, than those who did not.
According to Stephen Tankel, America's (often imperfect) commitment to human rights had, in some cases, served as a
restraint, incentivising allies not to embarrass their patron or
engage in abuses that were so blatant that America felt compelled to censor them.[100]

With Trump, it was the exact opposite. There was no embarrassment or censure. He enthusiastically embraced dictatorships
over democracies, praised strongmen for being strongmen, and
explicitly gave them *carte blanche* to treat their populations in
whatever way they wished—as long as it seemed like they were
doing a "great job" in countering terrorism. Rather than promoting healthy political systems, his preference and admiration
for autocrats invited allies to repress (and thereby radicalise)
their political opponents.[101] Instead of furthering "stability",
Trump's policy was sowing the seeds of future conflict.

While Trump's foreign policy may have sounded "tough", it
fuelled conflicts and made counter-terrorism efforts less effective. The hollowing out of the State Department, combined
with Trump's idiosyncrasies and the empowerment of "know-
nothings", left America incapable of pulling off foreign "deals",
allowed partners like Saudi Arabia to take advantage, and
undermined America's "exceptionalism". Far from being

"respected",[102] there was little in Trump's foreign policy that lived up to the promise of making America great again. If anything, it systematically eroded the structures and foundations on which American power, global leadership, and security had been built.

8

HOMELAND

For more than a week in mid-August 2017, the small city of Charlottesville, Virginia, dominated the national news. On 11 August, hundreds of right-wing extremists gathered in the university town to protest against the removal of the statue of a Confederate general. The event brought together supporters from the entire far-right spectrum: hardened neo-Nazis and members of the Ku Klux Klan as well as the supposedly less racist, more "identitarian" groups that are often referred to as Alternative Right. In the evening, they lit torches and walked across the campus of the University of Virginia, chanting "White lives matter" and "Jews will not replace us".[1] The following day, a twenty year old white nationalist rammed his car into a crowd of counter-protesters, killing a woman and injuring 39 other people, in what Trump's Attorney General, Jeff Sessions, called an act of "domestic terrorism".[2]

Many of the protesters who came to Charlottesville supported Trump. Next to marchers who had draped themselves in Swastikas or dressed in Ku Klux Klan robes, there were dozens who wore the red "Make America Great Again" hats that became famous during Trump's campaign. David Duke, a white nationalist, Holocaust denier, and former Grand Wizard of the Ku Klux Klan, described the event as a "turning point", arguing that Trump's election had been the reason why so many far-right activists felt empowered to make a stand. Referencing Trump's inaugural address, he said: "We are going to fulfil the promises of Donald Trump… [W]e voted for Donald Trump, because he said he's going to take our country back".[3]

For most modern Presidents, condemning a violent demonstration like the one at Charlottesville, which had resulted in the loss of life, would have been a given. Many, in fact, might have considered it a duty. Yet, Trump not only avoided condemning the protest and never called the car ramming an act of terrorism, but spent most of the following days attributing blame to "both sides", defending white nationalists, and justifying their narrative. In his first comment, he condemned "hatred, bigotry, and violence on many sides", suggesting that the car attack had been a response to left-wing violence. After practically every mainstream politician—including the Republican Party's entire leadership, and even Senator Ted Cruz—denounced him, he read out a statement, which declared that racism was "evil", and that hate groups such as the Ku Klux Klan and neo-Nazis were "repugnant".[4] But little more than twenty-four hours later, he returned to his original position. Speaking at a press conference on 15 August, Trump repeated the claim that "many sides" had been responsible for the violence, and singled out the "very, very violent… alt-left", while pointing out that "not all of [the extreme right protesters] were white supremacists".[5] He concluded by saying that "you had some very fine people on both sides".[6]

As this chapter will show, Trump's attitude towards right-wing extremism is one of the most disturbing aspects of his War on Terror. Although substantive changes to domestic counter-terrorism laws and policies have been relatively minor, Trump has radically transformed the political environment in which homegrown radicalisation and terrorism have played out. Contrary to previous administrations, who went out of their way to condemn all forms of extremism, Trump has actively promoted far-right narratives, making it clear that he considers the enemy to be "radical Islam" rather than terrorism per se. In doing so, he has empowered the extreme right and "enabled" a rising number of hate crimes and terrorist attacks, while undermining the trust of Muslim communities. More so than any other modern President, he has deepened divisions, furthered polarisation, and created the political environment in which domestic terrorism has been able to thrive.

Prosecuting Jihadists

In a previous book, I described jihadist radicalisation in the United States as "the American exception",[7] because it never developed the dense structures that existed in Western European countries like France, Britain, or Germany. Despite America being a far greater—and more important—object of hate for jihadists than Europe, American Muslims have largely resisted their call to arms. In the ten years prior to the outbreak of the Syrian conflict in 2011, 205 people in America were charged with jihadist-related offences—less than half of the number in Britain. The majority were accused of fund-raising, propaganda, or wanting to fight in a foreign conflict. Only ninety had any intention of carrying out attacks on American soil.[8]

In terms of their origin and radicalisation, they could be divided into three clusters. The first consisted of American individuals who had been radicalised abroad. This included many of the potentially most significant terrorists, such as Najibullah Zazi, an Afghan-American who wanted to blow up the New York subway in 2009; or Faisal Shahzad, a Pakistani-American who attempted to explode a car bomb on Times Square in 2010. The second group was Somali-Americans, mostly from Minnesota, who experienced high levels of deprivation, and were, in many cases, motivated by the civil war in their country of origin. (The first—and only—American suicide bombers blew themselves up on the battlefields of Somalia.) The final cluster consisted of Americans who had been inspired by the Yemeni-American preacher Anwar al-Awlaki and his protégé, Samir Khan, the editor of al-Qaeda's online magazine *Inspire*. Their terrorist "legacy" extended to the so-called Fort Hood shooting in 2009, whose perpetrator, Major Nidal Hassan, had communicated with al-Awlaki, and the 2013 Boston bombings, which were based on bomb-making instructions drawn from *Inspire*.[9]

In America, like everywhere else, the conflict in Syria and the rise of Islamic State led to a significant mobilisation of jihadists, albeit at a much lower rate than in Europe. By February 2019, the George Washington University's Program on Extremism counted charges against 177 American residents or citizens in relation to Islamic State and/or the Syrian conflict. Over 40 per cent related to travelling (or wanting to travel) to Syria, while a third concerned terrorist attacks in America. (By comparison, the number of travellers from Britain was 900, and from France nearly 2,000.) Like earlier periods of jihadist recruitment, the "ISIS wave" involved several dozen Somali-Americans as well as large numbers of individuals who were inspired by online propaganda and communication. Unlike previous mobilisations, however, it extended to a wider demographic range, including women (over 10 per cent), very young people (as young as fifteen) and middle-aged recruits (the oldest Syria traveller was fifty-eight).

Islamic State also inspired several terrorist attacks on American soil, most significantly the shootings in San Bernardino, which killed fourteen, and the Pulse nightclub in Orlando, Florida, which killed forty-nine.[10] Taken together, these two attacks accounted for nearly two thirds of the 102 fatalities of jihadist terrorism in American since the September 11, 2001, attacks. Neither of them, nor any of the previous attacks, were directed by Islamic State, or could be shown to have any direct, operational link to any foreign terrorist organisation.[11] American jihadism has not just been comparatively rare; it is also a mostly homegrown phenomenon.

There are many explanations for why America has seen less jihadist recruitment than other Western countries. Some have to do with the history of Muslim immigration to America, the diverse origins of American Muslim communities, and the resulting lack of "Muslim ghettos".[12] Others relate to the American "ethos", and American Muslims' strong belief in fundamentally American ideas such as "the melting pot, the American Dream, individualism, and grassroots voluntarism".[13] Arguably the least "glamorous" explanation is the large amount of attention and resources that American governments have devoted to counter-terrorism, and the tough and proactive way in which jihadist threats have consequently been tackled. Since 2001, the counter-terrorism offices at the FBI and large police forces like the New York Police Department (NYPD) and the Los Angeles Police Department (LAPD) have been well-funded and generously staffed. With the Joint Terrorism Task Forces (JTTF) and regional fusion centres, they had effective structures for cooperation and information-sharing at their disposal. Meanwhile, the FBI has used controversial tactics such as "sting operations" through which confidential informants have involved would-be jihadists in plotting attacks or travelling to Syria. (Half of the Syria-related cases resulted from "stings",[14] which civil rights and Muslim groups condemned for inflating terrorist numbers and undermining the trust of Muslim communities.)[15] Not least, law enforcement agencies have been successful in bringing court cases and getting judges to impose long sentences of ten, or often twenty or thirty years.

While this system has come under occasional criticism, most of the people involved in domestic counter-terrorism believe it has worked. As Seamus Hughes, a former official at the National Counter-Terrorism Center, explained:

> We have processes in place that don't allow for the in-person recruitment you would see [in Britain]. Like, there is not going to be a "Sharia for U.S." [group] handing out leaflets in [New York City]. It's just not how we do business here. And that is because the FBI usually interjects pretty early in the process and does not allow these networks to form.

> I don't think much has changed between the Obama and the Trump administration when it comes to [this]. You still have

the JTTFs, you still have fusion centres, you still have everybody playing in the same spaces.[16]

Indeed, even after the shock of the San Bernardino and Orlando attacks, there was no appetite for change among Trump's domestic "generals". As far as is known, none of Trump's most radical ideas, such as creating a "Muslim registry" or the blanket surveillance of mosques, has been seriously considered.

"Terrorism Prevention"

Changes to the countering violent extremism (CVE) programme have been more significant. Ever since the Obama administration published its domestic CVE strategy in 2011,[17] and expanded federal programmes in the wake of the 2013 Boston bombing, the CVE approach has been controversial. Several Muslim organisations were reluctant to partner with the FBI and other federal agencies, which they associated with the hated "sting operations".[18] Civil liberties groups, such as the American Civil Liberties Union (ACLU), and some of the President's own allies on the Left regarded the entire "CVE paradigm" as a sinister plot to stigmatise and "securitise" Muslim communities.[19] As a consequence, three pilot programmes, which had been launched by DHS in 2015, experienced numerous difficulties and delays, and have long been "on life support".[20] Even Obama officials conceded: "[We haven't quite] cracked the code on how to get this totally right".[21]

Meanwhile, Obama's opponents on the Right rejected CVE too—albeit for different reasons. In their view, there was no need for engagement, outreach, or trust-building with Muslim communities, except for programmes that countered "radical Islamic" ideology. Gorka, for example, routinely mocked CVE programmes as "jobs for jihadis", arguing that it was neither useful nor necessary to understand—or address—the social or political "root causes" of radicalisation.[22] Another factor was conservatives' deep suspicion of American Muslim organisations, which they believed were linked to Palestinian terrorists and the Muslim Brotherhood (an Islamist organisation that the Trump administration has repeatedly considered designating a terrorist group).[23] Frank Gaffney, the President of the Center for Security Policy, spent much of Obama's Presidency trying to prove the existence of a vast Islamist conspiracy, which he believed extended beyond community groups to practically every Muslim official in the Obama administration—including Huma Abedin, Hillary Clinton's personal assistant.[24]

Not least, hard-right conservatives resented the idea that Obama's CVE strategy sought to counter *all* forms of violent extremism, including right-wing extremism. In their view, doing so was not just an exercise in political correctness, but an excuse for targeting friends and allies. As far as they were concerned, the War on Terror was—ultimately—about countering "radical Islam", and it made no sense, therefore, to support programmes that involved partnering with the "enemy". Shortly after Trump won the election, Gorka said: "I predict with absolute certainty the jettisoning of concepts such as CVE".[25]

Initially, it seemed like Gorka's wish would be granted. One of the first decisions by John Kelly, Trump's first DHS Secretary, was to pull $10 million in CVE grants which had been allocated by the Obama administration. Kelly announced that grantees would have to meet additional conditions, including a willingness to support law enforcement.[26] This was followed by several months of internal debate about the title of the programme. Gorka's wife Katharine, a fellow "true believer", whom Trump appointed as a Senior Advisor to DHS,[27] was reportedly one of the key individuals arguing for radical change.[28] One of the first ideas was to call it "Countering Radical Islam", and focus exclusively on law enforcement training and public education. When officials pointed out that it was inappropriate—and possibly illegal—for an American government agency to get involved in theological arguments, Trump appointees came up with "Countering *Islamist* Extremism", which emphasised the ideological—rather than purely religious—character of the threat.[29] After this was rejected as well, they settled on "terrorism prevention", which was different (enough) from CVE, but made no explicit reference to Islam.

While, in many ways, frivolous, the discussion about the title of the programme offered insight into the true believers' mindset and intentions. Rather than as partnership and trust-building, they conceived of "terrorism prevention" as a law enforcement tool that would help the FBI and other police forces in dealing with "Islamic" aspects of their investigations. This was reflected in the nature of the organisations that were (eventually) given CVE grants. Fifteen of the twenty-six grantees were government agencies—mainly local police forces and offices of public safety—who received more than $6 million of the $10 million that had been allocated. Another three grantees, accounting for nearly $1.5 million, were closely involved with, or working for, government agencies. None of the twenty-six focused exclusively on right-wing extremism, and only five took an "all forms of extremism approach".[30] Grants that exclusively dealt with far-right extremism or involved American-Muslim organisations were cancelled without explanation.[31] While DHS spokespeople denied that anything had changed, or that Katharine Gorka had pushed the Department towards "an Islamist-only approach",[32] the evidence suggested otherwise.[33] In a recently leaked email, she wrote to a fellow "true believer": "God I hate this program".[34]

Though widely debated, the impact of these changes has been difficult to gauge. Although Trump officials drastically cut the CVE budget,[35] it was relatively small to begin with, and right-wing extremism had never been a priority. Even Obama's DHS had wanted to move away from broad-based community engagement towards a narrower emphasis on so-called "interventions" and closer links with law enforcement.[36] Most importantly, Trump's rhetoric left the government no choice. As Hughes explained:

> As a Trump administration official, you are not going to be able to go in and talk about prevention in most mosques. You

are going to have to get through the concerns that people had on the travel ban, the campaign, and all of those things. It's like you are not going to get your foot in the door to begin with.[37]

Right Turn

More consequential than his actual policies was Trump's increasingly right-wing rhetoric, whose origins and development can be traced back to the time of the 2008 financial crisis. During this period, the Republican Party experienced the rise of the Tea Party movement—a populist "insurgency" that articulated people's discontent with the political and economic elites, as well as a broader conservative agenda, especially on the issue of immigration. It was precisely at this time that Trump—once again—contemplated entering politics, and the Tea Party seemed like a natural fit for his populist inclinations. Green claimed that it was through his friendship with the owner of the *National Enquirer*, a supermarket tabloid, that Trump embraced one of the wildest rumours that was circulating on Tea Party websites at the time—the so-called birther conspiracy—according to which Obama, the country's first African-American President, was not a natural-born American.[38] Practically overnight, Trump became the country's most prominent "birther", raising doubts about Obama's citizenship and demanding to see his birth certificate. It is doubtful whether, at this point, Trump had developed a fully-fledged conservative worldview, or even understood what many of the Tea Party's ideas and policies were about,[39] but the birther issue clearly positioned him as a conservative and gave him access to hard-right blogs, websites, and talk radio shows, where he quickly became a star.[40]

Part of this subculture was a group of anti-Islam activists, whom Trump increasingly relied on for his views on "radical Islam". Coalescing around Gaffney, and activists such as Robert Spencer and Pamela Geller, their central argument was that terrorist attacks like those on September 11, 2001, were just the tip of the iceberg, and that all practising Muslims, not just their most extreme brethren, were involved in "civilizational jihad"—the systematic undermining of Western societies on all fronts and by all means, including through the building of mosques, demands for rights and recognition, and—of course—migration.[41] From their perspective, the root of the problem was not terrorism, or any specific interpretation of "jihad", but what they portrayed as the aggressive, expansionist "ideology" of Islam. In other words, while mainstream politicians were desperately trying to draw distinctions between Islam and jihadism, Gaffney sought to convince people of the opposite, namely that they were one and the same. Although Gaffney's views have remained on the outer fringes of the conservative movement, his network extended across Washington, DC, and included "uber-hawks" such as Pompeo, Bolton, as well as Ted Cruz, whom he initially supported in the Presidential race.[42]

More so than anyone else, however, it was Bannon who "connected the dots" and provided Trump with a (more or less) coherent intellectual *Überbau*—or superstructure—that unified the Tea Party's populism with Gaffney's hostility towards Islam and the more explicit forms of racism that could be found in the virtual subcultures of the alt-right and organisations like the Ku Klux Klan. Though Bannon was no intellectual, he had long been fascinated by philosophers of the European extreme right, like René Guénon (1886–1951) and Julius Evola (1898–1974), an "esoteric, spiritual Aryan", who had influenced Italy's fascist leader, Benito Mussolini, during the final, most radical phase of his reign.[43] Bannon was also familiar with their contemporary successors, such as the French philosophers Alain de Benoist (1943–) Renaud Camus (1946–), and Guillaume Faye (1949-2019), who claimed that "European civilisation" was in decline, and that the principal threats to "European identity" were Islam and (Islamic) immigration.[44] As Green points out, "[a]nyone steeped in… [these ideas] would recognize the terrifying spectre Trump conjured of marauding immigrants, Muslim terrorists, and the collapse of national sovereignty and identity".[45]

The combination of these ideas offered a powerful bridge between those who were within—albeit on the outer fringes of—the conservative movement and the extreme, anti-democratic Right, which had come to define itself in opposition to the system. Arguably, it was precisely their ambiguity that allowed them to co-exist in Trump's broad ideological tent. The concept of identity, for instance, could be perceived in cultural and nationalist terms, while also accommodating views that were based on race, religion, and ethnicity. The same applied to violence. Not only had Trump encouraged his supporters to beat up counter-protesters,[46] his rhetoric of conflict and "invasion" created a sense of urgency and existential threat, which could be used to justify violence against immigrants, Muslims, "politically correct" elites, the mainstream media, or whoever else he identified as "enemies of the people".[47]

In summary, it was precisely the absence of red lines or boundaries in relation to the extreme right—the fact that Trump (knowingly) allowed racists and potentially violent extremists to feel like they were part of his movement[48]—that made his political brand unique and fundamentally different from his predecessors.

In Office

Though rarely dominant, Gaffney and Bannon's ideas spread to all parts of the administration. One of the best-known examples was Richard Higgins, a National Security Council staffer, who drafted a 7-page memo titled "POTUS [President of the United States] & POLITICAL WARFARE" in which he tried to convince his colleagues that Trump was surrounded by "enemies", including the mainstream media, the leaderships of both political parties, "global corporations", "the deep state", "Islamists", and "cultural Marxists".[49] When it was leaked, much of the media portrayed him as "crazy", but failed to recognise that his ideas were those of the "identitarian" extreme right, which had for years presented Muslim immigration ("Islamists") and multi-culturalism ("cultural Marxists") as forms of "political warfare" against "Western civilization".[50] In fact, both Anders Breivik, the Norwegian terrorist, who killed sixty-eight people in July 2011, and Brenton Tarrant, who killed forty-nine Muslims in Christchurch, New Zealand, in March 2019, had used the exact same concepts in order to justify terrorism.[51] While Higgins did not call for actual warfare, his paper concluded by saying that "the defense of President Trump is the defense of America".[52]

Another example was Frank Wuco, a Tea Party conservative and retired naval intelligence officer, who had worked under Michael Flynn at CENTCOM. After leaving the military, he spent years hosting a radio show in Florida, in which he promoted the birther theory, and claimed that Obama's autobiography had been ghost-written by a left-wing terrorist.[53] He also created a fake jihadist persona by the name of Wasul, whom he role-played at public events. His core message was identical to that of Gaffney—that Islam was at "war" with the West, and that Western Muslims were seeking to "subjugate and humiliate non-Muslim members of their societies".[54] Trump not only gave him a job, but put him in charge of implementing the "Muslim travel ban" at DHS.

By far the most influential far-right supporter, however, has been Stephen Miller, one of Trump's closest policy advisors. He represented "Generation Breitbart" whose political views had been shaped by social media, and for whom "'melting the snowflakes' and 'triggering the libs'" were "first principles".[55] Miller has denied being part of the alt-right, and distanced himself from violence and white supremacism. Yet, he strongly opposed both legal and illegal immigration, has rejected the idea of America as a "nation of immigrants", and claimed that "millions of radical Muslims" were engaged in "holy war" against America.[56] Perhaps more so than any other official, he represented the conflation of Islam, immigration, and terrorism which has characterised Trump's approach towards countering terrorism. David Sterman, a researcher at the New America Foundation, told me that, "for [Miller], these are really one and the same issue".[57]

It was no accident, therefore, that Trump has consistently articulated far-right narratives. One of the most subtle ways of doing so was by excluding Muslims from the national narrative. Trump often speaks of "churches and synagogues", but never mentions mosques. When he talks about "faith leaders", he refers to "pastors, priests, and rabbis", but not imams. He acknowledges Christian and Jewish holidays, but not Islamic ones. Most importantly, he posts hysterical tweets whenever there are attacks *by* Muslims,[58] but rarely highlights attacks *against* them. A rare exception was the attack in Christchurch, after which Trump tweeted about "the horrible massacre in the Mosques" and "senseless" deaths,[59] but failed to mention the attacker's motivation, or that Muslims had been targeted because of their faith.[60]

On many occasions, Trump's support for right-wing extremists has been explicit. During the election campaign, he repeatedly re-tweeted accounts that were recognisable as "white supremacist". (One of them had a Twitter handle that included the words "white genocide".)[61] As President, he promoted the videos of a British far-right group,[62] expressed his concern about the fate of "white farmers" in South Africa, and re-tweeted the messages of conspiracy theorists and "identitarians".[63] In each case, Trump's defence was to claim ignorance, saying that he had been unaware of the accounts or their racist content.[64]

Yet, there are many instances in which Trump has enthusiastically expressed similar ideas. Examples include the election campaign, during which he claimed that Muslim immigrants had "taken over [Paris] and destroyed it" (see Chapter 2); his framing of the Mexican border "crisis" as an "invasion";[65] or an interview with the British newspaper *The Sun*, in which he linked immigration with the loss of identity:

"[A]llowing millions of people to come into Europe is very, very sad", he said, "I think you are losing your culture".[66] As many experts have pointed out,[67] the cumulative effect of these statements has been to shift the political discourse, push the limits of "acceptable" speech, and—in doing so— "normalise" extreme right narratives that seek to portray Muslims as "un-American" and (re-)define immigration as a source of weakness and decline.

Impact

Following his election, many commentators speculated that Trump's anti-Muslim rhetoric would cause more Muslim Americans to turn to terrorism. While surveys have shown that their attitudes towards the state have indeed worsened,[68] there is no evidence for increased radicalisation. In fact, the number of individuals that were charged with jihadism-related offences in 2018 was lower than in any of the preceding five years, reflecting an overall decline in Islamic State related radicalisation and recruitment.[69]

Nevertheless, there have been deep—and ongoing—concerns about Trump's impact on the relationship between security agencies and Muslim communities. Contrary to his allegation that American Muslims were refusing to cooperate with law enforcement, tip-offs from community members accounted for more than 20 per cent of jihadism-related arrests in the decade following 2001.[70] Trump's rhetoric has not just worsened Muslim Americans' perception of the US government, but led to greater fears about being seen to cooperate with law enforcement. In a recent study of Somali-American communities, for example, the researcher Melissa Salyk-Virk showed that Trump was mentioned in nearly a quarter of her interviews, and that his perceived hostility towards Muslims was strongly correlated with fears of law enforcement, especially the FBI.[71]

Virtually every law enforcement and intelligence officer I have spoken to believed that, over time, this would reduce the flow of information and result in "blind spots", making it harder to detect instances of radicalisation and recruitment. Michael Downing, a former chief of LAPD's Counter-Terrorism Bureau, told me that years of outreach by his police force have been jeopardised:

> Our whole effort was to build partnerships and trust, so that [Muslim communities] would... contribute to youth programmes and crimes strategies, [and generally work with us]. What we're afraid of [with the rise of Trump and his statements about Muslims] is that they will no longer share anything. Who are they going to go to now? ... Down the line we are going to pay for this, and that's just a matter of time.[72]

Nick Rasmussen, who was director of the National Counter-Terrorism Center (NCTC) until late 2017, made a similar point:

> I don't know that there's any one statement or any one event that you can point to that you could say, "Aha, all of a sudden, now things are worse". I tend to look at these things as being more environmental. Anything that... contributes over time to a sense that the authorities are inexorably set in conflict with particular communities makes our work more difficult...
>
> [FBI] Director [Christopher] Wray often talks about... how much we need community help... [T]hose conversations are harder when the environment is contaminated by mutual suspicion and questioning of motives.[73]

Michael Hayden, the former CIA and NSA Director, emphasised the impact on the work of American intelligence agencies abroad:

> In the places where [our...] officers operate, rumor, whisper, and conspiratorial chatter rule people's lives. And it doesn't take paranoia to connect actions [such as the travel ban] with the broader hateful anti-Islamic language of the campaign...
>
> CIA will be left with more of the weak and the merely avaricious, agents who will cut a deal just for the money, the worst kind of sources—and ISIS and al-Qaeda will (with more justi-

fication than they once had) claim that America and Islam are inevitable enemies.[74]

While sounding "tough", therefore, Trump's rhetoric undermined his government's efforts to track down and disrupt terrorist networks.

Enabler

The other side of the equation was an increase in hate crime and extreme right terrorism. Although the number of far-right activists in America remains modest when compared to European countries,[75] violent attacks against minorities have increased since the early 2010s, and grown steeply since Trump entered the political arena. According to the FBI, incidents of hate crime (defined as "criminal offense[s] against a person or property motivated in whole or in part by an offender's bias") increased by 5–6 per cent in each year between 2014 and 2016, but grew by 17 per cent in 2017.[76] "Violent far-right attacks" increased from an average of 11 in the years 2012–16 to more than 30 in 2017.[77] The number of "right-wing extremist murders" rose from 22 in 2016 to 29 in 2017. In 2018, it reached 50—the highest number in any year since 1995, when Timothy McVeigh killed 168 people in the Oklahoma City bombings.[78]

Given the notoriously complex relationship between political rhetoric and violent action,[79] it is difficult to determine how much of this increase can be attributed to Trump. As far as is known, no member of Trump's administration is personally involved in extreme right violence, nor has he called on his supporters to engage in terrorism, or stopped his Justice Department from "arresting or prosecuting individuals [that are] involved in illegal activities".[80] Yet, as Stephen Tankel argues, Trump is responsible for creating a political environment in which right-wing extremism has been able to thrive.[81] In his view, Trump is guilty of engaging in divisive and polarising rhetoric, "mainstreaming" extreme right narratives, giving credibility to conspiracy theories, and "[fuelling] right-wing recruitment… by validating their messaging and emboldening them". Moreover, his actions, such as the "Muslim travel ban", have created an exaggerated sense of crisis around the issue of immigration, prompting "even people who are not inspired by Trump… to commit acts of extremist violence". Trump, in other words, "may not be deliberately trying to enable far-right violence, but his rhetoric and actions are having that effect".[82]

Part of this argument is Trump's consistent refusal to distance himself from the extreme right. In an analysis of 30,000 Twitter accounts that were linked to white supremacists and supporters of the alt-right, the researcher J.M. Berger found that "[s]upport for Trump was shared by virtually all parts of the [alt-right] network and reflected in nearly every metric, including tabulations of the most followed, most retweeted, and most influential accounts".[83] Yet, despite many requests from within his own party, Trump has never repudiated this part of his base, or made any attempt to moderate their views.[84]

Trump has also failed to address—or even acknowledge— the numerous attacks that have been committed in his name. According to a detailed survey by South Asian Americans Leading Together, an advocacy organisation, 20 per cent of hate violence perpetrators in 2017 "referenced President Trump, a Trump policy, or a Trump campaign slogan" during their attacks.[85] Furthermore, vocal Trump supporters have been responsible for a dozen terrorist attacks (and attempted attacks) since 2016.[86] This included a terrorist plot against Somali refugees in Garden City, Kansas, which involved three militia members planning to launch attacks on the day after the Presidential election in November 2016. Two of them were enthusiastic Trump fans, who had repeatedly declared their allegiance to the President on social media and asked the judge in their trial "to boost the number of pro-Trump jurors".[87] Another case was the Charlottesville attacker, a twenty year old from Ohio who "idolized Hitler and Nazism" and was active in alt-right forums on the internet, but registered as a Republican when Trump declared his candidacy. According to a former teacher, he was "a big Trump supporter because of what he believed to be Trump's views on race".[88] The best-known example was the October 2018 mail bomber, Cesar Sayoc, who targeted CNN, prominent Democrats, and other individuals that Trump had previously singled out as enemies of the people. Known as "the MAGA bomber" because of Trump's campaign slogan "Make America Great Again", he was a fifty-six year old fitness instructor who had registered as a Republican when Trump became the party's nominee, and attended his campaign events.[89]

The most controversial case was the terrorist who killed eleven worshippers at the Tree of Life synagogue in Pittsburgh, Pennsylvania, in October 2018. An avowed anti-Semite, Robert Bowers was no fan of Trump, whom he dismissed as "a globalist, not a nationalist". Yet, as Tankel showed, he was clearly influenced by the President's hysterical warnings about "migrant caravans", and strongly supported his (verbal) attacks against the Jewish philanthropist George Soros. According to Tankel, he may not have acted on Trump's behalf, but Trump had contributed to the paranoid political climate in which he became convinced that it was necessary to "take matters into his own hands".[90]

Extreme Events

The expectation that Trump's election victory would reconcile far-right extremists with the system—and therefore make violence unnecessary—turned out to be mistaken,[91] as it underestimated the extent to which his base held deeply conspiratorial views. Like Higgins, many Trump supporters believed that their President was surrounded by enemies who sabotaged his agenda and tried to get him removed from office.[92] Support for Trump, therefore, has never translated into backing for the system or government institutions. If anything, Trump's difficulties in implementing election promises such as "The Wall" and the

"Muslim travel ban" increased their suspicion that the government was corrupt and undemocratic, and that violence might, at some point, become justified and necessary.

Many of my interviewees believed that such a scenario could be triggered by an extreme event. A good illustration was the case of Christopher Hasson, a Coast Guard lieutenant from Maryland, who plotted a series of assassinations and terrorist attacks, expressing a desire to kill "almost every last person on earth".[93] Court documents showed that he had long held "white supremacist" views, and wanted to emulate Anders Breivik, the Norwegian terrorist. They also suggested that he was planning to launch his terrorist campaign in the event of Trump's impeachment. Just before compiling a list of targets, he had searched the internet for terms like "what if trump illegally impeached", "best place in dc to see congress people", and "civil war if trump impeached".[94]

Another trigger could be a jihadist attack.[95] Based on Trump's electoral logic (see Chapter 2), his frantic responses to jihadist terrorism in other countries (see above), and the hysterical Tweets he posted after the 2017 Halloween attack (see Introduction), there is every reason to believe that his response to another attack would again be polarising and divisive, and might cause his supporters to "retaliate" by targeting Muslims and other ethnic minorities. From a counter-terrorism perspective, the government's greatest potential liability in this kind of situation would be the President himself.[96]

In domestic counter-terrorism, therefore, Trump's record has been far from positive. Although the long-standing formula of domestic prosecutions, early interventions and tough sentences remained the same, and changes in CVE policy were less consequential than they seemed, Trump fundamentally changed the political environment in which domestic radicalisation has played out. With Trump, America elected a President whose political brand relied on division and polarisation, and whose words and actions sought to accommodate people with explicitly racist views. Far from being tough on terrorism, he has undermined cooperation between Muslim communities and security agencies, while enabling a resurgence of far-right hate crime and terrorism. Although the institutions that combat terrorism continue to function, their President has made it harder for them to succeed.

CONCLUSION

At first sight, the National Strategy for Counterterrorism, which the White House published in October 2018,[1] seemed like a "Trumpian" document. It boldly talked about "victory", declared that "America remains at war", and named Islamic State and "radical Islamists" as enemies. It also devoted much attention to Iran—the world's "most prominent state sponsor of terrorism"—and placed greater emphasis than Obama on kinetic power, substituting the idea of tackling "conditions conducive to terrorism" for the more aggressive sounding concept of "pursuing terrorist threats to their source".

Yet, despite such "flavours", the strategy remained what Christopher Fonzone and Luke Hartig called "utterly conventional".[2] None of its "strategic objectives", "end states", or "lines of effort" represented anything that members of the Obama administration would have objected to. Most of the content was factual, concise, and built on previous counterterrorism strategies, articulating similar aims and using the same anodyne language of "protecting the homeland", "building societal resilience", and "promoting partnerships".[3] Contrary to Trump's dislike for democracy promotion, it even talked about America's "special role among nations as a vanguard of freedom, democracy, and constitutional governance".[4]

What it described was "the generals'" version of the War on Terror—a war in which smart, patriotic people put aside their political differences to "keep the American people safe", and whose course was determined not by tweets, but "the troops, the money, and the substance of the policies".[5] It was the kind of war that I frequently heard about when speaking to mainstream appointees and career officials, who told me that I should ignore the President's words, his tweets, and "the whole circus" coming out of the West Wing.

But was this accurate? Did it reflect all of the changes that have taken place since Trump's election? This book has attempted to make sense of the tension between "utterly conventional" documents like the counter-terrorism strategy and Trump's radical rhetoric. Rather than "ignoring Trump", I took the President, his ideas, politics, and ways of "doing business" seriously, and tried to find out how—and to what extent—he has imposed his will on America's War on Terror.

Ignorance, Idiosyncrasy, Ideology

In contrast to Fonzone and Hartig, my conclusion is that Trump's impact has been tangible. Some of the damage he has inflicted was the result of ignorance and incompetence. The best example is America's relationship with Saudi Arabia, which Bannon and Kushner—a "true believer" and a "know-nothing"—have turned into one of dependency. At the time of writing, Saudi Arabia had failed to deliver on most of the commitments it made at the May 2017 Riyadh summit, and repeatedly used its privileged relationship with America to advance its own, often misguided, interests in the region. Practically every major foreign policy decision by Crown Prince Mohammed bin Salman has increased sectarian tensions, heightened the risk of regional conflict, and created the potential for more terrorism.

Another factor has been idiosyncrasy and ill-discipline. This could be seen in Syria and Afghanistan, where Trump's impatience and desire for a "quick win" caused him to torpedo his own government's policies, creating precisely the kind of chaos that his "generals" had been working hard to resolve. Equally destructive has been his fascination with foreign "strongmen", such as Egypt's al-Sisi, Libya's Haftar, or the Philippines' Duterte. Far from acting like a "vanguard of freedom", he has applauded their excessive use of violence, and—in doing so— helped sow the seeds of future conflict and instability.

CONCLUSION

The most disturbing impact, however, has been ideological. Trump is the first President in recent history who has openly accommodated racists and the extreme right, both in terms of language, ideas, people, and his consistent refusal to acknowledge the growing right-wing terrorist threat. At the same time, the systematic conflation of jihadist terrorism, Islam, and immigration, which has been part of his political "brand", has not just undermined the idea of America as a religiously and ethnically diverse nation, alienated Muslim Americans, and polarised the country, but created significant opportunity costs, such as "extreme vetting" and the "travel ban" whose utility in counter-terrorism terms remains completely unproven.

This is not to say that American counter-terrorism has become totally dysfunctional. The military campaign against Islamic State in Syria and Iraq has been decisive and successful—at least in the short-term. There is no indication that his election has increased the threat from jihadist terrorism, or caused large numbers of Muslims to radicalise, as some of his opponents had predicted.[6] Although naming Islamic State or talking about "radical Islam" has not—in and of itself—defeated terrorism, there is no evidence that it has caused significant harm. Most importantly, the institutions and agencies that are responsible for operational counter-terrorism have remained strong and continue to do their jobs. In this respect, there is a great deal of continuity between Trump and his predecessors.

For the most part, however, this has not been because of Trump, but despite him. As I have shown throughout the book, his outsider status and the radicalism of his doctrine—which called for "killing terrorists" and "keeping Muslims out of the country"—meant that he arrived in office with few actual policies and not enough people to fill the thousands of politically appointed positions that enable newly elected Presidents to extend their will across government. Much of Trump's War on Terror has been run by career officials and mainstream Republicans—"the generals"—whose commitment to his doctrine was limited.

In summary, Trump has claimed to be tougher on terrorism than anyone, but there is no reason why Americans should feel safer now than they were under his predecessors. If anything, his approach has caused America to be more vulnerable: in the short-term, because his response to another jihadist attack would almost certainly be unhinged and deepen divisions in an already divided country; and in the long-term, because he has provided no strategic direction or shown that he understands the security implications of his domestic and foreign policy decisions. While much of his War on Terror has been bluster, its effect has been to leave America and the world more exposed to terrorist threats.

The Very Idea of America

At closer inspection, of course, much of Trump's War on Terror had little to do with countering terrorism. From his perspective, terrorism was politically useful, because it validated the narrative of external threat through which he mobilised his "base". Even more importantly, it allowed him to advance a radical ideological agenda that has challenged widely accepted definitions of America, and attempted to overturn the mainstream consensus on immigration and America's role in the world—the two claims on which contemporary explanations of American "exceptionalism", and the counter-terrorism policies of his predecessors, have rested.[7]

Regarding immigration, the mainstream consensus postulated that America was a multi-cultural "nation of immigrants", and that anyone—regardless of race, ethnicity, or religion—could, in principle, become part of it. Both as a candidate and as President, Trump has consistently made it clear that his idea of America was different. Although he rarely expressed his opposition to multi-culturalism in explicitly racist terms, he has consistently associated immigration—and, especially, Muslim immigration—with decline, chaos, and terror, and used terms like "culture" and "identity" as dog whistles which many of his supporters understood as references to religion and ethnicity.

Trump also disagreed with mainstream ideas about American global leadership and the liberal international order through which America had established and maintained its quasi-hegemonic position in the post-war era. In Trump's view, none of these arrangements were needed, as America could safeguard its commercial interests through deals and protect its security by projecting overwhelming military power—that is, by "killing terrorists" and "bombing the shit" out of countries. Trump seemed to offer greatness, respect and national revival, but with no commitments and at virtually no cost.

None of these ideas were unprecedented[8] or un-American,[9] nor did Trump have to "manufacture" the fears of decline and sense of insecurity about the rapidly changing nature of society, which they sought to leverage. But, like in other historical instances of populist nationalist mobilisations,[10] he skilfully exploited them, channelling people's grievances into a radical political project, for which the War on Terror provided a powerful instrument and justification. It would be naïve, therefore, to look at Trump's ideas on counter-terrorism only—and exclusively—as if they were about countering terrorism. Discussing Trump's War on Terror is also—and always—a debate about the very idea of America.

NOTES

INTRODUCTION

1. @realDonaldTrump, *Twitter*, 31 October 2017.
2. @realDonaldTrump, *Twitter*, 1 November 2017.
3. Ibid.
4. Mike Pence, quoted in Peter Baker, "Trump Abandons Idea of Sending Terrorism Suspect to Guantanamo", *New York Times*, 2 November 2017; available at https://www.nytimes.com/2017/11/02/us/politics/trump-new-york-terror-attack.html.
5. "Trump say US will hit ISIS '10 times harder' after NYC attack", *Associated Press*, 3 November 2017; available at https://www.bostonglobe.com/news/nation/2017/11/03/military-carries-out-airstrikes-against-islamic-state-somalia/wmOOZovnLPZkbDUj4oHH0I/story.html.
6. See, for example, Kim Barker, Joseph Goldstein, and Michael Schwirtz, "Finding a Rootless Life in U.S., Sayfullo Saipov Turned to Radicalisam", *New York Times*, 1 November 2017; available at https://www.nytimes.com/2017/11/01/nyregion/sayfullo-saipov-truck-attack-manhattan.html.
7. In fact, Trump eventually said so himself when he tweeted: "Would love to send the NYC terrorist to Guantanamo but statistically that process takes much longer than going through the Federal system". See @realDonaldTrump, *Twitter*, 2 November 2017.
8. Will Pavia, "Trump's tweets calling for death penalty 'helping accused New York terrorist' Sayfullo Saipov", *The Times*, 3 November 2017; available at https://www.thetimes.co.uk/article/trump-s-tweets-calling-for-death-penalty-helping-accused-new-york-terrorist-sayfullo-saipov-v3ntv9d96. See also "Defence

cites Trump's death penalty tweets in New York City terror attack trial", *The Guardian*, 6 September 2018; available at https://www.theguardian.com/us-news/2018/sep/06/terrorist-attack-new-york-trump-tweet-death-penalty.

9. Joshua A. Geltzer and Stephen Tankel, "What Happened to Trump's Counterterrorism Strategy", *The Atlantic*, 1 March 2018; available at https://www.theatlantic.com/international/archive/2018/03/trump-terrorism-iraq-syria-al-qaeda-isis/554333/.

10. Ibid.

11. See Jacob T. Levy, "The Weight of the Words", *Niskanen Centre*, 7 February 2018; available at https://niskanencenter.org/blog/the-weight-of-the-words/. See also Andrew Restuccia and Christopher Cadelago, "West Wing aides perfect a Trump survival skill: Ignoring the tweets", *Politico*, 13 September 2018; available at https://www.politico.com/story/2018/09/13/trump-inflated-hurricane-maria-death-toll-822236.

12. Quoted in Edward-Isaac Dovere, "David Petraeus would still work for Trump, under 'certain conditions'", *Politico*, 12 December 2017; available at https://www.politico.com/magazine/story/2017/12/12/david-petraeus-would-still-work-for-trump-under-certain-conditions-216065.

13. Levy, "The Weight", op. cit.

14. Derek Thompson, "Donald Trump's Language is Reshaping American Politics", *The Atlantic*, 15 February 2018; available at https://www.theatlantic.com/politics/archive/2018/02/donald-trumps-language-is-reshaping-american-politics/553349/.

15. Bronwen Maddox, *In Defence of America* (London: Duckworth Overlook, 2009). See also Kenneth Roth, "The Law of War in the War on Terror", *Foreign Affairs*, January 2004.

16. Michael J. Glennon, *National Security and Double Government* (New York: Oxford University Press, 2014); Jason Ralph, *America's War on Terror: The State of the 9/11 Exception from Bush to Obama* (Oxford: Oxford University Press, 2013).

17. See, for example, Sanjay Gupta, "The Doctrine of Pre-Emptive Strike: Application and Implications during the Administration of President George W. Bush", *International Political Science Review*,

29 (2) (2008); Richard H. Schultz and Andreas Vogt, "The Real Intelligence Failure on 9/11 and the Case for a Doctrine of Striking First" in Russell D. Howard and Reid L. Sawyer (eds), *Terrorism and Counterterrorism* (Boston: McGraw-Hill, 2003), pp. 367–90; Mary Ellen O'Connell, "The Legal Case against the Global War on Terror," *War Crimes Research Symposium* (2004).

18. See, for example, Daniel Byman, "The Foreign Policy Essay: Thoughts on Counterterrorism and 'Blowback,'" *Lawfare*, 30 November 2014; available at https://www.lawfareblog.com/foreign-policy-essay-thoughts-counterterrorism-and-blowback.

19. See, for example, William Lee Eubank and Leonard Weinberg, "Does democracy encourage terrorism?", *Terrorism and Political Violence*, 6 (4) (1994); Michael Freeman, "Democracy, Al Qaeda, and the Causes of Terrorism: A Strategic Analysis of US Policy", *Studies in Conflict and Terrorism*, 31 (1) (2008); David Beetham, "The Contradictions of Democratization by Force: The Case of Iraq", *Democratization*, 16 (3) (2009).

20. See Donna G. Starr-Deelen, *Presidential Policies on Terrorism: From Ronald Reagan to Barack Obama* (New York: Palgrave Macmillan, 2014); Aqil Shah, "Do U.S. Drone Strikes Cause Blowback? Evidence from Pakistan and Beyond", *International Security*, 42 (4) (2018). See also David Kilcullen and Andrew McDonald Exum, "Death from Above, Outrage Down Below," *The New York Times*, 16 May 2009; available at https://www.nytimes.com/2009/05/17/opinion/17exum.html.

21. See, for example, Sean Oliver-Dee, "Started but Contested: Analyzing US and British counter-extremism strategies", *The Review of Faith & International Affairs*, 16 (2) (2018).

22. See, for example, Laurie O'Connor, "Legality of the use of force in Syria against Islamic State and the Khorasan Group", *Journal on the Use of Force and International Law*, 3 (1) (2016); Louise Arimatsu and Michael N. Schmitt, "Attacking 'Islamic State' and the Khorasan Group: Surveying the International Law Landscape", *Columbia Journal of Transnational Law*, 53 (1) (2014).

23. See, for example, Trevor McCrisken, "Ten Years On," *International Affairs*, 87 (4) (2011); Jane Mayer, *The Dark Side: The Inside Story of How the War on Terror Turned into a War on American Ideals* (New York: Doubleday, 2008).

24. Walter M. Brasch, *America's Unpatriotic Acts: The Federal Government's Violation of Constitutional and Civil Rights* (New York: Peter Lang, 2005); Adam Liptak, "Civil Liberties Today", *The New York Times*, 7 September 2011; available at https://www.nytimes.com/2011/09/07/us/sept-11-reckoning/civil.html.

25. See Khaled A. Beydoun, *American Islamophobia: Understanding the Roots and Rise of Fear* (Oakland: University of California Press, 2018).

26. See, for example, Daniel Byman and Benjamin Wittes, "Reforming the NSA: How to Spy after Snowden", *Foreign Affairs*, 93 (3) (2014); David P. Fidler (ed.), *The Snowden Reader* (Bloomington: Indiana University Press, 2015).

27. See, for example, Trever Aaronson, *The Terror Factory: Inside the FBI's Manufactured War on Terrorism* (Brooklyn: IG Publishing, 2013); Antony Field, "Ethics and entrapment: Understanding Counterterrorism Stings", *Terrorism and Political Violence*, 28 (1) (2016).

28. See, for example, Erica Chenoweth and Pauline L. Moore, *The Politics of Terror* (Oxford: Oxford University Press, 2018); Ronald Crelinsten, *Counterterrorism* (Cambridge: Polity, 2009); Martha Crenshaw and Gary Lafree, *Countering Terrorism: No Simple Solutions* (Washington DC: Brookings, 2017); Richard English, *Terrorism: How to Respond* (Oxford: OUP, 2010); Richard Wilkinson, *Terrorism and the Liberal State* (London: Macmillan, 1977).

29. For more widely focused books with chapters on Trump, see Donna G. Starr-Deelen, *Counter-Terrorism from the Obama Administration to President Trump* (Basingstoke: Palgrave Macmillan, 2018); Michael B. Kraft and Edward Marks, *U.S. Counterterrorism: From Nixon to Trump* (Washington, DC: CRC Press, 2017). For shorter articles, see Geltzer and Tankel, "Whatever Happened to Trump's Counterterrorism Strategy?"; Christopher Fonzone and Luke Hartig, "The More Things Stay the Same: Why the Trump Administration's Counterterrorism Strategy Is Surprisingly Conventional", *Just Security*, 13 November 2018; available at https://www.justsecurity.org/61452/stay-same-trump-administrations-counterterrorism-strategy-surprisingly-conventional/; Matthew Kroenig, "The Case for Trump's Foreign Policy", *For-*

eign Affairs, May 2017; available at https://www.foreignaffairs.
com/articles/world/2017–04–17/case-trump-s-foreign-policy.
For journalistic accounts with significant chapters on Trump's
early decisions, see Bob Woodward, *Fear: Trump in the White House*
(London: Simon & Schuster, 2018); Michael Wolff, *Fire and Fury*
(New York: Little and Brown, 2018).

30. For a rare exception, see Philip Bobbitt, *Terror and Consent: The
Wars For the Twenty-First Century* (New York: Penguin, 2009). See
also Gary J. Schmitt, "US Counterterrorism in Perspective", in
Gary J. Schmitt (ed.), *Safety, Liberty, and Islamist Terrorism* (Washington: The AEI Press, 2010).

31. Interviewees were offered the chance to speak either on- and
off-the-record. The King's College London War Studies Group
Research Ethics Panel granted permission to conduct interviews
for this project ("Donald Trump's War on Terrorism") in
November 2017. The reference is LRS-17/18–5312.

32. This is what Christopher Fonzone and Luke Hartig have labelled
"a rough bipartisan (and nonpartisan) consensus on how to
approach what might be termed 'first generation' counterterrorism issues". See Fonzone, "The More Things", *Just Security*. For
a wider, academic perspective, see Peter M. Haas, "Introduction:
epistemic communities and international policy coordination",
International Organization, 46 (1) (1992), pp. 1–35.

1. THE TRUMP DOCTRINE

1. "National Security Strategy of the United States of America",
The White House, December 2018; available at https://www.
whitehouse.gov/wp-content/uploads/2017/12/NSS-Final-12-
18-2017-0905.pdf.

2. Ibid.

3. "Remarks by President Trump on the Administration's National
Security Strategy", *The White House*, 18 December 2017; available
at https://www.whitehouse.gov/briefings-statements/remarks-
president-trump-administrations-national-security-strategy/. For
fascism and the "myth of national rebirth", see Roger Griffin,
"The Palingenetic Core of Fascist Ideology" in Alessandro Campi

(ed.), *Che cos'è il fascismo? Interpretazioni e prospecttive di richerche* (Rome: Ideazione editrice, 2003), pp. 97–122; available at https://www.libraryofsocialscience.com/ideologies/resources/griffin-the-palingenetic-core/.

4. Ilan Goldenberg, "Trump's National Security Strategy Is Dead on Arrival", *Newsweek*, 18 December 2017; available at http://www.newsweek.com/trump-national-security-strategy-dead-arrival-751514.

5. Thomas Wright, "The National Security Strategy Papers Over a Crisis", *The Atlantic*, 19 December 2017; available at https://www.theatlantic.com/international/archive/2017/12/trump-national-security-strategy/548756/.

6. Patrick Radden Keefe, "McMaster and Commander", *New Yorker*, 30 April 2018; available at https://www.newyorker.com/magazine/2018/04/30/mcmaster-and-commander.

7. Ellen Mitchell, "WH official: 'I can't say' Trump has read entire national security strategy", *The Hill*, 18 December 2017; available at http://thehill.com/policy/defense/365516-wh-official-i-cant-say-trump-has-read-entire-national-security-strategy.

8. Quoted in Zack Beauchamp, "The case for Trump's foreign policy", *Vox*, 11 January 2018; available at https://www.vox.com/world/2018/1/11/16875344/trump-foreign-policy-randall-schweller.

9. Joshua Green, *Devil's Bargain: Steve Bannon, Donald Trump, and the Nationalist Uprising* (New York: Penguin, 2017), p. 241.

10. Marc Fisher, "Donald Trump doesn't read much. Being president probably wouldn't change that", *Washington Post*, 17 July 2016; available at https://www.washingtonpost.com/politics/donald-trump-doesnt-read-much-being-president-probably-wouldnt-change-that/2016/07/17/d2ddf2bc-4932-11e6–90a8-fb84201e0645_story.html?noredirect=on&utm_term=.67da581d7159.

11. This was not the first War on Terror, however. The expression was first used by Ronald Reagan in 1984. See interview with Bruce Hoffman, 9 April 2018.

12. "Remarks by the President upon Arrival", *The White House*, 16 September 2001; available at https://georgewbush-whitehouse.archives.gov/news/releases/2001/09/20010916–2.html.

13. For an overview, see "Defeating Terrorists, not Terrorism", *Bipartisan Policy Center*, September 2017, pp. 15–22; available at https://bipartisanpolicy.org/wp-content/uploads/2017/09/BPC-National-Security-Defeating-Terrorist-Not-Terrorism.pdf.

14. Quoted in "In full: President Bush's speech", *BBC News*, 20 January 2005; available at http://news.bbc.co.uk/1/hi/world/americas/4192773.stm.

15. "Obama West Point Speech in Full with Analysis", *BBC News*, 29 May 2014; available at https://www.bbc.co.uk/news/world-us-canada-27606537.

16. "National Security Strategy", *The White House*, May 2010; available at http://nssarchive.us/NSSR/2010.pdf.

17. Glennon, *National Security*, pp. 1–4.

18. Geltzer and Tankel, "Whatever Happened to Trump's Counterterrorism Strategy".

19. Robert Malley and Stephen Pomper, "Accounting for the Uncounted", *The Atlantic*, 16 December 2017; available at https://www.theatlantic.com/international/archive/2017/12/isis-obama-civilian-casualties/548501/.

20. John Brennan, Obama's (then) counter-terrorism advisor, at White House Press Briefing, 2 June 2011; quoted in "Defeating Terrorists", *Bipartisan Policy Center*, p. 43.

21. Quoted in Shreeya Sinha, "Obama's evolution on ISIS", *New York Times*, 9 June 2015; available at https://www.nytimes.com/interactive/2015/06/09/world/middleeast/obama-isis-strategy.html. Four months later, his commencement speech at West Point, which set out key foreign policy and security challenges, failed to mention Islamic State at all. See "Obama West Point Speech", BBC News.

22. Bush, quoted in "In full: President", BBC News.

23. Ibid. According to Obama, "When violent extremists operate in one stretch of mountains, people are endangered across an ocean". See "Remarks by the President at Cairo University, 6–04–09", *The White House*, 4 June 2009; available at https://obamawhitehouse.archives.gov/the-press-office/remarks-president-cairo-university-6-04-09.

24. "'Islam is Peace', Says President", The White House, 17 Sep-

tember 2001; available at https://georgewbush-whitehouse.
archives.gov/news/releases/2001/09/20010917-11.html.

25. "Remarks by the President at Cairo", The White House.

26. Walter Russell Mead, "The Jacksonian Tradition", *The National Interest*, 59(4) (1999), pp. 5–29

27. "Trump hangs portrait of Andrew Jackson in Oval Office", *The Hill*, 25 January 2017; available at https://thehill.com/home-news/administration/316115-trump-hangs-portrait-of-andrew-jackson-in-oval-office.

28. Quoted in "That Time Trump Spent Nearly $100,000 on an Ad Criticizing U.S. Foreign Policy in 1987", *Buzzfeed*, 10 July 2015; available at https://www.buzzfeednews.com/article/ilanben-meir/that-time-trump-spent-nearly-100000-on-an-ad-criticiz-ing-us.

29. "Transcript: Donald Trump's Foreign Policy Speech", *New York Times*, 27 April 2016; available at https://www.nytimes.com/2016/04/28/us/politics/transcript-trump-foreign-policy.html.

30. See Charlie Laderman and Brendan Simms, *Donald Trump: The Making of a World View* (London: Endeavour Press, 2017), chapter 2.

31. Marc Fisher and Michael Kranish, *Trump Revealed* (New York: Simon & Shuster, 2016), p. 275.

32. Quoted in "Donald Trump: How I'd Run the Country (Better)", *Esquire*, August 2004; available at https://www.esquire.com/news-politics/a37230/donald-trump-esquire-cover-story-august-2004/.

33. See "Trump hits Bush: Invading Iraq 'the single worst decision ever made'", *The Hill*, 3 March 2018; available at http://thehill.com/homenews/administration/376605-trump-hits-bush-invading-iraq-the-single-worst-decision-ever-made.

34. Quoted in "Full Text—U.S. President Trump announces strikes on Syria", Reuters, 13 April 2018; available at https://www.reuters.com/article/us-mideast-crisis-syria-trump-text/full-text-u-s-president-trump-announces-strikes-on-syria-idUSK-BN1HL040.

35. See Maureen Dowd, "Donald the Dove, Hillary the Hawk", *New York Times*, 30 April 2016; available at https://www.nytimes.

com/2016/05/01/opinion/sunday/donald-the-dove-hillary-the-hawk.html.

36. Mead, "The Jacksonian", p. 6.

37. As with Iraq, Trump's positions on Kosovo and Libya have shifted according to events on the ground. See Laderman, *Donald Trump*, p. 46.

38. See Ben Geier, "Donald Trump Won't Rule Out Using Nukes Against ISIS", *Fortune*, 23 March 2016.

39. Stephen M. Walt, "Welcome to the Dick Cheney Administration", *Foreign Policy*, 23 March 2018; available at https://foreign-policy.com/2018/03/23/welcome-to-the-dick-cheney-administration/.

40. Quoted in Laderman, *Donald Trump*, pp. 50–2.

41. "Transcript: Donald Trump Expounds on His Foreign Policy Views", *New York Times*, 26 March 2016; available at https://www.nytimes.com/2016/03/27/us/politics/donald-trump-transcript.html.

42. Trump, quoted in "Trump defends idea of shutting down mosques", *CBS News*, 19 November 2015; available at https://www.cbsnews.com/news/donald-trump-defends-idea-of-shutting-down-mosques-talks-about-ben-carson/.

43. In fact, he repeatedly called for the targeting of terrorists' families. See "Donald Trump Says He'd Take Out Terrorists' Families", *Time*, 2 December 2015; available at http://time.com/4132368/donald-trump-isis-bombing/.

44. Quoted in "Donald Trump: I would bomb the s*** out of them", #MAGA, 12 November 2015; available at https://www.youtube.com/watch?v=aWejiXvd-P8.

45. Quoted in Bob Woodward, *Fear: Trump in the White House* (New York: Simon and Schuster, 2018), p. 221.

46. Quoted in Nick Gass, "Trump: We'd be better off with Qaddafi, Saddam in power", *Politico*, 25 February 2016; available at https://www.politico.com/blogs/2016-gop-primary-live-updates-and-results/2016/02/donald-trump-qaddafi-saddam-219834.

47. "Transcript: Donald Trump", *New York Times*.

48. "Transcript: Second Debate", *New York Times*, 10 October 2016;

available at https://www.nytimes.com/2016/10/10/us/poli-tics/transcript-second-debate.html.

49. Quoted in Dan Mercia, "Trump on waterboarding: 'We have to fight fire with fire'", CNN, 26 January 2017; available at https://edition.cnn.com/2017/01/25/politics/donald-trump-water-boarding-torture/index.html.

50. Mead, "The Jacksonian", pp. 12–13, 17–18.

51. Quoted in Jenna Johnson, "Donald Trump on Waterboarding", *Washington Post*, 23 November 2015; available at https://www.washingtonpost.com/news/post-politics/wp/2015/11/23/donald-trump-on-waterboarding-if-it-doesnt-work-they-deserve-it-anyway/?utm_term=.2d61026e04b8.

52. Laderman, *Donald Trump*, Ch 3.

53. Ibid.

54. The "birther movement" alleged that President Obama was born outside the United States and secretly practised Islam. See Michael Barbaro, "Donald Trump Clung to 'Birther' Lie for Years, and Still Isn't Apologetic", *New York Times*, 16 September 2016; available at https://www.nytimes.com/2016/09/17/us/politics/donald-trump-obama-birther.html. See also Woodward, *Fear*, pp. 1–2.

55. Green, *Devil's Bargain*, p. xxvii.

56. "Donald Trump Sits Down with Bill O'Reilly", *Fox News*, 30 March 2011; available at https://www.foxnews.com/tran-script/2011/03/30/donald-trump-sits-down-bill-oreilly.html.

57. Ibid.

58. Ibid.

59. Ibid.

60. George Hawley, *Making Sense of the Alt-Right* (New York: Columbia University Press, 2017), p. 11.

61. David Neiwert, *Alt-America: The Rise of the Radical Right in the Age of Trump* (London: Verso, 2017).

62. See "Alt-Right", Southern Poverty Law Center, undated; available at https://www.splcenter.org/fighting-hate/extremist-files/ideology/alt-right.

63. J.M. Berger, "Trump Is the Glue That Binds the Far Right", *The Atlantic*, 29 October 2018; available at https://www.theatlantic.com/ideas/archive/2018/10/trump-alt-right-twitter/574219/.

64. Ibid., Ch 6.

65. See "DavidDuke.com", David Duke, undated; available at https://davidduke.com/.

66. Sarah Churchwell, "End of the American Dream? The Dark History of 'America First'", *Guardian*, 21 April 2018; available at https://www.theguardian.com/books/2018/apr/21/end-of-the-american-dream-the-dark-history-of-america-first.

67. "Former Klan Leader David Duke on His Senate Run and Donald Trump", *NPR*, 5 August 2016; available at https://www.npr.org/2016/08/05/488793451/former-klan-leader-david-duke-on-his-senate-run-and-donald-trump.

68. Quoted in Green, *Devil's Bargain*, p. 191.

69. Quoted in Jenna Johnson and Abigail Hauslohner, "'I think Islam hates us': A timeline of Trump's comments about Islam and Muslims", *Washington Post*, 20 May 2017; available at https://www.washingtonpost.com/news/post-politics/wp/2017/05/20/i-think-islam-hates-us-a-timeline-of-trumps-comments-about-islam-and-muslims/?utm_term=.dd4927dc6914.

70. Quoted in David Weigel, "Donald Trump's current take on Muslims: they're not Swedes", *Washington Post*, 22 September 2015; available at https://www.washingtonpost.com/news/post-politics/wp/2015/09/22/donald-trumps-current-take-on-muslims-theyre-not-swedes/?utm_term=.2ae1b497b394.

71. Ibid.

72. "Donald Trump: I think Islam hates us", CNN, 9 March 2016; available at https://www.youtube.com/watch?v=C-Zj0tfZY6o.

73. Quoted in Jenna Johnson, "Trump calls for 'total and complete shutdown of Muslims entering the United States'", *Washington Post*, 7 December 2015; available at https://www.washingtonpost.com/news/post-politics/wp/2015/12/07/donald-trump-calls-for-total-and-complete-shutdown-of-muslims-entering-the-united-states/?utm_term=.c9daeabd310b.

74. Mead, "The Jacksonian Tradition", pp. 8–9, 20.

75. Quoted in Melanie Garunay, "President Obama to Muslim Americans: 'You're a Valued Part of the American Family'", The White House, 21 July 2016; available at https://obam-

awhitehouse.archives.gov/blog/2016/07/25/president-obama-hosts-eid-reception.

2. THE CAMPAIGN

1. The breakup process started with Islamic State's (unilateral) declaration that the Syrian jihadist group Jabhat al-Nusra was under its command, and resulted in two entirely separate—and competing—jihadist groups in Syria twelve months later. Peter R. Neumann, *Radicalized: New Jihadists and the Threat to the West* (London: IB Tauris, 2016), pp. 60–4.

2. This, however, included deserts and unpopulated areas. See "Islamic State territory down 60 percent and revenue down 80 percent on Caliphate's third anniversary", IHS Markit, 29 June 2017.

3. See Neumann, *Radicalized*, Ch 3.

4. See, for example, J.M. Berger and Jonathon Morgan, "The ISIS Twitter Census: Defining and Describing the Population of ISIS Supporters on Twitter", Brookings, 5 March 2015; available at https://www.brookings.edu/research/the-isis-twitter-census-defining-and-describing-the-population-of-isis-supporters-on-twitter/.

5. "Foreign Fighters: An Updated Assessment of the Flow of Foreign Fighters into Syria and Iraq", The Soufan Group, December 2015; available at http://soufangroup.com/wp-content/uploads/2015/12/TSG_ForeignFightersUpdate3.pdf.

6. Quoted in Ralph Ellis, "ISIS releases message from al-Baghdadi calling for recruits", CNN, 14 May 2015; available at https://edition.cnn.com/2015/05/14/asia/al-baghdadi-audio/index.html.

7. See, for example, Alison Smale, "Terrorism Suspects Are Posing as Refugees, Germany Says", *New York Times*, 5 February 2016; available at https://www.nytimes.com/2016/02/06/world/europe/germany-refugees-isis.html; "Paris attack terrorists used refugee chaos to enter France, says PM Valls", France 24, 20 November 2015; available at https://www.france24.com/en/20151119-paris-attackers-slip-refugee-migrant-crisis-terrorism.

8. See "European Union Terrorism Situation and Trend Report", Europol, yearly editions; available at https://www.europol.europa.eu/activities-services/main-reports/eu-terrorism-situation-and-trend-report#fndtn-tabs-0-bottom-2.

9. See Peter Bergen, David Sterman, Albert Ford, and Alyssa Sims, "Jihadist Terrorism 16 Years after 9/11", New America, September 2017; available at https://www.newamerica.org/documents/1981/Terrorism_9-11_2017.pdf.

10. See, for example, Kathy Frankovic, "A nation divided over terrorism, immigration, and the courts", YouGov, 16 February 2017; available at https://today.yougov.com/topics/politics/articles-reports/2017/02/16/immigration-terrorism-courts-nation-divided.

11. See Steven Shepard, "Who has the upper hand on terrorism, Clinton or Trump?", *Politico*, 19 September 2016; available at https://www.politico.com/story/2016/09/clinton-trump-terrorism-leaders-228376.

12. Mark Leibovich, "Look Out for the Trump Pivot!", *The New York Times*, 25 March 2016; available at https://www.nytimes.com/2016/03/24/magazine/look-out-for-the-trump-pivot.html.

13. See, for example, "Bush 2004 Campaign Ad—Mi Familia", YouTube, 9 November 2006; available at https://www.youtube.com/watch?v=wN0njltQkPE.

14. See Jennifer Rubin, "GOP autopsy report goes bold", *Washington Post*, 18 March 2013; available at https://www.washingtonpost.com/blogs/right-turn/wp/2013/03/18/gop-autopsy-report-goes-bold/?noredirect=on&utm_term=.1635ed652180.

15. Salena Zito and Brad Todd, *The Great Revolt: Inside the Populist Coalition Reshaping American Politics* (New York: Crown Forum, 2018), pp. 16–17.

16. Green, *Devil's Bargain*, p. 97. As a businessman, Trump had a mixed history when it comes to race relations. See Kranish, *Trump Revealed*, pp. 279–82.

17. Zito, *The Great Revolt*, p. 45.

18. Green, *Devil's Bargain*, p. 106.

19. When asked what time had been America's "greatest", Trump

chose the 1950s, saying that "we were not pushed around [back then], we were respected by everybody, we had just won a war, we were pretty much doing what we had to do". Quoted in "Transcript: Donald Trump", *New York Times*.

20. Edward Ashbee, *The Trump Revolt* (Manchester: Manchester University Press, 2017), p. 75.

21. Ibid., pp. 61–6.

22. Matt Grossmann, "Racial Attitudes and Political Correctness in the 2016 Presidential Election", *Niskanen Center*, 10 May 2018; available at https://niskanencenter.org/blog/racial-attitudes-and-political-correctness-in-the-2016-presidential-election/.

23. Victor Davis Hanson, *The Case for Trump* (New York: Basic Books, 2019), pp. 108–9.

24. See Oren Tsur (et al.), "The Data Behind Donald Trump's Twitter Takeover", *Politico*, 29 April 2016; available at https://www.politico.com/magazine/story/2016/04/donald-trump-2016-twitter-takeover-213861.

25. Green, *Devil's Bargain*, p. 104.

26. See Ed Pilkington, "How the Drudge report ushered in the age of Trump", *Guardian*, 24 January 2018; available at https://www.theguardian.com/us-news/2018/jan/24/how-the-drudge-report-ushered-in-the-age-of-trump.

27. Hawley, *Making Sense*, pp. 116, 119. Also see Andrew Marantz, "Trolls for Trump", *New Yorker*, 31 October 2016; available at https://www.newyorker.com/magazine/2016/10/31/trolls-for-trump.

28. Emily Stewart, "Donald Trump Rode $5 Billion in Free Media to the White House", The Street, 20 November 2016; available at https://www.thestreet.com/story/13896916/1/donald-trump-rode-5-billion-in-free-media-to-the-white-house.html.

29. Trump regularly ordered printouts of his tweets in order to understand which ones had gained the most traction, concluding that "the most effective tweets were often the most shocking". See Woodward, *Fear*, p. 207.

30. "Trump: Being Presidential Would Be Boring", *YouTube*, 4 April 2016; available at https://www.youtube.com/watch?v=cGZzXH94uMk.

31. This is how Senator John McCain once described Trump's campaign. Quoted in Kranish, *Trump Revealed*, p. 313.

32. Thomas B. Edsall, "What Motivates People More Than Loyalty? Loathing", *The New York Times*, 1 March 2018; available at https://www.nytimes.com/2018/03/01/opinion/negative-partisanship-democrats-republicans.html.

33. See Rupert Brown, "Social identity theory: past achievements, current problems and future challenges", *European Journal of Social Psychology*, 30 (2000), pp. 745–78.

34. "Remarks by the President at the Summit on Countering Violent Extremism", *The White House*, 19 February 2015; available at https://obamawhitehouse.archives.gov/the-press-office/2015/02/19/remarks-president-summit-countering-violent-extremism-february-19-2015.

35. "Remarks by the President in Closing of the Summit on Countering Violent Extremism", *The White House*, 18 February 2015; available at https://obamawhitehouse.archives.gov/the-press-office/2015/02/18/remarks-president-closing-summit-countering-violent-extremism.

36. See, for example, Maajid Nawaz, "We Treat Radical Islam Like Voldemort", *Big Think*, June 2016; available at https://bigthink.com/videos/maajid-nawaz-on-the-voldemort-effect.

37. See, for example, Mark Juergensmeyer, *Terror in the Mind of God: The Global Rise of Religious Violence* (Oakland, CA: University of California Press, 1998); Shiraz Maher, *Salafi-Jihadism: The History of an Idea* (London: Hurst, 2016); Peter Mandaville, *Islam and Politics*, 2nd edn (London: Routledge, 2014).

38. Nawaz, "We Treat Radical".

39. @RealDonaldTrump, *Twitter*, 4 July 2016.

40. Gorka was commissioned to write papers for Trump's campaign. See Jacey Fortin, "Who Is Sebastian Gorka?", *New York Times*, 17 February 2017; available at https://www.nytimes.com/2017/02/17/us/politics/dr-sebastian-gorka.html. For the bigger picture, see Wajahat Ali (et al.), "Fear Inc.: The Roots of the Islamophobia Network in America", *Center for American Progress*, August 2011; available at https://cdn.americanprogress.org/wp-content/uploads/issues/2011/08/pdf/islamophobia.pdf.

41. See "Gaffney defiant in the face of mainstream media attacks", *The Counter Jihad Report*, 21 March 2017; available at https://counterjihadreport.com/category/frank-gaffney/.

42. Lauren Carroll and Louis Jacobson, "Trump cites shaky survey in call to ban Muslims from entering US", *Politifact*, 9 December 2015; available at https://www.politifact.com/truth-o-meter/statements/2015/dec/09/donald-trump/trump-cites-shaky-survey-call-ban-muslims-entering/.

43. Ibid.

44. Quoted in "Rubio to Trump: 'I Want to Be Correct, not Politically Correct'", YouTube, 10 March 2016; available at https://www.youtube.com/watch?v=-xZRb86Drrw&feature=youtu.be&t=8s.

45. See Mead, "The Jacksonian", p. 20.

46. Farah Pandith, interview with the author, June 2018.

47. Quoted in "Donald Trump in Birmingham: Full Speech at the BJCC", YouTube, 21 November 2015; available at https://www.youtube.com/watch?v=IgvPoFo1zPY.

48. Quoted in "'This Week' Transcript", ABC News, 22 November 2015; available at https://abcnews.go.com/Politics/week-transcript-donald-trump-ben-carson/story?id=35336008.

49. Ibid.

50. See Mark Mueller, "Some Jersey City Muslims Did Celebrate 9/11", NJ.com, 22 December 2015; available at https://www.nj.com/news/index.ssf/2015/12/exclusive_jersey_city_cop_residents_say_some_musli.html. Bill Riales, "Credible Source on 9–11 Muslim Celebrations: FBI", WKRG, 25 November 2015; available at https://www.wkrg.com/news/credible-source-on-9-11-muslim-celebrations-fbi/957001459.

51. See Costas Panagopoulos, "Trends: Arab and Muslim Americans and Islam in the Aftermath of 9/11", *The Public Opinion Quarterly*, 70 (4) (2006), pp. 608–24.

52. Quoted in Salvador Hernandez, "Trump Falsely Claims Muslims Knew in Advance Of San Bernardino Terror Plot", Buzzfeed News, 30 March 2016; available at https://www.buzzfeednews.com/article/salvadorhernandez/trump-falsely-claims-muslims-knew-in-advance-of-san-bernardi.

53. Ibid.

54. Quoted in @asmamk, *Twitter*, 29 December 2015.

55. Trump made contradictory statements about whether he believed Muslim Americans should be registered too. See Sabrina Siddiqui, "Trump and a Muslim registry: does he want one, and is it even possible?", *Guardian*, 27 November 2016; available at https://www.theguardian.com/us-news/2016/nov/27/donald-trump-muslim-registry-policy-possibility.

56. See, for example, Emily Stephenson and Amanda Becker, "Trump backs surveillance of mosques despite criticism of rhetoric", *Reuters*, 15 June 2016; available at https://www.reuters.com/article/us-usa-election-idUSKCN0Z12AS.

57. Quoted in Jon Street, "Trump Gets Blunt with Anchor on Radical Islam", *The Blaze*, 22 March 2016; available at https://www.theblaze.com/news/2016/03/22/trump-gets-blunt-with-anchor-on-radical-islam-you-have-to-deal-with-the-mosques-whether-you-like-it-or-not.

58. Quoted in "Full text: Khizr Khan's speech to the 2016 Democratic National Convention", *ABC News*, 1 August 2016; available at https://abcnews.go.com/Politics/full-text-khizr-khans-speech-2016-democratic-national/story?id=41043609.

59. Quoted in: "Donald Trump to Father of Fallen Soldier: 'I've Made a Lot of Sacrifices'", ABC News, 30 July 2016; available at https://abcnews.go.com/Politics/donald-trump-father-fallen-soldier-ive-made-lot/story?id=41015051.

60. Quoted in "Full text: Donald Trump announces a presidential bid", *Washington Post*, 16 June 2015; available at https://www.washingtonpost.com/news/post-politics/wp/2015/06/16/full-text-donald-trump-announces-a-presidential-bid/?utm_term=.303d57d9ab65.

61. Quoted in "Transcripts: State of the Union", *CNN*, 28 June 2015; available at http://edition.cnn.com/TRANSCRIPTS/1506/28/sotu.01.html.

62. @RealDonaldTrump, *Twitter*, 30 May 2016.

63. Quoted in "What Trump Has Said About Judge Curiel", Indystar, 11 June 2016; available at https://eu.indystar.com/story/news/2016/06/11/what-trump-has-said-judge-curiel/85641242/.

64. See "Donald Trump: Refugees could be the ultimate Trojan horse", Fox News, 3 October 2015; available at https://www.youtube.com/watch?v=K9Pr6a_nMU4.

65. Kranish, *Trump Revealed*, p. 317.

66. Quoted in Johnson, "Trump calls".

67. @RealDonaldTrump, Twitter, 13 June 2016.

68. Quoted in "Meet the Press—July 24, 2016", NBC News, 24 July 2016; available at https://www.nbcnews.com/meet-the-press/meet-press-july-24-2016-n615706.

69. Quoted in Lauren Carroll, "Donald Trump says hundreds of immigrants and their children have been implicated in U.S. terrorism", *Politifact*, 16 June 2016; available at https://www.politifact.com/truth-o-meter/article/2016/jun/14/donald-trump-says-hundreds-migrants-and-their-chil/.

70. Jessica Estepa, "'Preventing Muslim immigration' disappears from Trump website", *USA Today*, 9 May 2017; available at https://eu.usatoday.com/story/news/politics/onpolitics/2017/05/08/preventing-muslim-immigration-statement-disappears-donald-trump-campaign-site/101436780/.

71. Quoted in: "Exclusive: Donald Trump talks immigration, terrorism, and campaign's future", *Time*, 9 December 2015; available at http://time.com/4140698/donald-trump-interview/.

72. Quoted in "Read Donald Trump's Ohio Speech on Immigration and Terrorism", *Time*, 15 August 2016; available at http://time.com/4453110/donald-trump-national-security-immigration-terrorism-speech/.

73. McKay Coppins, "Trump's Right-Hand Troll", The Atlantic, 28 May 2018; available at https://www.theatlantic.com/politics/archive/2018/05/stephen-miller-trump-adviser/561317/.

74. See, for example, @RealDonaldTrump, *Twitter*, 21 December 2015; @RealDonaldTrump, *Twitter*, 22 March 2016.

75. However, when dozens of military leaders criticised his position on torture, he stopped referring to "the generals", claiming that "I know more about ISIS than the generals do, believe me!" See "Donald Trump: I know more than the generals on ISIS", *YouTube*, 12 November 2015; available at https://www.youtube.com/watch?v=kul34O_yMLs.

76. Quoted in "Transcript: Donald Trump's Foreign Policy Speech", *New York Times*, 27 April 2016; available at https://www.nytimes.com/2016/04/28/us/politics/transcript-trump-foreign-policy.html.

77. Quoted in Raf Sanchez, "Donald Trump has a 'very beautiful' plan to defeat Isil", *Telegraph*, 1 June 2015; available at https://www.telegraph.co.uk/news/worldnews/northamerica/usa/11644926/Donald-Trump-has-a-very-beautiful-plan-to-defeat-Isil-but-he-cant-tell-anyone-about-it.html.

78. Quoted in Gideon Resnick, "Donald Trump's New Foreign Policy: Say Nothing", *The Daily Beast*, 21 September 2015; available at https://www.thedailybeast.com/donald-trumps-new-foreign-policy-say-nothing.

79. The clearest indication that there had never been any plan was that one of his first actions in office was to order his officials to come up with one.

80. Quoted in "Transcript of the Republican Presidential Debate", *New York Times*, 14 February 2016; available at https://www.nytimes.com/2016/02/14/us/politics/transcript-of-the-republican-presidential-debate.html.

81. Katie Glueck, "Cruz pledges relentless bombing to destroy ISIL", *Politico*, 12 May 2015; available at https://www.politico.com/story/2015/12/cruz-isil-bombing-216454.

82. Quoted in Geier, "Donald Trump".

83. Quoted in "Transcript of".

84. Quoted in "Donald Trump Won't Take Nuclear Weapons Off the Table", NBC News, 31 March 2016; available at http://www.msnbc.com/hardball/watch/donald-trump-won-t-take-nukes-off-the-table-655471171934?v=raila&.

85. @RealDonaldTrump, Twitter, 9 February 2016.

86. He also promoted it in tweets following the terrorist attacks in Barcelona in August 2017. See Jacob Pramuk, "Trump promotes unfounded story about mass killing of terrorists", CNBC, 17 August 2017; available at https://www.cnbc.com/2017/08/17/trump-promotes-unfounded-story-about-mass-killing-of-terrorists.html.

87. Quoted in Jenna Johnson and Josie DelReal, "Trump tells story

about killing terrorists with bullets dipped in pigs' blood", *Washington Post*, 20 February 2016; available at https://www.washingtonpost.com/news/post-politics/wp/2016/02/20/trumps-story-about-killing-terrorists-with-bullets-dipped-in-pigs-blood-is-likely-not-true/?utm_term=.bd2db43ae7c2.

88. Louis Jacobson, "Donald Trump cites dubious legend about Gen. Pershing, pigs' blood and Muslims", Politifact, 23 February 2016; available at https://www.politifact.com/truth-o-meter/statements/2016/feb/23/donald-trump/donald-trump-cites-dubious-legend-about-gen-pershi/.

89. Robert Paxton, *The Anatomy of Fascism* (London: Penguin, 2004), p. 205.

3. POLICY AND PEOPLE

1. See Robert O'Harrow and Shawn Boburg, "Behind the chaos: Office that vets Trump appointees plagued by inexperience", *Washington Post*, 30 March 2018; available at https://www.washingtonpost.com/investigations/behind-the-chaos-office-that-vets-trump-appointees-plagued-by-inexperience/2018/03/30/cde31a1a-28a3-11e8-ab19-06a445a08c94_story.html?utm_term=.e3e6e6a960df.

2. Michael Lewis, "'This guy doesn't know anything': the inside story of Trump's shambolic transition team", *Guardian*, 27 September 2018; available at https://www.theguardian.com/news/2018/sep/27/this-guy-doesnt-know-anything-the-inside-story-of-trumps-shambolic-transition-team. For a similar account, see Nathal Toosi, "Inside the Chaotic Early Days of Trump's Foreign Policy", *Politico Magazine*, 1 March 2019; available at https://www.politico.com/magazine/story/2019/03/01/trump-national-security-council-225442 https://www.politico.com/magazine/story/2019/03/01/trump-national-security-council-225442.

3. Michael V. Hayden, *The Assault on Intelligence: American National Security in an Age of Lies* (New York: Penguin Press, 2018), p. 82.

4. Woodward, *Fear*, pp. 1–5.

5. See, for example, Eliot A. Cohen, "Is Trump Ending the American

Era?", *The Atlantic*, October 2017; available at https://www. theatlantic.com/magazine/archive/2017/10/is-trump-ending-the-american-era/537888/.

6. See Matt Taibbi, "How America Made Donald Trump Unstoppable", *Rolling Stone*, 24 February 2016; available at https://www.rollingstone.com/culture/culture-news/how-america-made-donald-trump-unstoppable-162952/.

7. Fisher, *Trump Revealed*, pp. 316–30.

8. Hayden, *The Assault*, pp. 82–3.

9. National Security Council official #1, interview with the author, May 2018.

10. Mead, "The Jacksonian", pp. 18–22.

11. See Rory Carroll, "'I'm, like, a really smart person': Donald Trump exults in outsider status", *Guardian*, 12 July 2015; available at https://www.theguardian.com/us-news/2015/jul/12/im-like-a-really-smart-person-donald-trump-exults-in-outsider-status.

12. Donald J. Trump with Tony Schwartz, *Trump: The Art of the Deal* (New York: Ballantine Books, 1987).

13. Trump talked about running the country like his business in interviews as early as 1980. See Laderman, *Donald Trump*, p. 27.

14. Michael Wolff, *Siege: Trump under Fire* (New York: Little Brown, 2019), p. 11.

15. In other policy areas, however, Heritage became one of Trump's most significant suppliers of policy and personnel. See "Tracking how many key positions Trump has filled so far", *Washington Post*, last updated at 27 July 2018; available at https://www. washingtonpost.com/graphics/politics/trump-administration-appointee-tracker/database/?utm_term=.4f6ea613c252.

16. Jacob Heilbrunn, "Donald Trump's Brains", *New York Review of Books*, 21 December 2017; available at https://www.nybooks. com/articles/2017/12/21/donald-trump-brains/.

17. Ryan William, quoted in "Tom Cotton Speech—Claremont's 2018 Annual Dinner", *YouTube*, 8 May 2018; available at https://www.youtube.com/watch?v=Gij9-dXYsOw.

18. Publius Decius Mus (Michael Anton), "The Flight 93 Election", *Claremont Review of Books*, 5 September 2016; available at http:// claremont.org/crb/basicpage/the-flight-93-election/.

19. Ibid. For an updated version of his essay, see Michael Anton, *After the Flight 93 Election: The Vote that Saved America and what We Still Have to Do* (New York: Encounter, 2019).

20. Green, *Devil's Bargain*, p. 6.

21. Fazia Patel, Matthew Duss, and Amos Toh, "Foreign Law Bans", *Center for American Progress*, 16 May 2013; available at https://www.americanprogress.org/issues/security/reports/2013/05/16/63540/foreign-law-bans/.

22. Kerry McDermott, "Barack Obama's choice for CIA director 'converted to Islam', former FBI agent claims", *Daily Mail*, 12 February 2013; available at http://www.dailymail.co.uk/news/article-2277524/Obamas-choice-CIA-chief-converted-Islam-says-FBI-agent.html.

23. Gregory Krieg, "Ted Curz defends foreign policy adviser Frank Gaffney", CNN, 22 March 2016; available at https://edition.cnn.com/2016/03/21/politics/ted-cruz-frank-gaffney-national-security/index.html.

24. See Joel Gunter, "Trump's Muslim Lockdown: What is the Center for Security Policy", BBC News, 8 December 2015; available at https://www.bbc.co.uk/news/world-us-canada-35037943.

25. See "Tracking how many", *Washington Post*.

26. Lorraine Woellert, "The cost of Donald Trump's deserted government", *Politico*, 27 April 2018; available at https://www.politico.com/story/2018/04/27/trump-deserted-government-552971.

27. Kathryn Dunn Tenpas, et al., "Tracking turnover in the Trump administration", Brookings, last updated 20 July 2018; available at https://www.brookings.edu/research/tracking-turnover-in-the-trump-administration/.

28. "Donald Trump: 'My primary consultant is myself'", NBC Morning Joe, 16 March 2016; available at https://www.youtube.com/watch?v=W7CBp8lQ6ro.

29. See, for example, Ishaan Tharoor, "The dark controversial past of Trump's counterterrorism advisor", *Washington Post*, 22 March 2016; available at https://www.washingtonpost.com/news/worldviews/wp/2016/03/22/the-dark-controversial-past-of-trumps-counterterrorism-adviser/?utm_term=.6792ceb4a6e2.

30. William Boykin et al., *Sharia: The Threat to America* (Washington: Center for Security Policy, 2010).

31. Robert S. Mueller III, "Report on the Investigation into Russian Interference in the 2016 Election, Volume I of II", Department of Justice, March 2019, p. 91; available at https://www.justice.gov/storage/report.pdf.

32. Quoted in Michael Crowley, "Trump's foreign policy team baffles GOP experts", *Politico*, 21 March 2016; available at https://www.politico.com/story/2016/03/donald-trump-foreign-policy-advisers-221058.

33. "Open Letter on Donald Trump from GOP Security Leaders", War on the Rocks, 2 March 2016; available at https://warontherocks.com/2016/03/open-letter-on-donald-trump-from-gop-national-security-leaders/; Damian Paletta, "GOP National Security Veterans: Trump Would Be 'Dangerous President'", *Wall Street Journal*, 8 August 2016; available at https://blogs.wsj.com/washwire/2016/08/08/gop-national-security-veterans-trump-would-be-dangerous-president/?mod=e2tw; Karen De Young, "75 retired senior diplomats sign letter opposing Trump for president", *Washington Post*, 22 September 2016; available at https://www.washingtonpost.com/world/national-security/75-retired-senior-diplomats-sign-letter-opposing-trump-for-president/2016/09/21/5c5dff10–8046–11e6-b002–307601806392_story.html?utm_term=.dc01dd57ec88.

34. The way I use the term implies no reference to the 19th century nativist political party of the same name.

35. See "Transcript: Donald Trump", *New York Times*.

36. See, for example, Lewis, "'This guy'"; Henry Mance, "Academic touted as Trump's EU envoy embellished autobiography", *Financial Times*, 9 February 2017; available at https://www.ft.com/content/239d378e-ee20-11e6-ba01-119a44939bb6.

37. Harrow, "Behind the chaos", *Washington Post*.

38. Maggie Haberman, Michael S. Smith, Adam Goldman, and Annie Karni, "Trump Ordered Officials to Give Jared Kushner a Security Clearance", *New York Times*, 28 February 2019; available at https://www.nytimes.com/2019/02/28/us/politics/jared-kushner-security-clearance.html.

39. Wolff, *Siege*, p. 126.
40. Quoted in "Trump to Kushner: If you can't make Mideast peace, no one can", *The Times of Israel*, 20 January 2017; available at https://www.timesofisrael.com/trump-to-kushner-if-you-cant-make-mideast-peace-no-one-can/.
41. Ibid., p. I.
42. Hayden, *The Assault*, p. 63.
43. Ibid.
44. James Kitfeld, "How Mike Flynn Became America's Angriest General", *Politico*, 16 October 2016; available at https://www.politico.com/magazine/story/2016/10/how-mike-flynn-became-americas-angriest-general-214362.
45. Hayden, *The Assault*, p. 64.
46. Michael T. Flynn and Michael Ledeen, *The Field of Fight* (New York: St Martin's Press, 2016), p. 76.
47. Hayden, *The Assault*, p. 65.
48. Keefe, "McMaster and Commander".
49. For the full memo, see "Here's the memo that blew up the Security Council", *Business Insider*, 11 August 2017; available at http://uk.businessinsider.com/heres-the-memo-that-blew-up-the-national-security-council-2017–8?r=US&IR=T.
50. See Rosie Gray, "The Man McMaster Couldn't Fire", *The Atlantic*, 23 July 2017; available at https://www.theatlantic.com/politics/archive/2017/07/ezra-cohen-watnick/534615/.
51. Senior Trump appointee #2, conversation with author, 19 October 2017.
52. See Mckay Coppins, "Trump's Right-Hand Troll", *The Atlantic*, 28 May 2018.
53. Trump appointee #3, interview with the author, April 2018.
54. Eliot Cohen, quoted in Keefe, "McMaster and Commander". See also Anonymous, "I am Part of the Resistance Inside the Trump Administration", *New York Times*, 6 September 2018; available at https://www.nytimes.com/2018/09/05/opinion/trump-white-house-anonymous-resistance.html?action=click&module=Top%20Stories&pgtype=Homepage.
55. For Mattis, see Susan Glasser, "How Jim Mattis Became Trump's 'Last Man Standing'", *The New Yorker*, 20 April 2018; available at https://www.newyorker.com/news/letter-from-trumps-wash-

ington/how-jim-mattis-became-trumps-last-man-standing; Keefe, "McMaster and Commander"; Robert F. Worth, "Can Jim Mattis Hold the Line in Trump's 'War Cabinet'", *New York Times Magazine*, 26 March 2018; available at https://www.nytimes.com/2018/03/26/magazine/can-jim-mattis-hold-the-line-in-trumps-war-cabinet.html.

56. See Ryan Evans, "Mattis the Great, Mattis the Exploited", War on The Rocks, 28 January 2017; available at https://warontherocks.com/2017/01/mattis-the-great-mattis-the-exploited/.

57. See, for example, Spencer Ackerman, "Fear Mounts as Mattis Quits Pentagon", *Daily Beast*, 21 December 2018; available at https://www.thedailybeast.com/fear-mounts-as-mattis-quits-pentagon.

58. See Wesley Morgan, "How Mattis Tried to Contain Trump", *Politico*, 20 December 2018; available at https://www.politico.com/story/2018/12/20/how-mattis-tried-to-contain-trump-1049741.

59. Mattis, quoted in "Read: James Mattis' Resignation Letter", CNN, 20 December 2018; available at https://edition.cnn.com/2018/12/20/politics/james-mattis-resignation-letter-doc/index.html.

60. Chris Costa, interview with the author, June 2018.

61. Sebastian Gorka, *Why We Fight: Defeating America's Enemies—With No Apologies* (New York: Regnery, 2018), Ch 5.

62. See, for example, Sebastian Gorka, quoted in "The Point is You're Out", YouTube, 1 September 2017; available at https://www.youtube.com/watch?v=LDR3_1Fofschttps://www.youtube.com/watch?v=LDR3_1Fofsc.

63. See, for example, John Hudson, Shane Harris, Josh Dawsey, and Anne Gearan, "Trump, frustrated by advisers, is not convinced the time is right to attack Iraq", *Washington Post*, 15 May 2019; available at https://www.washingtonpost.com/world/national-security/trump-frustrated-by-advisers-is-not-convinced-the-time-is-right-to-attack-iran/2019/05/15/bbf5835e-1fbf-4035-a744-12799213e824_story.html?utm_term=.e621ed185bc3. See also Victor David Hanson, *The Case for Trump* (New York: Basic Books, 2019), p. 81.

64. "Tracking how many", *Washington Post*.

4. BANNING MUSLIMS

1. Quoted in Justin Moyer, "Dick Cheney slams Trump's Muslim entry ban", *Washington Post*, 8 December 2015; available at https://www.washingtonpost.com/news/morning-mix/wp/2015/12/08/dick-cheney-slams-trumps-muslim-entry-ban-and-suggests-u-s-re-invade-middle-east/.

2. @GovPenceIN, *Twitter*, 8 December 2015.

3. Hawley, *Making Sense*, p. 21.

4. Samuel Huntington, *Who Are We? The Challenges to America's National Identity* (New York: Simon and Schuster 2005). Fukuyama pointed out that these "values served as the basis for national identity but were also accessible to people who were not white and Christian or in some way 'blood and soil' related to the Anglo-Saxon Protestant founders of the country". See "The Challenge of Positive Freedom", *NPQ*, Spring 2007; available at https://onlinelibrary.wiley.com/doi/abs/10.1111/j.1540-5842.2007.00885.x.

5. Mead, "The Jacksonian", pp. 8–9.

6. Ibid., p. 10.

7. Even if there was evidence that America had engaged in similar practices in the past. Examples mentioned by Hawley are the Chinese Exclusionary Act (1882), the Immigration Act (1924), and Operation Wetback, "which forcibly deported undocumented immigrants" as recently as the 1950s. See Hawley, *Making Sense*, p. 22.

8. For an overview, see Muzzaffar Chishti and Claire Bergeron, "Post-9/11 Policies Dramatically Alter the U.S. Immigration Landscape", *Migration Policy Institute*, 8 September 2011; available at https://www.migrationpolicy.org/article/post-911-policies-dramatically-alter-us-immigration-landscape.

9. Zack Beauchamp, "Trump Says Obama Banned Refugees Too. He's Wrong", *Vox*, 31 January 2017; available at https://www.vox.com/world/2017/1/31/14444862/obama-refugee-ban-2011.

10. "Protecting the Nation from Foreign Terrorist Entry Into the United States", Executive Order 13769, *White House*, 27 January

2017; available at https://www.whitehouse.gov/presidential-actions/executive-order-protecting-nation-foreign-terrorist-entry-united-states/.

11. "provided that the religion of the individual is a minority religion in the individual's country of nationality".

12. Quoted in "Trump Urges 'Shutdown' on Muslims Entering US", *YouTube*, 7 December 2015; available at https://www.youtube.com/watch?v=YUK2aMYGMCg.

13. David Bier, "A Dozen Times Trump Equated His Travel Ban with a Muslim Ban", *Cato At Liberty*, 14 August 2017; available at https://www.cato.org/blog/dozen-times-trump-equated-travel-ban-muslim-ban.

14. "'Trump asked for a Muslim ban', Giuliani says", *Washington Post*, 29 January 2017; available at https://www.washingtonpost.com/news/the-fix/wp/2017/01/29/trump-asked-for-a-muslim-ban-giuliani-says-and-ordered-a-commission-to-do-it-legally/?utm_term=.c0d00629664b.

15. Ron Nixon, "Travel Ban Caught Homeland Security By Surprise, Report Concludes", *New York Times*, 19 January 2018; available at https://www.nytimes.com/2018/01/19/us/politics/homeland-security-travel-ban-inspector-general.html.

16. Ashley Parker, Philip Rucker, and Robert Costa, "From order to disorder: How Trump's immigration directive exposed GOP rifts", *Washington Post*, 30 January 2017; available at https://www.washingtonpost.com/politics/from-order-to-disorder-how-trumps-immigration-directive-exposed-gop-rifts/2017/01/30/b4e42044-e70f-11e6-b82f-687d6e6a3e7c_story.html?utm_term=.8fd86f0dccaa.

17. Kyle Cheney and Louis Nelson, "DHS chief promises to carry out Trump's immigration order 'humanely'", *Politico*, 31 January 2017; available at https://www.politico.com/story/2017/01/trump-immigration-order-john-kelly-234435; Nixon, "Travel Ban Caught".

18. Quoted in Wolff, *Fire and Fury*, p. 65.

19. Senior Trump appointee #1, interview with the author, May 2018.

20. Alberto Fernandez, interview with the author, April 2018.

21. @rcallimachi, *Twitter*, 8 February 2017.
22. See "Cabinet members lobby Trump to remove Iraq from new travel ban", *Reuters*, 2 March 2017; available at https://www.reuters.com/article/us-usa-immigration-iraq-idUSKBN169015; Kevin Liptak, "Why Iraq was removed from the revised travel ban", *CNN*, 6 March 2017; available at https://edition.cnn.com/2017/03/06/politics/iraq-travel-ban/index.html.
23. "Face the Nation Transcript, January 29, 2017", *CBS News*, 29 January 2017; available at https://www.cbsnews.com/news/face-the-nation-transcript-january-29-2017-priebus-mccain-ellison/.
24. "Around the World and the U.S., New Travel Ban Draws Anger, Applause and Shrugs", *New York Times*, 25 September 2017; available at https://www.nytimes.com/2017/09/25/us/travel-ban-reaction.html.
25. "Immigrant Visas Issued: Fiscal Year 2016", *State Department*, undated; available at https://travel.state.gov/content/dam/visas/Statistics/AnnualReports/FY2016AnnualReport/FY16AnnualReport-TableIII.pdf; "Immigrant Visas Issued: Fiscal Year 2017", *State Department*, undated; available at https://travel.state.gov/content/dam/visas/Statistics/AnnualReports/FY2017AnnualReport/FY17AnnualReport-TableIII.pdf.
26. "Around the World", New York Times.
27. Ibid.
28. "Protecting the Nation from Foreign Terrorist Entry Into the United States", Executive Order 13780, *White House*, 6 March 2017; available at https://www.gpo.gov/fdsys/pkg/FR-2017-03-09/pdf/2017-04837.pdf.
29. @RealDonaldTrump, *Twitter*, 5 June 2017; @RealDonald Trump, *Twitter*, 15 September 2017.
30. Quoted in "Trump's travel is unconstitutional religious discrimination, US court rules", *Associated Press*, 15 February 2018; available at https://www.theguardian.com/us-news/2018/feb/15/trump-travel-ban-unconstitutional-appeals-court-ruling-virginia.
31. "Presidential Declaration Enhancing Vetting Capabilities and Processes for Detecting Attempted Entry Into the United States by Terrorists or Other Public-Safety Threats", *The White House*,

24 September 2017; available at https://www.whitehouse.gov/
presidential-actions/presidential-proclamation-enhancing-vet-
ting-capabilities-processes-detecting-attempted-entry-united-
states-terrorists-public-safety-threats/.

32. Organisations like the American Civil Liberties Union have
pointed out that Venezuelan citizens were not banned "in any
meaningful sense", as the ban only applied to a small number of
senior officials and their families, while the number of visas
issued for North Koreans had always been very small. See
"Timeline of the Muslim Ban", *ACLU Washington*, no date; available at https://aclu-wa.org/pages/timeline-muslim-ban.

33. "Presidential Declaration", *White House*.

34. Trump vs. Hawaii, 17 U.S. 585 (2018).

35. See Hal Brands, "U.S. Grand Strategy in an Age of Nationalism: Fortress America and its Alternatives", *The Washington Quarterly*, 40(1) (2017), pp. 73–94.

36. See Julian Borger, "US to slash refugee admission to historic low
of 30,000, Pompeo confirms", *Guardian*, 17 September 2018;
available at https://www.theguardian.com/us-news/2018/
sep/17/us-refugees-immigration-mike-pompeo-cap.

37. Quoted in "Face the Nation", *CBS News*.

38. See "Shariah, the Threat to America: An Exercise in Competitive Analysis", *Center for Security Policy*, 2010; available at http://
www.voltairenet.org/IMG/pdf/Shariah_-_The_Threat_to_
America_Team_B_Report_.pdf.

39. See Maher, *Salafi-Jihadism*.

40. In a December 2015 interview, Trump suggested that immigration officials would ask a person "Are you a Muslim?", and if
their response was "Yes", they would be denied entry. He did not
seem to consider that potential terrorists may not answer this
question truthfully. Quoted in "Donald Trump on Muslim
Travel Ban", *MSNBC*, 8 December 2015, available at https://
www.youtube.com/watch?v=5I3E3-U-1jc&feature=youtu.
be&t=14m05s.

41. Julia Ruschchenko, "Converts to Islam and Home Grown Jihadism", *Henry Jackson Society*, October 2017; available at http://
henryjacksonsociety.org/wp-content/uploads/2017/10/HJS-
Converts-to-Islam-Report.pdf.

42. Peter R. Neumann, "Foreign fighter total in Syria/Iraq now exceeds 20,000", *ICSR Insight*, 26 January 2015; available at https://icsr.info/2015/01/26/foreign-fighter-total-syriairaq-now-exceeds-20000-surpasses-afghanistan-conflict-1980s/.

43. This is based on an estimate of 1.5 billion Muslims and 60,000 jihadists. See Neumann, *Radicalized*, Ch 3.

44. Twenty-one per cent of the world's population are estimated to be Muslim, while 15 per cent are males between the age of 15 and 34. See "World Age Structure", *Index Mundi*, undated; available at https://www.indexmundi.com/world/age_structure.html.

45. "Protecting the Nation", Executive Order 13769.

46. Quoted in "Trump's Speech to Congress: Video and Transcript", *New York Times*, 28 February 2017; available at https://www.nytimes.com/2017/02/28/us/politics/trump-congress-video-transcript.html.

47. See "DOJ, DHS Report: Three Out of Four Individuals Convicted of International Terrorism and Terrorism-Related Offenses were Foreign-Born", *Department of Justice*, 16 January 2018; available at https://www.justice.gov/opa/pr/doj-dhs-report-three-out-four-individuals-convicted-international-terrorism-and-terrorism.

48. Ibid.

49. According to David Bier, for example, only 55 per cent of "terrorism-related" convictions actually involved terrorism. See David Bier, "Very Few Immigration Vetting Failures Since 9/11", *Cato At Liberty*, 31 August 2017; available at https://www.cato.org/blog/very-few-immigration-vetting-failures-terrorists-911. Also David Sterman, "Under Trump, Can We Trust the Government's Terrorism Data", *CNN*, 17 January 2018; available at https://edition.cnn.com/2018/01/17/opinions/under-trump-can-we-trust-the-governments-terrorism-data-opinions-sterman/index.html; Miriam Valverde, "Donald Trump's team misleads in tying international terrorism report to immigration", *Politifact*, 22 January 2018; available at https://www.politifact.com/truth-o-meter/article/2018/jan/22/donald-trumps-team-misleads-tying-international-te/.

50. According to the U.S. Extremist Crime Database, between September 12, 2001, and the end of 2016, far-right extremists caused 106 deaths, while jihadists caused 119. Quoted in Miriam Valverde, "A look at the data on domestic terrorism and who's behind it", *Politifact*, 16 August 2017; available at https://www.politifact.com/truth-o-meter/article/2017/aug/16/look-data-domestic-terrorism-and-whos-behind-it/.

51. Quoted in Benjamin Wittes, "Case Closed: The Justice Department Won't Stand Behind Its Report on Immigrants and Terrorism", *Lawfare*, 7 January 2019; available at https://www.lawfareblog.com/case-closed-justice-department-wont-stand-behind-its-report-immigrants-and-terrorism.

52. Ibid.

53. Senior former counter-terrorism official, interview with the author, May 2018.

54. If lawful permanent residents were added to the total, the share of "non-immigrants" was 87 per cent. "Citizenship Likely an Unreliable Indicator of Terrorist Threat to the United States", *Department of Homeland Security*, undated (leaked in March 2017).

55. Brian Michael Jenkins, "The Origins of America's Jihadists", *RAND*, December 2017; available at https://www.rand.org/pubs/perspectives/PE251.html.

56. "Who are the terrorists?", *New America*, undated; available at https://www.newamerica.org/in-depth/terrorism-in-america/who-are-terrorists/. For the full report, see Peter Bergen, David Sterman, Albert Ford, and Alyssa Sims, "Jihadist Terrorism 16 Years After 9/11", *New America Foundation*, September 2017; available at https://na-production.s3.amazonaws.com/documents/Terrorism_9-11_2017.pdf.

57. Senior former counter-terrorism official, interview with the author, May 2018.

58. Quoted in "Meet the Press", *NBC News*.

59. Quoted in "Read Donald Trump's", *Time*.

60. Quoted in "Remarks by President", *White House*.

61. See Chishti, "Post-9/11 Policies". Also Nadeem Muaddi, "The Bush-era Muslim registry failed", *CNN*, 22 December 2016; available at https://edition.cnn.com/2016/11/18/politics/nseers-muslim-database-qa-trnd/index.html.

62. See Chishti, "Post-9/11 Policies".

63. Ibid.

64. Jeremy Scahill and Ryan Devereaux, "Watch Commander: Barack Obama's Secret Terrorist-Tracking System by the Numbers", *The Intercept*, 5 August 2014; available at https://theintercept.com/2014/08/05/watch-commander/.

65. Seamus Hughes, interview with the author, April 2018.

66. Leon Rodriguez, speaking at a 2015 Congressional hearing; cited in Peter Bergen, "Trump's big mistake on Syria refugees", CNN, 28 January 2017; available at https://edition.cnn.com/2017/01/28/opinions/trumps-big-mistake-on-syrian-refugees-bergen/index.html.

67. See Alex Nowrasteh, "Terrorism and Immigration: A Risk Analysis", *CATO Institute Policy Analysis*, Number 798, 13 September 2016; available at https://www.cato.org/publications/policy-analysis/terrorism-immigration-risk-analysis.

68. Bier, "Very Few Immigration", *Cato*.

69. Nowrasteh, "Terrorism and Immigration", *Cato*.

70. Ibid., p. 1.

71. See Franco Odonez, "Trump officials exaggerate terrorist threat on southern border in tense briefing", *McClatchy*, 4 January 2019; available at https://www.mcclatchydc.com/news/policy/immigration/article223944055.html.

72. Robin Simcox, "The Asylum-Terror Nexus: How Europe Should Respond", *Heritage Backgrounder*, 18 June 2018; available at https://www.heritage.org/sites/default/files/2018-06/BG3314.pdf.

73. Peter Bergen, David Sterman, et al., "Stephen Miller's Kitchen Sink Approach to Justifying the Travel Ban", *New America*, 21 February 2017; available at https://www.newamerica.org/international-security/blog/stephen-millers-kitchen-sink-approach-justifying-travel-ban/.

74. See, for example, Jenkins, "The Origins", p. 2.

75. Alexander Nowrasteh, interview with the author, May 2018.

76. Quoted in "Read Donald Trump's", *Time*.

77. See Dara Lind, "Donald Trump's plan to subject immigrants to "ideological tests", explained", *Vox*, 16 August 2016; available at

https://www.vox.com/2016/8/16/12491000/trump-extreme-vetting-test-immigrant.

78. Alexander Guittard, correspondence with the author, October 2018.

79. Mark Krikorian, a Trump adviser who heads the Center for Immigration Studies, suggested that applicants should be asked: "Do you think it's okay to kill apostates? Do you think it's okay to throw gays off of buildings?" Quoted in Deborah Amos, "Trump Backers Want Ideology Text for Extreme Vetting", NPR, 4 February 2017; available at https://www.npr.org/sections/parallels/2017/02/04/513289953/trump-backers-want-ideology-test-for-extreme-vetting.

80. "Extreme Vetting Initiative: Statement of Objectives (SOO)", ICE, 12 June 2017; available at https://www.brennancenter.org/sites/default/files/Extreme%20Vetting%20Inititate%20-%20Statement%20of%20Objectives.pdf.

81. Ibid.

82. "Technology Experts Letter to DHS", 16 November 2017; available at https://www.documentcloud.org/documents/4243211-Technology-Experts-Letter-to-DHS-Opposing-the.html. For a discussion of radicalisation and specificity, see Peter R. Neumann, *Der Terror ist unter uns: Dschihadismus und Radikalisierung in Europa* (Berlin: Ullstein, 2016), Ch 2.

83. "Technology Experts Letter".

84. See "Coalition Letter to DHS", 16 November 2017; available at https://www.brennancenter.org/sites/default/files/Coalition%20Letter%20to%20DHS%20Opposing%20the%20Extreme%20Vetting%20Initiative%20-%2011.15.17.pdf.

85. See Nicole Kobie, "The complicated truth about China's social credit system", *Wired.com*, 21 January 2019; available at https://www.wired.co.uk/article/china-social-credit-system-explained.

86. See "Extreme Vetting Initiative", *ICE*.

87. Senior former counter-terrorism official, interview with the author, May 2018.

88. George Joseph, "Extreme Digital Vetting of the Visitors to the U.S. Moves Forward Under New Name", *Pro Publica*, 22 November 2017; available at https://www.propublica.org/article/

extreme-digital-vetting-of-visitors-to-the-u-s-moves-forward-under-a-new-name.

89. Juan Zarate, interview with the author, May 2018; senior former counter-terrorism official, interview with the author, May 2018.

90. See Matt Apuzzo, Michael S. Schmidt, and Julian Preston, "U.S. Visa Process Missed San Bernardino Wife's Online Zealotry", *New York Times*, 12 December 2015; available at https://www.nytimes.com/2015/12/13/us/san-bernardino-attacks-us-visa-process-tashfeen-maliks-remarks-on-social-media-about-jihad-were-missed.html.

91. Natasha Duarte, Emma Llanso, and Anna Loup, "Mixed Messages? The Limits of Automated Social Media Content Analysis", Center for Democracy and Technology, November 2017; available at https://cdt.org/files/2017/11/Mixed-Messages-Paper.pdf.

92. Seamus Hughes, interview with the author, April 2018.

93. Quoted in Nick Miroff, "Trump is creating a vetting center. Is it 'extreme' enough to end his travel ban?", *Washington Post*, 23 April 2018; available at https://www.washingtonpost.com/world/national-security/trump-is-creating-a-vetting-center-is-it-extreme-enough-to-end-his-travel-ban/2018/04/22/6ab109fa-43fd-11e8-baaf-8b3c5a3da888_story.html?utm_term=.3183852890d9.

94. Matt Levitt, correspondence with the author, April 2019.

95. Ibid.

96. Ibid.

97. Senior former counter-terrorism official, interview with the author, May 2018.

98. Jenkins, "The Origins", p. 2.

5. RULES OF ENGAGEMENT

1. Carl von Clausewitz, *On War*, edited and translated by Michael Howard and Peter Paret (Princeton: Princeton University Press, 1984), p. 75.

2. Ibid., p. 87.

3. Quoted in Alan Mallinson, *Too Important for the Generals* (London: Penguin, 2017), p. 1.

4. Though largely civilian, Homeland Security is also responsible for Coast Guard, which is considered part of the United States Armed Forces.

5. Colin S. Gray, *Modern Strategy* (Oxford: Oxford University Press, 1999), p. 60.

6. The general in question was Curtis May. Quoted in Mead, "The Jacksonian", p. 23.

7. Quoted in Seth Harp, "Why Trump Has Nothing to Say About ISIS", *Rolling Stone*, 18 October 2017; available at https://www.rollingstone.com/politics/politics-news/why-trump-has-nothing-to-say-about-isis-127733/.

8. Glennon, *National Security*.

9. See, for example, Helene Cooper, "Trump Gives Military New Freedom. But With That Comes Danger", *New York Times*, 5 April 2017; available at https://www.nytimes.com/2017/04/05/us/politics/rules-of-engagement-military-force-mattis.html.

10. According to Fonzone and Hartig, it consisted of: "the fact that we are in an armed conflict with certain terrorist groups; that this armed conflict can spill across national borders in certain circumstances; that working by, with, and through partners is the preferred strategy, such that large footprint military deployments should be avoided if at all possible; that the Executive Branch uses an 'all tools' approach to fighting terrorism, with discretion to choose the appropriate tool as the circumstances require and law allows; that domestic and international law binds our counterterrorism activities, with significant work being done to develop our positions on certain issues (*e.g.*, detainee treatment, targeting); and that ethical and moral considerations, and the strategic need to win over local populations, lead us to generally apply standards above and beyond those legally required". See Fonzone, "The More Things", *Just Security*.

11. See Micah Zenko, "Obama's Final Drone Strike Data", *Council on Foreign Relations*, 20 January 2017; available at https://www.cfr.org/blog/obamas-final-drone-strike-data.

12. See Peter Bergen, "A gripping glimpse into Bin Laden's decline and fall", CNN, 11 March 2015; available at https://edition.

cnn.com/2015/03/10/opinions/bergen-bin-laden-al-qaeda-decline-fall/index.html.

13. "Procedures for Approving Direct Action against Terrorist Targets Located Outside the United States and Areas of Active Hostilities", *National Security Council*, 22 May 2013; available at https://www.aclu.org/sites/default/files/field_document/presidential_policy_guidance.pdf.

14. "Summary of Information Regarding U.S. Counterterrorism Strikes Outside Areas of Active Hostilities", *Director of National Intelligence*, 1 July 2016; available at https://www.dni.gov/files/documents/Newsroom/Press%20Releases/DNI+Release+on+CT+Strikes+Outside+Areas+of+Active+Hostilities.PDF.

15. See Charlie Savage and Eric Schmitt, "Trump eases combat rules in Somalia intended to protect civilians", *New York Times*, 30 March 2017; available at https://www.nytimes.com/2017/03/30/world/africa/trump-is-said-to-ease-combat-rules-in-somalia-designed-to-protect-civilians.html.

16. Charlie Savage, "Obama Relaxes Rules for Striking ISIS in Afghanistan", *New York Times*, 20 January 2016; available at https://www.nytimes.com/2016/01/21/world/asia/obama-relaxes-rules-for-striking-isis-in-afghanistan.html.

17. Ibid.

18. Wolff, *Fire and Fury*, p. 7.

19. Quoted in Greg Jaffe, "For Trump and his generals, 'victory' has different meanings", *Washington Post*, 5 April 2018; https://www.washingtonpost.com/world/national-security/for-trump-and-his-generals-victory-has-different-meanings/2018/04/05/8d74eab0–381d-11e8–9c0a-85d477d9a226_story.html?noredirect=on&utm_term=.8e5709bd3223.

20. Quoted in Woodward, *Fear*, p. 73.

21. Quoted in Mallory Shelbourne, "Al Qaeda leader calls Trump 'White House's New Fool'", *The Hill*, 5 February 2017; available at https://thehill.com/policy/defense/317986-aqap-leader-calls-trump-white-houses-new-fool.

22. White House spokesman Sean Spicer, quoted in Eric Schmitt and David Sanger, "Devices Seized in Yemen Raid Offer Some Clues to Qaeda Tactics", *New York Times*, 1 March 2017; avail-

able at https://www.nytimes.com/2017/03/01/world/middlee-ast/yemen-intelligence-raid.html.

23. See Cynthia McFadden, William Arkin and Ken Dilanian, "Officials: Still No Actionable Intel from Yemen SEAL Raid", *NBC News*, 1 March 2017; available at https://www.nbcnews.com/news/us-news/officials-still-no-actionable-intel-yemen-seal-raid-n727866.

24. Quoted in "'Mission started before I got here': Trump asked about criticism over Yemen raid", *Fox News*, 28 February 2017; available at http://insider.foxnews.com/2017/02/28/trump-navy-seal-ryan-owens-death-generals-wanted-do-yemen-r aid.

25. Charlie Savage and Eric Schmitt, "Trump Administration Is Said to Be Working to Loosen Counterterrorism Rules", *New York Times*, 12 March 2017; available at https://www.nytimes.com/2017/03/12/us/politics/trump-loosen-counterterrorism-rules.html.

26. Senior Trump appointee #2, interview with the author, June 2018.

27. Savage, "Trump Eases".

28. Juan Zarate, interview with the author, May 2018.

29. See Defense Secretary James Mattis, quoted in "Political and Security Situation in Afghanistan—Stenographic Transcript", *Committee on Armed Services, United States Senate*, 3 October 2017, p. 40; available at https://www.armed-services.senate.gov/imo/media/doc/17-82_10-03-17.pdf.

30. Ibid., pp. 33–4.

31. Alexander Bick, interview with the author, May 2018.

32. National Security Council official #1, interview with the author, May 2018.

33. Charlie Savage and Eric Schmitt, "Trump Poised to Drop Some Limits on Drone Strikes and Commando Raids", *New York Times*, 21 September 2017; available at https://www.nytimes.com/2017/09/21/us/politics/trump-drone-strikes-commando-raids-rules.html.

34. Daniel Byman, interview with the author, May 2018.

35. See Dave Philipps, "Trump May Be Preparing Pardons for Ser-

vicemen Accused of War Crimes", *New York Times*, 18 May 2019; available at https://www.nytimes.com/2019/05/18/us/trump-pardons-war-crimes.html.

36. In various iterations, it may even be traced back to the 1950s. See Diana Dalphonse, Chris Townsend, and Matthew Weaver, "Shifting Landscape: The Evolution of By, With, and Through", *Real Clear Defense*, 1 August 2018; available at https://www.real-cleardefense.com/articles/2018/08/01/shifting_landscape_the_evolution_of_by_with_and_through_113676.html.

37. Mattis quoted in "Political and Security", *Committee on Armed Services*, p. 16.

38. Savage, "Trump Poised".

39. Flynn, *The Field*, p. 38.

40. Chris Costa, correspondence with author, April 2019.

41. Mattis quoted in "Political and Security", *Committee on Armed Services*, p. 40.

42. See "Presidential Memorandum Plan to Defeat the Islamic State of Iraq and Syria", *The White House*, 28 January 2017; available at https://www.whitehouse.gov/presidential-actions/presidential-memorandum-plan-defeat-islamic-state-iraq-syria/.

43. Andrew Newbrander, "Collateral Damage in Afghanistan: A Policy Failure, or a Failure to Follow Policy", *Johns Hopkins University*, Baltimore, MA, 2018, p. 21.

44. See "Department of Defense Press Briefing on U.S. Africa Command", *U.S. Department of Defense*, 24 March 2017; available at https://dod.defense.gov/News/Transcripts/Transcript-View/Article/1130131/department-of-defense-press-briefing-on-us-africa-command-by-general-thomas-d-w/.

45. Hanson, *The Case for*, p. 72.

46. Maggie Haberman, "Donald Trump Reverses Position on Torture and Killing Terrorists' Families", *New York Times*, 4 March 2016; available at https://www.nytimes.com/politics/first-draft/2016/03/04/donald-trump-reverses-position-on-torture-and-killing-terrorists-families/.

47. See, for example, Jaffe, "For Trump and his generals".

48. Chris Costa, interview with the author, June 2018.

49. Quoted in "Trump: Load Guatanamo Bay up with 'Bad

Dudes'", *Associated Press*, 23 February 2016; available at https://
www.youtube.com/watch?v=j7dmMI3CtKI.

50. Charlie Savage, "Ordering Guantanamo to Stay Open Is One
Thing, but Refilling It Is Another", *New York Times*, 31 January
2018; available at https://www.nytimes.com/2018/01/31/us/
politics/trumps-order-to-keep-guantanamo-open-faces-familiar-
obstacles-to-refilling-it.html?module=inline.

51. Charlie Savage, "U.S. Transfers First Guantanamo Detainee
Under Trump, Who Vowed to Fill It", *New York Times*, 2 May
2018; available at https://www.nytimes.com/2018/05/02/us/
politics/guantanamo-detainee-transferred-trump-al-darbi.html.

52. Phil Stewart and Idrees Ali, "U.S. advancing towards first Guantanamo repatriation under Trump", *Reuters*, 20 March 2018;
available at https://uk.reuters.com/article/uk-usa-trump-guan-
tanamo-exclusive/exclusive-u-s-advancing-toward-first-guanta-
namo-repatriation-under-trump-idUKKBN1GW07D.

53. Savage, "U.S. Transfers".

54. Juan Zarate interview with the author, May 2018.

55. Savage, "U.S. Transfers".

56. Juan Zarate interview with the author, May 2018.

57. See "Trump's First Year in Numbers: Strikes Triple in Somalia
and Yemen", *Bureau of Investigative Journalism*, 19 January 2018;
available at https://www.thebureauinvestigates.com/stories/
2018-01-19/strikes-in-somalia-and-yemen-triple-in-trumps-first-
year-in-office.

58. Ibid. Also Thomas Gibbons-Neff, "U.S. airstrikes in Afghanistan
are at levels not seen since Obama troop surge", *Washington Post*,
17 July 2017; available at https://www.washingtonpost.com/
news/checkpoint/wp/2017/07/17/u-s-airstrikes-in-
afghanistan-are-at-levels-not-seen-since-obama-troop-
surge/?utm_term=.165cdb7e6ba6.

59. Newbander, "Collateral Damage", p. 28. Developments in Libya
and West Africa were harder to assess: while the U.S. has
expanded existing drone bases, and—in the case of Niger—built
an entirely new one, it also recently announced the withdrawal
of some troops. See Eric Schmitt, "Where Terrorism Is Rising
in Africa and the U.S. Is Leaving", New York Times, 1 March

2019; available at https://www.nytimes.com/2019/03/01/world/africa/africa-terror-attacks.html; Joe Penney, Eric Schmitt, and Rukmini Callimachi, "CIA Drone Mission, Curtailed by Obama, Is Expanded in Africa under Trump", New York Times, 9 September 2018; available at https://www.nytimes.com/2018/09/09/world/africa/cia-drones-africa-military.html. Eric Schmitt, "Under Trump, U.S. Launched 8 Airstrikes Against ISIS in Libya. It disclosed 4", *New York Times*, 8 March 2018; available at https://www.nytimes.com/2018/03/08/world/africa/us-airstrikes-isis-libya.html. Shawn Snow, "Niger is a central hub for counterterrorism ops in West Africa", *Military Times*, 24 October 2017; available at https://www.militarytimes.com/flashpoints/2017/10/24/niger-is-a-central-hub-for-us-counterterrorism-ops-in-west-africa/.

60. Chris Costa, interview with the author, June 2018.

61. Ibid.

62. See, for example, Pamela Engel, "Dropping 'the mother of all bombs' in Afghanistan sends a strong message about Trump's military strategy", *Business Insider*, 14 April 2017; available at https://www.businessinsider.com/mother-of-all-bombs-afghanistan-trump-military-strategy-2017–4?r=US&IR=T.

63. Robert F. Worth, "Can Jim Mattis Hold the Line in Trump's 'War Cabinet'?", *New York Times*, 26 March 2018; available at https://www.nytimes.com/2018/03/26/magazine/can-jim-mattis-hold-the-line-in-trumps-war-cabinet.html.

64. Mattis, quoted in "Political and Security", Committee on Armed Services, p. 34.

65. Zenko, "Obama's Final".

66. See Newbrander, p. 28.

67. Juan Zarate, interview with the author, May 2018.

68. See Newbrander, p. 34.

69. Greg Jaffe, "White House ignores executive order requiring count of civilian casualties in counterterrorism strikes", *Washington Post*, 1 May 2018; available at https://www.washingtonpost.com/world/national-security/white-house-ignores-executive-order-requiring-count-of-civilian-casualties-in-counterterrorism-strikes/2018/05/01/2268fe40–4d4f-11e8-af46-b1d6dc0d9bfe_story.html?noredirect=on&utm_term=.9b320179fc82.

70. See "Over 3,300 civilians killed in U.S.-led airstrikes: report", *The New Arab*, 23 September 2018; available at https://www. alaraby.co.uk/english/news/2018/9/23/over-3-300-syrian-civilians-killed-in-us-led-airstrikes-report.

71. "US-led coalition 'deeply in denial' about civilian casualties in Raqqa", *Amnesty International*, 17 July 2018; available at https:// www.amnesty.org/en/latest/news/2018/07/syria-us-led-coali-tion-deeply-in-denial-about-civilian-casualties-in-raqqa/.

72. See Eric Schmitt and Matthew Rosenberg, "CIA Wants Author-ity to Conduct Drone Strikes in Afghanistan for the First Time", *New York Times*, 15 September 2017; available at https://www. nytimes.com/2017/09/15/us/politics/cia-drone-strike-author-ity-afghanistan.html.

73. Chris Costa, interview with the author, June 2018.

74. Anthony Blinken, interview with the author, May 2018.

75. See, for example, Colin Kahl, "This is how easily the U.S. and Iran could blunder into war", *Washington Post*, 23 May 2019; available at https://www.washingtonpost.com/outlook/this-is-how-easily-the-us-and-iran-could-blunder-into-war/2019/05/23/40dbbcae-7c07–11e9–8ede-f4abf521ef17_story.html?utm_term=.63b216a0a5ac. Also Ian Bremmer, "These 5 Proxy Bat-tles Are Making Syria's Civil War Increasingly Complicated", *Time*, 16 February 2018; available at http://time.com/5162409/syria-civil-war-proxy-battles/.

76. For example, Senior Trump Appointee #2, interview with the author, June 2018.

77. William J. Burns, *The Back Channel: American Diplomacy in a Disor-dered World* (London: Hurst, 2019), p. 400.

78. Stephen Tankel, interview with the author, May 2018.

6. DEFEATING ISIS

1. Richard Iron, "Viewpoint: What Clausewitz (Really) Meant by 'Centre of Gravity'", *Defence Studies*, 1(3) (2001), p. 109.

2. Clausewitz, *On War*, p. 595.

3. See Stefan Heißner, Peter R. Neumann, John Holland McCowan, and Rajan Basra, *Caliphate in Decline: An Estimate of Islamic State's Financial Fortunes* (London: ICSR, 2017); available at https://icsr.

info/wp-content/uploads/2017/02/ICSR-Report-Caliphate-in-Decline-An-Estimate-of-Islamic-States-Financial-Fortunes.pdf.

4. Neumann, *Radicalized*, p. 87.

5. See Nicholas Glavin, "Remaining and Expanding: Why Local Violent Extremist Organizations Reflag to ISIS", *Small Wars Journal*, undated; available at https://smallwarsjournal.com/jrnl/art/remaining-and-expanding-why-local-violent-extremist-organizations-reflag-isis.

6. Daniel Byman, "What Happens When ISIS Goes Underground", *Brookings*, 18 January 2018; available at https://www.brookings.edu/blog/markaz/2018/01/18/what-happens-when-isis-goes-underground/.

7. Emerson, quoted in "Larry Interviews Steve Emerson on Trump's Impact on the War on Terror", *The Larry Elder Show*, 1 December 2017; available at https://www.larryelder.com/highlight/larry-interviews-steven-emerson-trumps-impact-war-terror/.

8. Quoted in "Remarks by President Trump at the National Republican Congressional Committee March Dinner", *The White House*, 20 March 2018; available at https://www.whitehouse.gov/briefings-statements/remarks-president-trump-national-republican-congressional-committee-march-dinner/.

9. @RealDonaldTrump, Twitter, 19 December 2018.

10. Obama, quoted in "Obama Syria speech: Full text", BBC News, 11 September 2013; available at https://www.bbc.co.uk/news/world-us-canada-24044553.

11. Obama quoted in Steve Contorno, "What Obama said about Islamic State as a 'JV' team", *Politifact*, 7 September 2014; available at https://www.politifact.com/truth-o-meter/statements/2014/sep/07/barack-obama/what-obama-said-about-islamic-state-jv-team/.

12. Obama, quoted in "Remarks by the president at the United States Military Academy Commencement Ceremony", *The White House*, 28 May 2014; available at https://obamawhitehouse.archives.gov/the-press-office/2014/05/28/remarks-president-united-states-military-academy-commencement-ceremony.

13. Ben Rhodes, *The World As It Is: Inside the Obama White House* (New York: Vintage, 2018), pp. 62–3.

14. See, for example, Lara Marlowe, "Obama turns focus to 'nation-building… at home'", *Irish Times*, 24 June 2011; available at https://www.irishtimes.com/news/obama-turns-focus-to-nation-building-at-home-1.604746.

15. Brian Fishman, *The Master Plan: ISIS, al-Qaeda, and the Jihadi Strategy for Final Victory* (New Haven: Yale University Press, 2016), p. 144.

16. See Joe Klein, "Yes He Did: Judging Obama's Legacy", *Foreign Affairs*, July/August 2017.

17. See, for example, James A. Piazza, "Draining the swamp: democracy promotion, state failure, and terrorism in 19 Middle Eastern countries", *Studies in Conflict and Terrorism*, 30(6) (2007), pp. 521–539.

18. Obama, quoted in "Remarks by the President on the Middle East and North Africa", The White House, 19 May 2011; available at https://obamawhitehouse.archives.gov/the-press-office/2011/05/19/remarks-president-middle-east-and-north-africa.

19. See "US 'within reach of strategic defeat of al-Qaeda'", BBC News, 9 July 2011; available at https://www.bbc.co.uk/news/world-south-asia-14092052.

20. Obama, quoted in "Remarks by the", White House, 19 May 2011.

21. See Rhodes, *The World*, Ch 23.

22. Ash Carter, "Behind the Plan to Defeat ISIS", *The Atlantic*, 31 October 2017; available at https://www.theatlantic.com/international/archive/2017/10/isis-plan-defeat/544418/.

23. Alexander Bick, interview with the author, May 2018.

24. Ibid.

25. Carter, "Behind the".

26. Alexander Bick, interview with the author, May 2018.

27. Trump, quoted in Aaron Stein, "The 'Adults in the Room' Need to Take Trump Seriously on Syria", *War on the Rocks*, 10 April 2018; available at https://warontherocks.com/2018/04/the-adults-in-the-room-need-to-take-trump-seriously-on-syria/.

28. "Obama to send up to 250 more troops to Syria to fight ISIS", *Reuters*, 25 April 2016; available at https://www.cnbc.com/2016/04/24/obama-to-send-up-to-250-more-us-troops-to-syria-to-fight-isis.html.

29. See *Global Coalition* website, undated; https://theglobalcoalition.org/en/home/.

30. Carter, "Behind the".

31. Ibid.

32. Lt. Gen. Stephen Townsend, quoted in Jim Michaels, "Iraqi forces in Mosul see deadliest urban combat since World War II", *USA Today*, 30 March 2017; available at https://eu.usatoday.com/story/news/world/2017/03/29/united-states-mosul-isis-deadly-combat-world-war-ii/99787764/. Another major victory was the campaign against Islamic State in Libya, where American forces helped local partners to reclaim the city of Sirte, where Islamic State had established a stronghold. See Alia Brahimi and Jason Pack, "Strategic Lessons from the Ejection of ISIS in Sirte", *Atlantic Council*, 16 May 2017; available at https://www.atlanticcouncil.org/blogs/menasource/strategic-lessons-from-the-ejection-of-isis-from-sirte.

33. Department of Defense figures, quoted in Jamie McIntyre, "Here's How Much Ground ISIS Has Lost Since Trump Took Over", *Washington Examiner*, 23 December 2017; available at https://www.washingtonexaminer.com/heres-how-much-ground-isis-has-lost-since-trump-took-over.

34. Mythili Sampathkumar, "Three quarters of 'unintentional' civilian deaths in Iraq and Syria have occurred during the Trump presidency", *The Independent*, 26 January 2018; available at https://www.independent.co.uk/news/world/middle-east/donald-trump-us-civilian-deaths-iraq-syria-isis-coalition-bombing-a8180331.html.

35. Inna Rudolf, interview with the author, August 2018.

36. For an overview, see Inna Rudolf, *From Battlefield to Ballot Box: Contextualising the Rise and Evolution of Iraq's Popular Mobilisation Units* (London: ICSR, 2017); available at https://icsr.info/wp-content/uploads/2018/05/ICSR-Report-From-Battlefield-to-Ballot-Box-Contextualising-the-Rise-and-Evolution-of-Iraq%E2%80%99s-Popular-Mobilisation-Units.pdf.

37. Ibid.

38. Tom Parker, interview with the author, April 2018.

39. @stcolumbia, Twitter, 25 January 2018.

40. See Joshua A. Geltzer, "The Perils of a Post-ISIS Middle East", *The Atlantic*, 27 December 2017; available at https://www.the-atlantic.com/international/archive/2017/12/middle-east-isis-syria-kurds-iran-iraq-turkey-trump/549227/.

41. Trump, quoted in "Trump Defends Idea", CBS News.

42. Trump, quoted in Rebecca Tan, "A timeline of Trump's clearly made-up 'secret plan' to fight ISIS", *Vox*, 3 July 2017; available at https://www.vox.com/world/2017/7/3/15904646/trump-syria-assad-russia-iran-secret-generals-military-isis-terrorism.

43. See "Presidential Memorandum Plan to Defeat the Islamic State of Syria and Iraq", The White House, 28 January 2017; available at https://www.whitehouse.gov/presidential-actions/presi-dential-memorandum-plan-defeat-islamic-state-iraq-syria/.

44. Kimberly Dozier, "U.S. Commandos Running Out of ISIS Targets", *Daily Beast*, 5 July 2017; available at https://www.thedai-lybeast.com/us-commandos-running-out-of-isis-targets.

45. Paul Szoldra, "'The strategy hasn't changed at all'—Trump's plan to defeat ISIS is the same as Obama's", *Business Insider*, 3 July 2017; available at https://www.businessinsider.my/trump-strategy-defeat-isis-obama-2017-7/.

46. McGurk, quoted in "Update on the D-ISIS Campaign", *State Department*, 21 December 2017; available at https://www.state.gov/update-on-the-d-isis-campaign/.

47. Chris Costa, interview with the author, June 2018.

48. "US to arm Kurdish fighters against Isis in Raqqa, despite Turk-ish opposition", *Associated Press*, 9 May 2017; available at https://www.theguardian.com/world/2017/may/09/us-arm-kurdish-fighters-syria-isis-raqqa-trump.

49. Chris Costa, interview with the author, June 2018.

50. McGurk, quoted in "Update on".

51. See Barbara Starr, Zachary Cohen, and Ryan Browne, "U.S. joins first air assault 'behind enemy lines' against ISIS in Syria", CNN, 23 March 2017; available at https://edition.cnn.com/2017/03/22/politics/syria-tabqa-dam/.

52. See Kieran Cooke, "Destruction of dams: will IS carry through with its threats?", *Middle East Eye*, 13 November 2016; available at https://www.middleeasteye.net/opinion/destruction-dams-will-carry-through-its-threats.

53. McGurk, quoted in "Update on".

54. Ibid.

55. Ibid.

56. Department of Defense figures, quoted in McIntyre, "Here's How". See also Jon Greenberg, "ISIS territory losses near 100 per cent", Politifact, 30 January 2018; available at https://www.politifact.com/truth-o-meter/statements/2018/jan/30/donald-trump/trump-isis-territory-losses-near-100/.

57. See James Dobbins and Seth G. Jones, "The End of a Caliphate", *Survival*, 59(3) (2017), pp. 55–71. Also "After the caliphate: Has IS been defeated?", BBC News, 7 February 2019; available at https://www.bbc.co.uk/news/world-middle-east-45547595.

58. Neumann, *Radicalized*, p. 70.

59. See Bethan McKernan, "Up to 30,000 Isis fighters remain in Iraq and Syria, says U.N.", *The Independent*, 15 August 2018; available at https://www.independent.co.uk/news/world/middle-east/isis-fighters-iraq-syria-un-report-jihadis-raqqa-iraq-a8492736.html. Lead Inspector General, "Operation Inherent Resolve and Other Overseas Contingency Operations", *Report to the United States Congress*, 30 September 2018, p. 17; available at https://www.stateoig.gov/system/files/fy2019_lig_oco_oir_q4_sep2018.pdf.

60. Department of Defense figures, quoted in McIntyre, "Here's How".

61. While former Obama officials said that it was their plan which had delivered the result, Trump and "the generals" emphasised the changes they had made. Others pointed out it was "not unusual for the most dramatic battlefield gains to come at the end of a conflict", when "cities [tend to] fall like dominos". See, for example, Ilan Goldenberg and Nicholas Heras, "Obama's ISIS policy is working for Trump", *Washington Post*, 25 January 2018; available at https://www.washingtonpost.com/news/posteverything/wp/2018/01/25/obamas-isis-policy-is-working-

for-trump/?utm_term=.562ba508c445. Also McIntyre, "Here's How".

62. McGurk, quoted in "Update on".

63. Hassan Hassan, interview with the author, May 2018. Also "'War on Annihilation': Devastating Toll on Civilians, Raqqa—Syria", Amnesty International, July 2018, p. 49; available at https://www.amnesty.org.uk/files/reports/War%20of%20anni-hiliation%20report.pdf.

64. The number of artillery rounds fired in Raqqa was larger than the number used during the entire 2003 Iraq war. See Shawn Snow, "These Marines in Syria fired more artillery than any battalion since Vietnam", *Marine Corps Times*, 6 February 2018; available at https://www.marinecorpstimes.com/news/your-marine-corps/2018/02/06/these-marines-in-syria-fired-more-artillery-than-any-battalion-since-vietnam/. Also "'War on Annihilation'", *Amnesty*, p. 8.

65. See Zachary Cohen, "US-led coalition admits airstrikes killed 77 civilians in Raqqa, Syria", CNN, 7 August 2018; available at https://edition.cnn.com/2018/08/06/politics/us-coalition-raqqa-civilians-killed/index.html. Also Richard Hall, "UK government in 'deep denial' over Syrian civilian deaths in Raqqa campaign", *The Independent*, 15 October 2018; available at https://www.independent.co.uk/news/world/middle-east/uk-syria-raqqa-isis-civilian-casualties-raf-air-strikes-deaths-a8584876.html.

66. Thomas Veale, quoted in Paul Sonne, "'No one will ever know' how many civilians U.S. has killed in fight against ISIS", *Washington Post*, 5 June 2018; available at https://www.washington-post.com/world/national-security/pentagonno-one-will-ever-know-how-many-civilians-us-has-killed-in-fight-against-isis/2018/06/05/4b3fec30–6900–11e8-bbc5-dc9f3634fa0a_story.html?utm_term=.adede92cfc9d.

67. Quoted in David Remnick, "The Tragic Legacy of Raqqa Is Being Slaughtered Silently", *The New Yorker*, 21 October 2017; available at https://www.newyorker.com/news/as-told-to/the-tragic-legacy-of-raqqa-is-being-slaughtered-silently.

68. Hassan Hassan, interview with the author, May 2018.

69. Quoted in "French colonel slams US tactics against Daesh in Syria", *Middle East Monitor*, 18 February 2019; available at https://www.middleeastmonitor.com/20190218-french-colonel-slams-us-tactics-against-daesh-in-syria/.

70. See Gil Barndollar, "A French Officer Speaks the Truth about the War in Syria", *Defense One*, 5 March 2019; available at https://cdn.defenseone.com/b/defenseone/interstitial.html?v=8.27.1&rf=https%3A%2F%2Fwww.defenseone.com%2Fideas%2F2019%2F03%2Ffrench-officer-speaks-truth-about-war-syria%2F155304%2F.

71. See Paul Sonne and Karen DeYoung, "Trump wants to get the U.S. out of Syria's war, so he asked the Saudi king for $4 billion", *Washington Post*, 16 March 2018; available at https://www.washingtonpost.com/world/national-security/trump-wants-to-get-the-us-out-of-syrias-war-so-he-asked-the-saudi-king-for-4billion/2018/03/16/756bac90-2870-11e8-bc72-077aa4dab9ef_story.html?utm_term=.30ced4938157.

72. See "U.S. cuts $230m in Syria aid, says no rebuilding funds until peace talks underway", Reuters, 17 August 2018; available at https://www.cbc.ca/news/world/syria-aid-us-cuts-1.4789383.

73. See Reber Kalo and Sirwan Kajjo, "Efforts to Rebuild Raqqa Continue after Islamic State", VOA, 1 December 2018; available at https://www.voanews.com/a/efforts-to-rebuild-raqqa-continue-after-islamic-state/4683176.html.

74. See ibid; Jonathan Beale, "Who will help to rebuild the city of Raqqa?", BBC News, 22 October 2018; available at https://www.bbc.co.uk/news/world-middle-east-45863457.

75. Hassan Hassan, interview with the author, May 2018.

76. Joshua Landis, correspondence with the author, July 2018.

77. Indeed, there is every reason to believe that it would have generated opportunity costs as well. See Mark Stout, correspondence with the author, May 2019.

78. See "Remarks on the Way Forward for the United States in Syria", *State Department*, 17 January 2018; available at https://https://al.usembassy.gov/remarks-secretary-tillerson-way-forward-united-states-regarding-syria/.

79. @RealDonaldTrump, Twitter, 19 December 2018.

80. @RealDonaldTrump, Twitter, 19 December 2018.

81. See @RealDonaldTrump, Twitter, 31 December 2018.

82. See Matthew J. Belvedere, "Secretary of State Mike Pompeo: US withdrawal from Syria doesn't change mission to destroy ISIS", CNBC, 7 January 2019; available at https://www.cnbc.com/2019/01/07/secretary-of-state-mike-pompeo-us-with-drawal-from-syria-doesnt-change-mission-to-destroy-isis-and-stop-irans-influence-in-the-mideast.html; "Remarks by Vice President Mike Pence at the 2019 Munich Security Conference", *White House*, 16 February 2019; available at https://www.white-house.gov/briefings-statements/remarks-vice-president-pence-2019-munich-security-conference-munich-germany/.

83. "Worldwide Threat Assessment of the US Intelligence Community", *Office of the Director of National Intelligence*, 29 January 2019, p. 11; available at https://www.intelligence.senate.gov/sites/default/files/documents/os-dcoats-012919.pdf.

84. Ibid.

85. "Statement for the record of retired Vice Adm. Joseph Maguire, nominee for Director of the National Counterterrorism Center", Office of the Director of National Intelligence, 25 July 2018; available at https://www.dni.gov/index.php/nctc-news-room/nctc-speeches-testimonies-and-interviews/item/1890-statement-for-the-record-of-retired-vice-adm-joseph-maguire-nominee-for-director-of-the-national-counterterrorism-center.

86. Ibid.

87. Petter Nesser, "Europe hasn't won the war on terror", *Politico*, 5 December 2018; available at https://www.politico.eu/article/europe-hasnt-won-the-war-on-terror/.

88. See Shane Harris, "Intelligence officials were 'misquoted' after public hearing, Trump claims", *Washington Post*, 31 January 2019; available at https://www.washingtonpost.com/world/national-security/intelligence-officials-were-misquoted-after-public-hearing-trump-claims/2019/01/31/339952ce-25a7-11e9-ad53-824486280311_story.html?utm_term=.1dde33dd6c43.

89. See, for example, Jeremy Diamond and Elise Labott, "Trump Told Turkey's Erdogan in Dec. 14 Phone call about Syria, 'It's all yours. We are done'", CNN, 24 December 2018; available at

https://edition.cnn.com/2018/12/23/politics/donald-trump-erdogan-turkey/index.html.

90. Matthew Lee and Josh Lederman, "Trump wants out of Syria, but don't say 'timeline'", *Associated Press*, 6 April 2018; available at https://apnews.com/4a710b330dc14c279efc3fc9bc527902. At a public rally in Ohio, which took place during the same period, he told his supporters: "We're knocking the hell out of ISIS. We'll be coming out of Syria like very soon. Let other people take care of it now". Quoted in Ryan Browne and Barbara Starr, "Trump says US will withdraw from Syria 'very soon'", *CNN*, 29 March 2018; available at https://edition.cnn.com/2018/03/29/politics/trump-withdraw-syria-pentagon/index.html.

91. Alexander Bick, interview with the author, May 2018.

92. Trump reportedly told the Turkish President: "it's all yours". Quoted in Diamon, "Trump Told Turkey's".

93. Ali Ertan Toprak, conversation with author, February 2019.

94. See Andrew Buncombe, "Top Republicans to probe resignation of 'livid' James Mattis", *The Independent*, 21 December 2018; available at https://www.independent.co.uk/news/world/americas/us-politics/james-mattis-trump-syria-troops-isis-resignation-rebels-sdf-letter-turkey-kurds-erdogan-phone-call-a8695491.html.

95. Eric Schmitt, "U.S. Troops Leaving Syria, but Some May Stay Longer Than Expected", *New York Times*, 29 March 2019; available at https://www.nytimes.com/2019/03/29/world/middleeast/us-troops-syria-isis.html.

96. "America says it will soon begin a full withdrawal from Syria", *al-Naba*, 20 December 2018 (in Arabic).

97. See Hassan Hassan, "Insurgents Again: Islamic State's Calculated Return to Attrition in the Syria-Iraq Region and Beyond", *CTC Sentinel*, December 2017; available at https://ctc.usma.edu/insurgents-again-the-islamic-states-calculated-reversion-to-attrition-in-the-syria-iraq-border-region-and-beyond/.

98. Matthew Levitt and Aaron Y. Zelin, "Mission Unaccomplished: The Tweet that Upended Trump's Counterterrorism and Iran Policies", War on the Rocks, 25 December 2018;

available at https://warontherocks.com/2018/12/mission-unaccomplished-the-tweet-that-upended-trumps-counterter-rorism-and-iran-policies/.

99. Ellen Francis, "Let Down by U.S., Syrian Kurdish Leaders Look to Russia and Assad", Reuters, 27 December 2019; available at https://www.reuters.com/article/us-mideast-crisis-syria-kurds/let-down-by-us-syrian-kurdish-leaders-look-to-russia-and-assad-idUSKCN1OQ18E.

100. Rebecca Collars, "With One Tweet, Trump May Have Given Assad a Path to Victory in Syria", *Time*, 21 December 2018; available at http://time.com/5485660/syria-trump-isis-assad/.

101. See Michael Rainey, "Cost of War in Syria Is Rising", *Fiscal Times*, 11 April 2018; available at http://www.thefiscaltimes.com/2018/04/11/Cost-War-Syria-Rising.

102. See Luis Martinez and Elisabeth McLaughlin, "What you need to know about US Military Involvement in Syria", ABC News, 20 December 2018; available at https://abcnews.go.com/Politics/us-military-involvement-syria-trump-orders-with-drawal/story?id=59930250.

103. See Bill Bostock, "ISIS could regroup in Syria and retake swathes of territory", Business Insider, 5 February 2019; available at https://www.businessinsider.com/isis-may-retake-syria-territory-in-6-months-pentagon-says-2019-2?r=US&IR=T.

104. Trump, quoted in "Transcript: President Trump on Face the Nation", CBS News, 3 February 2019; available at https://www.cbsnews.com/news/transcript-president-trump-on-face-the-nation-february-3-2019/.

105. See Kori Schake, "Trump Just Messed Up the One Thing He Did Better Than Obama", *The Atlantic*, 19 December 2018; available at https://www.theatlantic.com/ideas/archive/2018/12/withdrawal-syria-will-come-high-price/578608/.

106. Brett McGurk, "Hard Truths in Syria", *Foreign Affairs*, May 2019; available at https://www.foreignaffairs.com/articles/syria/2019-04-16/hard-truths-syria.

107. Joshua A. Geltzer, "When Diplomacy Disappears", *Foreign Policy*, 18 April 2018; available at https://foreignpolicy.com/2018/04/18/when-diplomacy-disappears-counterterrorism-isis-syria-turkey-kurds-ypg-pkk-erdogan-trump/.

108. Graham, quoted in "'Iraq on Steroids': senator in Syria warning as Trump receives remains", *Reuters*, 19 January 2019; available at https://www.theguardian.com/world/2019/jan/19/syria-lindsey-graham-iraq-on-steroids-trump.

7. FRIENDS AND FOES

1. In the words of former presidential candidate Mitt Romney, "God did not create this country to be a nation of followers. America must lead the world, or someone else will". Romney, quoted in Hilde Eliassen Restad, *American Exceptionalism: An idea that made a nation and remade the world* (London: Routledge, 2015), p. 2.

2. Lincoln, quoted in Paul E. Peterson, "Is America Still the 'Hope of Earth'?" in Thomas W. Gilligan (ed.), *American Exceptionalism in a New Era* (Stanford: Hoover Institution Press, 2017), p. 10.

3. Restad, *American Exceptionalism*, p. 7.

4. Kori Schake, "American Dominance of the International Order" in Gilligan, *American Exceptionalism*, p. 79.

5. Restad, *American Exceptionalism*, p. 6.

6. Trump, quoted in "Transcript: Donald Trump", *New York Times*.

7. Quoted in "Full text", *Washington Post*.

8. Tony Schwartz, quoted in Jane Mayer, "Donald Trump's Ghostwriter Tells All", *The New Yorker*, 25 July 2016; available at https://www.newyorker.com/magazine/2016/07/25/donald-trumps-ghostwriter-tells-all.

9. Even if Trump has not written the book—critics argue he might not even have read it—the content is clearly based on him and what he told his ghostwriter Tony Schwartz.

10. Trump, *Trump: The Art*, esp. Ch 2.

11. Ibid., pp. 51–2.

12. Ibid., p. 58.

13. Ibid., p. 1.

14. @RealDonaldTrump, Twitter, 11 December 2016.

15. Quoted in Worth, "Can Jim Mattis", *New York Times*.

16. Quoted in Shane Ryan, "Here Are All 30 Tweets Trump Made About Afghanistan", Paste, 22 August 2017; available at https://

www.pastemagazine.com/articles/2017/08/here-are-all-30-tweets-trump-made-about-afghanista.html.

17. Quoted in "Trump: US Must End 'Cycle of Intervention and Chaos'", *VOA News*, 7 December 2016; available at https://www.voanews.com/a/trump-us-must-end-cycle-of-intervention-and-chaos/3626252.html.

18. Trump, quoted in "Full Transcript and Video: Trump's Speech on Afghanistan", *New York Times*, 21 August 2017; available at https://www.nytimes.com/2017/08/21/world/asia/trump-speech-afghanistan.html.

19. Ibid.

20. Wolff, *Fire and Fury*, Ch 20. Also Kosh Sadat and Stan McChrystal, "Staying the Course in Afghanistan", *Foreign Affairs*, November/December 2017, p. 2.

21. Michael Kugelman, interview with the author, May 2018.

22. See William I. Zartman, "Ripeness: The Hurting Stalemate and Beyond" in Paul C. Stern and Daniel Druckman (eds), *International Conflict Resolution After the Cold War* (Washington, DC: National Academy Press, 2000).

23. See Ellen Mitchell, "Afghanistan war at a stalemate, top general tells lawmakers", *The Hill*, 4 December 2018; available at https://thehill.com/policy/defense/419739-afghanistan-war-at-a-stalemate-top-general-tells-lawmakers.

24. Mitchell, "Afghanistan war", *The Hill*.

25. See Krishnadev Calamur, "The Afghan government is missing from Afghanistan's peace process", *The Atlantic*, 12 February 2019; available at https://www.theatlantic.com/international/archive/2019/02/afghanistan-government-united-states-taliban/582487/.

26. Ibid., p. 52.

27. Dan Lamothe and Josh Dawsey, "Trump wanted a big cut in troops in Afghanistan", *Washington Post*, 8 January 2019; available at https://www.washingtonpost.com/world/national-security/new-plans-for-afghanistan-would-have-trump-withdrawing-fewer-troops/2019/01/08/ddf2858e-12a0–11e9-a896-f104373c7ffd_story.html?utm_term=.f7bf7d3d771c.

28. Daniel Byman, interview with the author, May 2018.

29. See Lamothe, "Trump wanted a", *Washington Post*.

30. Senior Defense Department official, conversation with author, February 2019.

31. Quoted in "The Inaugural Address", *The White House*, 20 January 2017; available at https://www.whitehouse.gov/briefings-statements/the-inaugural-address/.

32. Ibid.

33. See "Remarks by Vice President Pence at the 2019 Munich Security Conference", *The White House*, 16 February 2019; available at https://www.whitehouse.gov/briefings-statements/remarks-vice-president-pence-2019-munich-security-conference-munich-germany/.

34. Senior American official, intervention at Sir Bani Yas forum, December 2017.

35. See Martin Chulov, "I will return Saudi Arabia to moderate Islam, says crown prince", *The Guardian*, 24 October 2017; available at https://www.theguardian.com/world/2017/oct/24/i-will-return-Saudi Arabia-moderate-islam-crown-prince.

36. Bannon, quoted in Dexter Filkins, "A Saudi Prince's Quest to Remake the Middle East", *The New Yorker*, 9 April 2018; available at https://www.newyorker.com/magazine/2018/04/09/a-saudi-princes-quest-to-remake-the-middle-east.

37. Carol Leonnig, Shane Harris, Josh Dawsey, and Greg Jaffe, "How Jared Kushner forged a bond with the Saudi Prince", *Washington Post*, 19 March 2018; available at https://www.washingtonpost.com/politics/how-jared-kushner-forged-a-bond-with-the-saudi-crown-prince/2018/03/19/2f2ce398–2181–11e8-badd-7c9f29a55815_story.html?utm_term=.01a3311dc4d7.

38. Ibid.

39. Quoted in "President Trump's Speech to the Arab Islamic American Summit", *The White House*, 21 May 2017; available at https://www.whitehouse.gov/briefings-statements/president-trumps-speech-arab-islamic-american-summit/.

40. Ibid.

41. Ibid.

42. Ibid.

43. Bannon, quoted in Filkins, "A Saudi Prince's", *The New Yorker*.

44. Wolff, *Siege*, p. 132.

45. Jon Greenberg, "Donald Trump touts non-existent $450 billion in Saudi orders", *Politifact*, 23 October 2018; available at https://www.politifact.com/truth-o-meter/statements/2018/oct/23/donald-trump/donald-trump-touts-nonexistent-450-billion-saudi-o/.

46. See Julian Borger: "Syria: proposal to replace US troops with Arab force comes with grave risks", *The Guardian*, 18 April 2018; available at https://www.theguardian.com/us-news/2018/apr/18/us-syria-arab-force-replace-american-troops-saudi-arabia-egypt-uae.

47. Hassan Hassan, "The Arab Alliance Is a Circular Firing Squad", *Foreign Policy*, 3 June 2019; available at https://foreignpolicy.com/2019/06/03/the-arab-alliance-is-a-circular-firing-squad/.

48. Matthew Levitt, correspondence with author, March 2019.

49. Wahhabism is shorthand for the Saudi variant of what is often referred to as Salafism. See Roel Meijer (ed.), *Global Salafism: Islam's New Religious Movement* (London: Hurst, 2009).

50. See, for example, Ola Salem and Abdullah Alaoudh, "Mohammed bin Salman's Fake Anti-Extremism Campaign", *Foreign Policy*, 13 June 2019; available at https://foreignpolicy.com/2019/06/13/mohammed-bin-salmans-fake-anti-extremist-campaign/.

51. See Chulov, "I will return", *The Guardian*.

52. Daveed Gartenstein-Ross, correspondence with author, March 2019.

53. See Steve Simon and Daniel Benjamin, "Reckless in Riyadh", *The New York Review of Books*, 27 June 2019; available at https://www.nybooks.com/articles/2019/06/27/mohammad-bin-salman-reckless-riyadh/.

54. Filkins, "A Saudi Prince's", *New Yorker*.

55. @RealDonaldTrump, Twitter, 6 June 2017.

56. See Suzaane Kianpour, "Emails show UAE-linked effort against Tillerson", BBC News, 5 March 2018; available at https://www.bbc.co.uk/news/world-us-canada-43281519.

57. See Eric Schmitt and Nicholas Fandos, "Saudi Prince 'Com-

plicit' in Kashoggi's Murder, Senators Say after C.I.A. Briefing", *New York Times*, 4 December 2018; available at https://www. nytimes.com/2018/12/04/us/politics/cia-senate-khashoggi-. html.

58. "Statement from President Donald J. Trump on Standing with Saudi Arabia", The White House, 20 November 2018; available at https://www.whitehouse.gov/briefings-statements/statement-president-donald-j-trump-standing-saudi-arabia/.

59. Wolff, *Siege*, p. 248.

60. Neumann, *Radicalized*, pp. 78–84.

61. For an overview, see Marc Lynch, *The New Arab Wars: Uprisings and Anarchy in the Middle East* (New York: Public Affairs, 2016).

62. Daniel Benjamin, interview with the author, April 2018.

63. Quoted in "Yemen crisis: why is there a war?", BBC News, 18 December 2018; available at https://www.bbc.co.uk/news/world-middle-east-29319423.

64. Quoted in ibid.

65. Michael Knights, "Saudi Arabia's War in Yemen: A View from the Ground", *The Hill*, 26 March 2018; available at https://thehill.com/opinion/international/380046-saudi-arabias-war-in-yemen-a-view-from-the-ground.

66. For various reports on the Yemen crisis by the Crisis Group, see https://www.crisisgroup.org/middle-east-north-africa/gulf-and-arabian-peninsula/yemen. See also Lynch, *The New Arab Wars*, pp. 235–40.

67. Maggie Michael, Trish Wilson, and Lee Keath, "Yemen: US allies strike deals with al-Qaida in war on rebels", *Associated Press*, 6 August 2018; available at https://www.apnews.com/8863660 ca8684d5ca51ff58edd95b6de.

68. Nima Elbagir, Salma Abdelaziz, Mohammed Abo El Gheit, and Laura Smith, "Sold to an ally, lost to an enemy", CNN, 8 February 2019; available at https://edition.cnn.com/interactive/2019/02/middleeast/yemen-lost-us-arms/.

69. Quoted in Paul R, Pillar, "John Bolton's Middle East War Plans", *The National Interest*, 9 May 2019; available at https://nationalinterest.org/blog/paul-pillar/john-boltons-middle-east-war-plans-56722.

70. Ibid. For the wider debate, see also Vali Nasr, "Iran Among the Ruins", *Foreign Affairs*, March 2018; available at https://www.foreignaffairs.com/articles/middle-east/2018-02-13/iran-among-ruins. Eli Lake, "Regime Change in Iran? That's not Trump's Policy", *Bloomberg*, 23 April 2019; available at https://www.bloomberg.com/opinion/articles/2019-04-23/regime-change-in-iran-that-s-not-trump-s-policy.

71. See Kahl, "This is how easily".

72. Mark Lynch, interview with the author, April 2018.

73. Quoted in "Text of Bush's Address", CNN, 11 September 2001; available at http://edition.cnn.com/2001/US/09/11/bush.speech.text/.

74. Quoted in "Text: Obama's speech in Cairo", *New York Times*, 4 June 2009; available at https://www.nytimes.com/2009/06/04/us/politics/04obama.text.html.

75. Ibid.

76. See, for example, Muna Ndulo and Sara Lulo, "Free and Fair Elections, Violence and Conflict", *Harvard International Law Journal*, 51(2010), pp. 150–71. Also Eubank, "Does democracy encourage", *Terrorism*.

77. See, for example, Havard Hegre, "Democracy and armed conflict", *Journal of Peace Research*, 51(2) (2014), pp. 159–72.

78. See, for example, Beetham, "The Contradictions of", *Democratization*.

79. Brian Hook, "Note for the Secretary: Balancing Interests and Values", State Department, 17 May 2017; available at https://www.politico.com/f/?id=00000160-6c37-da3c-a371-ec3f13380001.

80. See Jeane J. Kirkpatrick, "Dictatorships & Double Standards", *Commentary*, November 1979; available at https://www.commentarymagazine.com/articles/dictatorships-double-standards/.

81. Hook, "Note for the", State Department.

82. Ibid.

83. Ibid.

84. See, for example; Katherine C. Gorka and Patrick Sookdheo (ed.), *Fighting the Ideological War: Winning Strategies from Communism to Islamism* (McLean, VA: Isaac Publishing, 2012).

85. Quoted in "Ambassador Nathan A. Sales on the State Department's Role in Countering Violent Extremism", *Hudson Institute*, 30 May 2018; available at https://s3.amazonaws.com/media. hudson.org/files/publications/SalesFINAL.pdf.

86. Ibid.

87. Trump, quoted in "Read Donald Trump's", *Time*.

88. "Egypt: repression now 'more extreme' than under Mubarak", Amnesty International, 20 September 2018; available at https:// www.amnesty.org.uk/press-releases/egypt-repression-now-more-extreme-under-mubarak.

89. Quoted in "Trump praises Sisi, says relations 'never been stronger'", *Egypt Today*, 25 September 2018; available at http://www. egypttoday.com/Article/2/58065/Trump-praises-Sisi-says-relations-never-been-stronger.

90. Quoted in Woodward, *Fear*, p. 324.

91. Stephanie Kirchgaessner and Ruth Michaelson, "General accused of war crimes courted by West in Libya", *The Guardian*, 25 September 2017; available at https://www.theguardian.com/ world/2017/sep/25/khalifa-haftar-libyan-general-accused-of-human-rights-abuses.

92. This followed a phone call with Haftar. See Ryan Browne, "Trump praises Libyan general as his troops march on US backed government in Tripoli", *CNN*, 19 April 2019; available at https://edition.cnn.com/2019/04/19/politics/us-libya-praise-haftar/index.html.

93. Peter Stubley, "Philippines president Rodrigo Duterte admits 'my only sin is the extrajudicial killings'", *The Independent*, 27 September 2018; available at https://www.independent.co.uk/ news/world/asia/rodrigo-duterte-philippines-sin-extrajudicial-killings-war-on-drugs-a8558116.html.

94. See Joe Sterling and Buena Bernal, "Duterte jokes about rape while rallying troops to fight militants", CNN, 14 August 2017; available at https://www.cnn.com/2017/05/26/asia/philippines-duterte-speech/index.html.

95. Quoted in "Duterte: Hitler killed millions of Jews, I will kill millions of drug addicts", *Washington Post*, 30 September 2016; available at https://www.washingtonpost.com/news/worldviews/

wp/2016/09/29/duterte-hitler-killed-3-million-jews-i-will-kill-3-million-drug-dealers/.

96. Jesscia Trisko Darden, "Trump's Dangerous Dance with Duterte", American Enterprise Institute, 23 January 2018; available at http://www.aei.org/publication/trumps-danger-ous-dance-with-duterte/.

97. Quoted in "Rodrigo Duterte: 'Give me salt and vinegar and I'll eat terrorists' livers'", *The Independent*, 24 April 2017; available at https://www.independent.co.uk/news/world/asia/rodrigo-duterte-terrorists-salt-vinegar-philippines-livers-50-times-bru-tal-isis-bad-mood-a7698706.html.

98. Quoted in Oliver Holmes, "Trump hails 'great relationship' with Philippines' Duterte", *The Guardian*, 13 November 2017; available at https://www.theguardian.com/us-news/2017/nov/13/trump-hails-great-relationship-with-philippines-duterte.

99. See Juile A. Mertus, *Bait and Switch: Human Rights and U.S. Foreign Policy* (New York: Routledge, 2004).

100. For an overview of these arguments, see Oz Hassan and Jason Ralph, "Democracy promotion and human rights in U.S. for-eign policy", *The International Journal of Human Rights*, 15(4) (2011), pp. 509–19. Also Stephen Tankel, *With Us and Against Us: How America's Partners Help and Hinder the War on Terror* (New York: Columbia University Press, 2018).

101. This is what my colleague M.L.R. Smith and I described as "repression of the moderates". See Peter R. Neumann and M.L.R. Smith, *The Strategy of Terrorism* (London: Routledge, 2009), pp. 40–1. In Egypt, for example, al Qaeda-affiliated jihadists have recently started recruiting supporters among the 60–70,000 imprisoned members of the Muslim Brotherhood. Issandr el Amrani, "Rethinking Extremism, Radicalization and the 'Global War on Terror'", Konrad Adenauer Foundation conference, Beirut, 2 May 2019.

102. Kristen Bialik, "How the World Views the U.S. and Its Presi-dent in 9 Charts", Pew Research Center, 9 October 2018; available at https://www.pewresearch.org/fact-tank/2018/10/09/how-the-world-views-the-u-s-and-its-president-in-9-charts/.

8. HOMELAND

1. Johnny Simon, "The story behind that photo of a screaming white nationalist", Quartz, 15 August 2017; available at https://qz.com/1054023/charlottesville-torch-photo-white-nationalist-peter-cytanovic-wants-people-to-know-he-is-not-an-evil-nazi/.
2. See Mark Berman, "Was the Charlottesville car attack domestic terrorism, a hate crime, or both?", *Washington Post*, 15 August 2017; available at https://www.washingtonpost.com/news/post-nation/wp/2017/08/14/was-the-charlottesville-car-attack-domestic-terrorism-a-hate-crime-or-both/?utm_term=.0b27d170f1db.
3. Quoted in Libby Nelson, "David Duke explains the white nationalist Charlottesville protests", Vox, 12 August 2017; available at https://www.vox.com/2017/8/12/16138358/charlottesville-protests-david-duke-kkk.
4. Jonathan Lemire, "Bowing to public pressure, Trump denounces hate group by name", Associated Press, 15 August 2017; available at https://apnews.com/395f6966223043babc448e9eae97c6b8.
5. Quoted in Meghan Keneally, "Trump lashes out at 'alt-left' in Charlottesville, says 'fine people on both sides'", ABC News, 15 August 2017; available at http://abcnews.go.com/Politics/trump-lashes-alt-left-charlottesville-fine-people-sides/story?id=49235032.
6. Quoted in ibid.
7. Neumann, *Radicalized*, Ch 6.
8. Ibid., pp. 139–42.
9. Ibid., pp. 141–2.
10. "GW Extremism Tracker: ISIS in America", GWU Program on Extremism, February 2019; available at https://extremism.gwu.edu/isis-america.
11. Peter Bergen and David Sterman, "The Real Terrorist Threat in America", *Foreign Affairs*, 30 October 2018; available at https://www.foreignaffairs.com/articles/united-states/2018-10-30/real-terrorist-threat-america.
12. Neumann, *Radicalized*, p. 139.

13. Marc Sageman, quoted in ibid.

14. "GW Extremism Tracker", *GWU Program*.

15. See Jesse J. Norris, "Why the FBI and the Courts Are Wrong about Entrapment and Terrorism", *Mississippi Law Journal*, 85(2014), pp. 1259–1289; Risa A. Brooks, "Muslim 'Homegrown' Terrorism in the United States: How Serious Is the Threat", *International Security*, 36(2) (2011), pp. 7–47; Peter Bergen, *United States of Jihad: Investigating America's Homegrown Terrorist* (New York: Crown, 2016), Ch 5. See also Heather Maher, "How the FBI Helps Terrorists Succeed", *The Atlantic*, 26 February 2013; available at https://www.theatlantic.com/international/archive/2013/02/how-the-fbi-helps-terrorists-succeed/273537/.

16. Seamus Hughes, interview with the author, April 2018.

17. "Empowering Local Partners to Prevent Violent Extremism in the United States", White House, August 2011; available at https://obamawhitehouse.archives.gov/sites/default/files/empowering_local_partners.pdf.

18. See Sahar F. Aziz, "Losing the 'War of Ideas': A Critique of Countering Violent Extremism Programs", *Texas International Law Journal*, 52 (2017); available at https://papers.ssrn.com/sol3/papers.cfm?abstract_id=2913571.

19. For an overview of different stakeholders' criticisms, see "Countering Violent Extremism (CVE): A Resource Page", *Brennan Center for Justice*, 12 February 2015; available at https://www.brennancenter.org/analysis/cve-programs-resource-page.

20. Former NCTC official, interview with the author, April 2018.

21. National Security Council Official #2, interview with the author, May 2018.

22. See, for example, Sebastian Gorka, "From Killing Terrorists to 'Ameliorating Upstream Factors'", *National Review*, 28 July 2010; available at https://www.nationalreview.com/corner/killing-terrorists-ameliorating-upstream-factors-sebastian-l-gorka/.

23. See Charlie Savage, Eric Schmitt, and Maggie Haberman, "Trump Pushes to Designate Muslim Brotherhood a Terrorist Group", *New York Times*, 30 April 2019; available at https://www.nytimes.com/2019/04/30/us/politics/trump-muslim-brotherhood.html.

24. See Frank Gaffney, *The Muslim Brotherhood in the Obama Administration* (Los Angeles: David Horowitz Freedom Foundation, 2012).

25. Quoted in Peter Beinart, "The U.S. Government's Fight against Violent Extremism Loses Its Leader", *The Atlantic*, 31 July 2017; available at https://www.theatlantic.com/politics/archive/2017/07/a-breaking-point-for-muslim-representation/535428/.

26. See "DHS Countering Violent Extremism Grants", U.S. Department of Homeland Security, 23 June 2017; available at https://www.dhs.gov/news/2017/06/23/dhs-awards-grants-counter-terrorist-recruitment-and-radicalization-us.

27. See John Hudson, "The Gorka that Matters Isn't Leaving the Trump Administration", *BuzzFeed*, 29 August 2017; available at https://www.buzzfeednews.com/article/johnhudson/the-gorka-that-matters-isnt-leaving-the-trump-administration.

28. Ibid.

29. Seamus Hughes, interview with the author, April 2018.

30. "DHS Countering Violent", *U.S. Department*.

31. See Ron Nixon and Eileen Sullivan, "Revocation of Grant to Help Fight Hate under New Scrutiny after Charlottesville", *New York Times*, 15 August 2017; available at https://www.nytimes.com/2017/08/15/us/politics/right-wing-extremism-charlottesville.html.

32. Quoted in Hudson, "The Gorka", *Buzzfeed*.

33. Recently leaked emails suggest that, if anything, Gorka at one point considered channelling money into countering "antifa"—a loose coalition of anarchists who confront far-right extremists, sometimes violently—arguing that left-wing extremists were "the actual threats". See Jessica Schulberg, "Trump Homeland Security Official Suggested Antifascists Were 'The Actual Threats'", *Huffington Post*, 5 April 2019; available at https://www.huffingtonpost.co.uk/entry/dhs-violent-extremism-katie-gorka-life-after-hate-mpac-antifa_n_5ca787d7e4b0a00f6d3f2e73.

34. Gorka email, quoted in "Trump Homeland Security", *Huffington Post*.

35. Ibid.

36. Seamus Hughes, interview with the author, April 2018.

37. Ibid.

38. Green, *Devil's Bargain*, p. 95–102.

39. See Woodward, *Fear*, p. 3.

40. Green, *Devil's Bargain*, p. 104.

41. See Matthew Duss et al., "Fear, Inc. 2.0: The Islamophobia Network's Effort to Manufacture Hate in America", Center for American Progress, February 2015, pp. 5–10; available at https://cdn.americanprogress.org/wp-content/uploads/2015/02/FearInc-report2.11.pdf.

42. For an overview, see Wajahat Ali et al., "Fear, Inc.: The Roots of the Islamophobia Network in America", Center for American Progress, August 2011; available at https://www.americanprogress.org/issues/religion/reports/2011/08/26/10165/fear-inc/.

43. See Robert S. Gordon, 'Race' in R.J.B. Bosworth, *The Oxford Handbook of Fascism* (Oxford: Oxford University Press, 2009), p. 310. Also Joshua Green, "Inside the Secret, Strange Origins of Steve Bannon's Nationalist Fantasia", *Vanity Fair*, 17 July 2017; available at https://www.vanityfair.com/news/2017/07/the-strange-origins-of-steve-bannons-nationalist-fantasia.

44. See Mark Sedgwick (ed.), *Key Thinkers of the Radical Right: Behind the New Threat to Liberal Democracy* (Oxford: Oxford University Press, 2019). Also Thomas Chatterton Williams, "The French Origins of 'You Will Not Replace Us'", *New Yorker*, 27 November 2017; available at https://www.newyorker.com/magazine/2017/12/04/the-french-origins-of-you-will-not-replace-us.

45. Green, *Devil's Bargain*, p. 223.

46. See Meghan Keneally, "A look back at Trump comments perceived by some as encouraging violence", *ABC News*, 19 October 2018; available at https://abcnews.go.com/Politics/back-trump-comments-perceived-encouraging-violence/story?id=48415766.

47. For the notion of "existential threat" and its role in radicalisation, albeit in a different context, see David Malet, *Foreign Fighters: Transnational Identity in Civil Conflicts* (Oxford: Oxford University Press, 2013), Ch 1.

48. In a March 2019 interview with *Breitbart*, Trump said: "I have the tough people, but they don't play it tough—until they get to a certain point, and then it would be very bad, very bad".

Quoted in "Exclusive: Trump on Campus Free Speech Order", *Breitbart*, 12 March 2019; available at https://www.breitbart. com/politics/2019/03/12/exclusive-trump-on-campus-free-speech-executive-order-were-going-to-do-a-very-big-number-probably-next-week/.

49. Richard Higgins, "POTUS & POLITICAL WARFARE", internal National Security Council memo, May 2017; available at https://unconstrainedanalytics.org/wp-content/uploads/2018/09/Political-Warfare.pdf.

50. See Alexander Hitchens and Hans Brun, "A Neo-Nationalist Network: The English Defence League and Europe's Counter-Jihad Movement" in Peter R. Neumann (ed.), *Radicalization—Major Works Collection* (London: Routledge, 2015), Vol. 3, pp. 289–320.

51. See Jacob Aasland Ravndal, "The Dark Web Enabled the Christchurch Killer", *Foreign Policy*, 16 March 2019 available at https://foreignpolicy.com/2019/03/16/the-dark-web-enabled-the-christchurch-killer-extreme-right-terrorism-white-nationalism-anders-breivik/.

52. Higgins, "POTUS &", internal memo.

53. Andrew Kaczynski, Andrew Massie, and Nathan McDermott, "Senior White House Adviser at Homeland Security Repeatedly Promoted Fringe Conspiracy Theories", CNN, 20 December 2017; available at https://edition.cnn.com/2017/12/20/politics/kfile-frank-wuco-conspiracy-theories/index.html.

54. Quoted in Noah Lanard, "A Fake Jihadist Has Landed a Top Job at Homeland Security", *Mother Jones*, 1 November 2017; available at https://www.motherjones.com/politics/2017/11/a-fake-jihadist-has-landed-a-top-job-at-homeland-security/.

55. McKay Coppins, "Trump's Right-Hand Troll", *The Atlantic*, 28 May 2018; available at https://www.theatlantic.com/politics/archive/2018/05/stephen-miller-trump-adviser/561317/.

56. Ibid. Rosalind Helderman, "Stephen Miller: A key engineer for Trump's 'America First' agenda", *Washington Post*, 11 February 2017; available at https://www.washingtonpost.com/politics/stephen-miller-a-key-engineer-for-trumps-america-first-agenda/2017/02/11/a70cb3f0-e809–11e6-bf6f-301b6b44

3624_story.html?utm_term=.69047ef9ccc4. Theresa Vargas, "Trump adviser Stephen Miller was right about the Statue of Liberty's famous inscription", *Washington Post*, 11 February 2017; available at https://www.washingtonpost.com/news/retropolis/wp/2017/08/02/a-trump-adviser-was-right-about-the-history-of-the-statue-of-libertys-famous-inscription/?utm_term=.b06e1f7c6486.

57. David Sterman, interview with the author, May 2018.

58. See, for example, @RealDonaldTrump, Twitter, 12 December 2018.

59. @RealDonaldTrump, Twitter, 15 March 2019.

60. David Frum, "Democrats Are Falling Into the Ilhan Omar Trap", *The Atlantic*, 14 April 2019; available at https://www.theatlantic.com/ideas/archive/2019/04/trumps-attack-ilhan-omar-trap-democrats/587128/.

61. Ben Mathis-Lilley, "Trump Has Retweeted at least Four White Nationalist Accounts", Slate, 18 March 2019; available at https://slate.com/news-and-politics/2019/03/trump-white-nationalist-accounts-suspended-retweets.html.

62. This later turned out to be inaccurate, and Trump offered to apologise to the British government. See Graham Ruddick and Peter Walker, "Donald Trump prepared to apologise for UK far-right video retweets", *The Guardian*, 26 January 2018; available at https://www.theguardian.com/us-news/2018/jan/26/donald-trump-prepared-to-apologise-for-retweeting-britain-first.

63. @RealDonaldTrump, Twitter, 23 August 2018. See James Pogue, "The Myth of White Genocide", *Harpers*, March 2019; available at https://harpers.org/archive/2019/03/the-myth-of-white-genocide-in-south-africa/. The far-right identitarian was Lauren Southern, while the conspiracy theorist was Paul Watson. See @RealDonaldTrump, Twitter, 2 May 2019.

64. See Ruddick, "Donald Trump", *The Guardian*.

65. See Alix Clubertson, "'This is an invasion': Trump sending 5,200 troops to US-Mexico border", Sky News, 29 October 2018; available at https://news.sky.com/story/this-is-an-invasion-trump-sending-5-200-troops-to-us-mexico-border-for-migrant-caravan-11539539.

66. Trump, quoted in "'Migrants Harm UK': Donald Trump says Britain is 'losing its culture' because of immigration", *The Sun*, 12 July 2018; available at https://www.thesun.co.uk/news/6766947/donald-trump-britain-losing-culture-immigration/. The closest he has come to making an openly racist statement was during a January 2018 White House meeting, in which he reportedly said: "Why do we want these from all these shithole countries [like Haiti] here? We should have more people from places like Norway!" Quoted in @christinawilkie, *Twitter*, 11 January 2018.

67. See, for example, Carole Gallagher, "Normalizing Hate", Big World podcast, undated; available at https://www.american.edu/sis/big-world/8-normalizing-hate.cfm. For a comparative context, see Isaac Stanley-Becker, "'Our country is full!': Trump's declaration carries far-right echoes that go back to the Nazi era", *Washington Post*, 18 April 2019; available at https://www.washingtonpost.com/nation/2019/04/08/our-country-is-full-trumps-declaration-carries-far-right-echoes-that-go-back-nazi-era/?utm_term=.426706222ed9.

68. See "U.S. Muslims Concerned About Their Place in Society", Pew Research Center, 26 July 2017; available at http://www.pewforum.org/2017/07/26/findings-from-pew-research-centers-2017-survey-of-us-muslims/.

69. "GW Extremism Tracker", GWU Program.

70. Peter Bergen and Andrew Lebovich, "1 in 5 terror cases started with tips from Muslims", CNN, 10 March 2011; available at http://edition.cnn.com/2011/POLITICS/03/09/bergen.king.hearing/index.html.

71. Melissa Salyk-Virk, "Building Community Resilience? Community Perspectives of the Countering Violent Extremism Pilot Program in Minneapolis/St. Paul", *Studies in Conflict and Terrorism*, 41 (2018); available at https://www.tandfonline.com/doi/abs/10.1080/1057610X.2018.1514054.

72. Michael Downing, interview with the author, April 2018.

73. Quoted in Paul Cruickshank, "A View from the CT Foxhole: Nicholas Rasmussen, Former Director, National Counterterrorism Center", *CTC Sentinel*, January 2018; available at https://ctc.

usma.edu/view-ct-foxhole-nicholas-rasmussen-former-director-national-counterterrorism-center/.

74. Hayden, *The Assault*, pp. 130–1.

75. For an overview, see Daniel Koehler, "Right-Wing Extremism and Terrorism in Europe: Current Developments and Issues for the Future", Prism, 6(2) (2016), pp. 85–104.

76. "2017 Hate Crime Statistics Released", FBI, 13 November 2018; available at https://www.fbi.gov/news/stories/2017-hate-crime-statistics-released-111318.

77. Seth G. Jones, "The Rise of Far-Right Extremism in the United States", CSIS Briefs, 7 November 2018; available at https://www.csis.org/analysis/rise-far-right-extremism-united-states.

78. "Murder and Extremism in the United States in 2018", Anti-Defamation League, 2019; available at https://www.adl.org/murder-and-extremism-2018. Also Evan Perez, "FBI has seen significant rise in white supremacist domestic terrorism in recent months", CNN, 23 May 2019; available at https://edition.cnn.com/2019/05/23/politics/fbi-white-supremacist-domestic-terror/index.html.

79. The link between radical rhetoric and extremist violence continues to be one of the most controversial—and complex—debates among social scientists. See Peter R. Neumann, "The Trouble with Radicalisation", *International Affairs*, 89(4) (2013), pp. 873–93.

80. Stephen Tankel, "Riding the Tiger: How Trump Enables Right-Wing Extremism", War on the Rocks, 5 November 2018; available at https://warontherocks.com/2018/11/riding-the-tiger-how-trump-enables-right-wing-extremism/.

81. Ibid.

82. Ibid.

83. J.M. Berger, "Trump is the glue that binds the far right", *The Atlantic*, 29 October 2018; available at https://www.theatlantic.com/ideas/archive/2018/10/trump-alt-right-twitter/574219/. For the full study, see J.M. Berger, *The Alt-Right Twitter Census: Defining and Describing the Audience for Alt-Right Content on Twitter* (Dublin: VOX-Pol Network of Excellence, 2018); available at https://www.voxpol.eu/download/vox-pol_publication/AltRightTwitterCensus.pdf.

84. See Sam Levin, "'It's a small group of people': Trump again denies white nationalism is a rising threat", *The Guardian*, 16 March 2019; available at https://www.theguardian.com/us-news/2019/mar/15/donald-trump-denies-white-nationalism-threat-new-zealand.

85. "Communities on Fire: Confronting Hate Violence and Xenophobic Political Rhetoric", South Asian Americans Leading Together, 2018, pp. 3, 21; available at http://saalt.org/report-communities-on-fire-confronting-hate-violence-and-xenophobic-political-rhetoric/.

86. For an overview, see Mehdi Hasan, "Here Is a List of Far-Right Attackers Trump Inspired", *The Intercept*, 27 October 2018; available at https://theintercept.com/2018/10/27/here-is-a-list-of-far-right-attackers-trump-inspired-cesar-sayoc-wasnt-the-first-and-wont-be-the-last/.

87. Hasan, "Here Is a", *The Intercept*. For the full story, see Jessica Pressler, "The Plot to Bomb Garden City, Kansas", *New York Magazine*, 11 December 2017; available at http://nymag.com/intelligencer/2017/12/a-militias-plot-to-bomb-somali-refugees-in-garden-city-ks.html?gtm=bottom&gtm=top.

88. Quoted in Dake Kang and Dan Sewell, "Crash suspect's ex-teacher said he idolized Hitler, Nazism", Associated Press, 14 August 2017; available at https://apnews.com/93d3cba12d134836ae243af285b27eaf.

89. Meg O'Connor and Jessica Lipscomb, "Social Media Posts Show Florida Bomber Cesar Sayoc Held Extremist Views", *Miami New Times*, 26 October 2018; available at https://www.miaminewtimes.com/news/cesar-sayocs-social-media-posts-show-florida-bomber-cesar-sayoc-held-extremist-views-1085 9874.

90. Tankel, "Riding the", War on the Rocks.

91. See, for example, Jacob Aasland Ravndal, "Right-wing terrorism and violence may actually have declined", *Washington Post*, 2 April 2019; available at https://www.washingtonpost.com/politics/2019/04/02/is-right-wing-terrorism-violence-rise/?utm_term=.7b4f6341e506.

92. See Julie Carrie Wong, "What is QAnon? Explaining the bizarre

right-wing conspiracy theory", *The Guardian*, 31 July 2018; available at https://www.theguardian.com/technology/2018/jul/30/qanon-4chan-rightwing-conspiracy-theory-explained-trump.

93. Quoted in Vegas Tenold, "The neo-Nazi plot against America is much bigger than we realize", *The Guardian*, 3 March 2019; available at https://www.theguardian.com/world/2019/mar/02/christopher-hasson-coast-guard-neo-nazi-far-right.

94. Lynh Bui, "'I am dreaming of a way to kill almost every last person on earth'", *Washington Post*, 21 February 2019; available at https://www.washingtonpost.com/local/public-safety/self-proclaimed-white-nationalist-planned-mass-terror-attack-government-says-i-am-dreaming-of-a-way-to-kill-almost-every-last-person-on-earth/2019/02/20/61daf6b8–3544–11e9-af5b-b51b7ff322e9_story.html?utm_term=.f434fffec3f8.

95. Researchers at California State University at San Bernardino found that Trump statements about the travel ban lead to "moderately increased" internet searches for terms like "kill Muslims". See "Hate Crime in the United States: 20 State Compilation of Official Data", *Center for the Study of Hate and Extremism*, 2016, p. 26; available at https://www.documentcloud.org/documents/3110202-SPECIAL-STATUS-REPORT-v5–9–16–16.html.

96. Daniel Byman, interview with the author, May 2018.

CONCLUSION

1. "National Strategy for Counterterrorism of the United States of America", *The White House*, October 2018; available at https://www.whitehouse.gov/wp-content/uploads/2018/10/NSCT.pdf. A first version of the strategy was leaked in May 2017. See Jonathan Landay and Warren Strobel, "Exclusive: Trump counterterrorism strategy urges allies to do more", Reuters, 5 May 2017; available at https://uk.reuters.com/article/uk-usa-extremism/exclusive-trump-counterterrorism-strategy-urges-allies-to-do-more-idUKKBN1812AH.

2. Fonzone, "The More Things", *Just Security*.

3. Ibid., p. 1.

4. "National Strategy for", White House, p. 1.

5. Petraeus, quoted in Dovere, "David Petraeus", Politico.

6. See Eugene Emery and Miriam Valverde, "Clinton Said Terror-ists Use Trump's Remarks About Muslims for Recruitment", *Politifact*, 10 October 2016; available at https://www.politifact.com/truth-o-meter/statements/2016/oct/10/hillary-clinton/clinton-said-terrorists-use-trumps-remarks-about-m/.

7. See Restad, *American Exceptionalism*.

8. Paxton, *The Anatomy of*, esp. Ch 2.

9. Mead, "The Jacksonian".

10. Paxton, "Comparisons and Definition" in Bosworth, *The Oxford Handbook*, pp. 554–5.

INDEX

INDEX

INDEX

INDEX

INDEX

INDEX